ROYAL CHILDREN

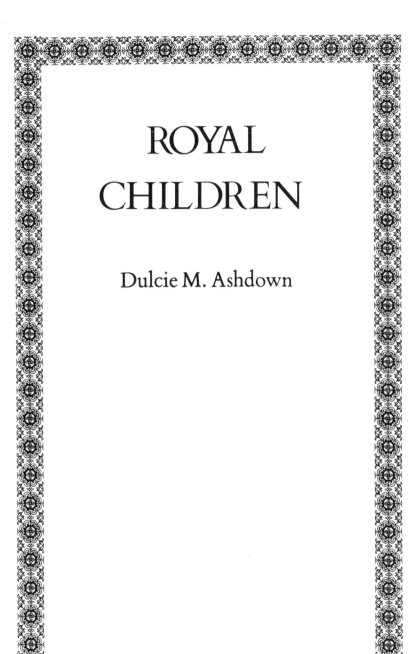

ROYAL
CHILDREN

Dulcie M. Ashdown

ROBERT HALE · LONDON

Robert Hale Limited
Clerkenwell House
Clerkenwell Green
London, EC1

Photoset, printed and bound
in Great Britain by
REDWOOD BURN LIMITED
Trowbridge & Esher

Contents

Illustrations

Life in the Victorian slums
(*Reproduced by permission of the* Mary Evans Picture Library)
'Many happy returns!' (Frith)
(*Reproduced by permission of the* Harrogate Art Gallery)
The future Queen Victoria, 1824
(*Reproduced by permission of* Dulwich College)

Between pages 144 and 145
Victoria with her mother, the Duchess of Kent
(*Reproduced by gracious permission of* Her Majesty the Queen)
Louise, Baroness Lehzen, Victoria's governess
(*Reproduced by gracious permission of* Her Majesty the Queen)
Victoria and Albert with their children
(*Reproduced by gracious permission of* Her Majesty the Queen)
The matriarch Victoria in the 1890s
(*Reproduced by gracious permission of* Her Majesty the Queen)
The three eldest children of the future King George V, with their
    mother
(*Reproduced by permission of* Popperfoto)
Gas-mask parade at a Dr Barnardo's nursery
(*Reproduced by permission of* Fox Photos Ltd)
Childhood 1970s-style: skate-boarding
(*Reproduced by permission of* Barnaby's Picture Library)
Coronation Day, 1937
(*Reproduced by permission of* Fox Photos Ltd)
Princesses Elizabeth and Margaret painting
(*Reproduced by courtesy of the* Radio Times Hulton Picture Library)
Christening Day, 1948
(*Reproduced by permission of* Fox Photos Ltd)
Coronation Day, 1953
(*Reproduced by permission of* Fox Photos Ltd)
The modern royal family
(*Reproduced by permission of* Syndication International)

Acknowledgements

The author acknowledges, with thanks, permission received from Earl Spencer to quote from manuscripts at Althorp, and from the Administrator of Blenheim Palace for material from the Duke of Marlborough's family papers.

The following publishers have given permission for reproduction of quotations from books in copyright:

W. H. Allen & Co. Ltd: H. Cathcart, *The Royal Bedside Book* (1969)

Associated Book Publishers Ltd: Lord Hervey, ed. R. Sedgwick, *Some materials towards memoirs of the reign of George II* (Eyre & Spottiswoode Publishers Ltd, 1931)

Benn Brothers: ed. A. Aspinall, *Letters of the Princess Charlotte, 1811–17* (Home & van Thal, 1949)

Cassell Ltd: M. Crawford, *The Little Princesses* (1950)

Chatto & Windus Ltd: ed. E. Rickert, *The Babees' Book* (1908) — with acknowledgement to the author's literary estate

Curtis Brown Ltd: ed. H. Bolitho, *Further Letters of Queen Victoria* (1938)

Evans Brothers Ltd: ed. R. Fulford, *Dearest Child* (1965)

Harvill Press/John Joliffe: ed. and trs. J. Joliffe, *Froissart's Chronicles* (1967)

Hutchinson Publishing Group Ltd: ed. J. Grieg, *The Faringdon Diary* (1922–8) and Mabel, Countess of Airlie, *Thatched with Gold* (1962)

Macmillan Ltd (London and Basingstoke): ed. L. Strachey and R. Fulford, *The Greville Memoirs, 1818–40* (1938)

Frederick Muller Ltd: David Duff, *Edward of Kent* (Stanley Paul, 1938)

John Murray Ltd: ed. A. C. Benson and Viscount Esher, *The Letters of Queen Victoria, 1837–61* (1907; ed. H. Wyndham, *The Correspondence of Sarah Spencer, Lady Lyttelton, 1787–1870* (1912) and Sir Clement Markham, *Richard III* (Smith Elder, 1906)

Oxford University Press: C. Oman, *The Great Revolt of 1381* (1906); L. Stone, *The Crisis of the Aristocracy* (1967); ed. F. H. Mares *The Memoirs of Robert Carey* (1972); R. L. Arkell, *Caroline of Anspach*

(1939); Sir George Young, *Poor Fred* (1940) and Flora Thompson, *Lark Rise to Candleford* (1939)
Pitkin Pictorials Ltd: C. Birt, *The Royal Sisters* (1949)

While the author of *Royal Children* has made every effort to trace the copyright owners of works from which text has been quoted, in a few cases this has been impossible (notably in those of Aspinall Oglander's *Admiral's Wife*, 1940, and M. Blundell's *Cavalier*, 1933, published by Longmans Green), and the author takes this opportunity to offer apologies to any authors/publishers whose rights may have been unwittingly infringed.

Introduction

The life of the royal family is like a great 'soap-opera', a view into the lives of others, a 'continuing story' embracing birth, marriage, death and incidents exciting, amusing, sometimes shocking – a story apparently without end.

Over the past thirty-odd years, a virtual industry has been created within the writing and journalistic profession around the lives of the members of the royal family. Not a day passes without reference to them in the mass media, not a year without the publication of royal biographies. And there are known to be royal devotees who amass large scrapbooks of cuttings from newspapers and magazines about their favourite royal personages.

It is a harmless cult for those who follow it, though those who pander to it are often guilty of crimes of bad taste and of intrusion into the privacy of royal lives, against which the ordinary citizen would rebel if it was carried into his own.

It was not always so. In the Middle Ages, news of any important event took weeks to reach the furthermost parts of the kingdom, and the birth of a royal child could go unmarked by all but those closest to the throne. Until royal children became old enough to go to war or to be given in marriage to foreign sovereigns, they went largely unnoticed by the vast majority of Englishmen, for most of whom the monarchy was a distant institution, encroaching on private lives only when armies were levied or taxes raised, or when a royal cavalcade passed through the countryside *en route* for one of the royal castles. Even in later eras, though from the eighteenth-century portraits of the royal family were available in cheap prints in provincial shops, it was not until the coming of mass literacy in the nineteenth century that news of any sort had wide currency, let alone that of the arrival and nurture of royal children.

For today's researcher into the history of royal children, there is a plethora of detail about the modern royal family to be found in newspapers and magazines, fascinating anecdotes to be gleaned from memoirs of courtiers of the past couple of centuries, evidence from letters and observations from the Tudor and Stuart ages – but before that only sparse references to royal children who, unless they grew up to reign, may have lived out their lives almost as anonymously as the peasantry.

And yet these children lived close to the centre of events and of national decision-making, were often brought dangerously close to the battlefields of civil and international wars, were bartered for the sake of national peace, had their whole lives enriched or marred by the vagaries of national policies. In eras in which the personality of a monarch could bring a kingdom to glory and prosperity or ignominy and ruin, the upbringing of a royal child, the development of its morals and talents, could be of importance to every royal subject, and it is easy to trace the fortunes of the nation (at least to the nineteenth century) through the personalities of its monarchs, moulded by childhood experiences.

This study of royal children has two main aims: first, to find out how royal children lived in past times, how they were educated, how they played, how they were treated by those with authority over them; secondly, to examine the place of royal children in national events and policies. And their lives have been set against the context of the lives of the thousands of 'ordinary' children who were their contemporaries.

In many cases, the rigours which royal children of the past endured, the harsh regimes to which they were submitted, the crimes (even murder) which were committed against them, seem distant and alien from the modern age, in which there is a national outcry when even the least of infants is ill-treated or exploited. Such royal children, abused and deprived or exalted and cosseted seem strange to us, 'unnatural' in their responses to life, precocious, arrogant, prematurely hardened. But time and again one comes across a chance reference or quoted word which brings these children, so long in their graves, to life again and reveals a nature not so far from that of the child of today.

Whatever else history is, it is certainly the study of the common humanity which we share with our ancestors, high and humble, the strongest bond between past and present.

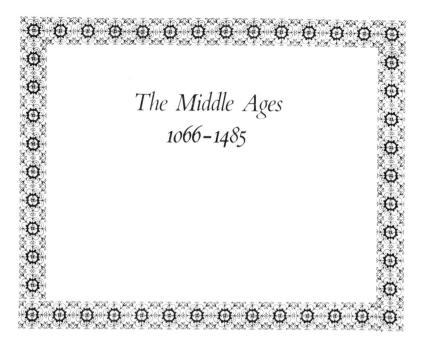

The Middle Ages
1066–1485

"They love an apple more than gold"

In the Middle Ages, childhood was a period to be hurried through, to be left as soon as possible. Farmers wanted hands for field and barn; tradesmen and artisans wanted workmen for their shops and benches; barons and kings needed warriors to swell their armies. Thus even the smallest children were put to work outdoors in every season of the year; boys were sent from home to take up craft apprenticeships even before they had entered their teens; and boys of rank were set on horses, swords in hand, when they were no more than ten years old, to practise for their dangerous careers.

And no one thought this cruel. Life was work, and work was life. Childhood was a training for both.

Nor would any parent be thought unkind for marrying off a daughter at puberty, to become a mother several times over before she was twenty. After all, with an average life expectancy of thirty to forty years, breeding was best begun young. Infant mortality was high, and out of every three or four babies born, only one might live to maturity.

Today it is hard to imagine the lives of medieval people, with their long hours of toil, their generally meagre diet, their rough housing, the painful illnesses they so often suffered – frequently worsened by the primitive doctoring they received. Social historians have painstakingly sifted thousands of documents which survive from the Middle Ages, but there remain whole areas of the 'human condition' in past centuries which are so sparsely covered that they must remain a mystery.

Childhood is one of these areas. No one was sentimental about children in the Middle Ages, nor was child development thought to be of much interest, so the subject rarely figures in contemporary works. One of the very few medieval treatises which touches on childhood, a manuscript written by the thirteenth-century Bartholomew de Glanville, well illustrates the attitude of detachment generally adopted:

Such children be nesh [soft] of flesh, lithe and pliant of body, able and light to moving, witty to learn and lead their lives without thought and

care. And set their courages only of mirth and liking, and dread no perils
more than beating with a rod: and they love an apple more than gold. . . .
They desire things that be to them contrary and grievous . . . and weep
more for the loss of an apple than for the loss of their heritage. They desire
all things that they see and pray and ask with voice and with hand. They
love talking and counsel of such children as they be and void company of old
men. . . . Suddenly they laugh, and suddenly they weep. Always they
cry, jangle and jape, that unneth [hardly] *they be still while they sleep.*
When they be washed of filth, anon they defile themselves again. When
their mother washeth and combeth them, they kick and sprawl, and put
with their feet and with hands, and withstand with all their might.[1]

But Bartholomew was a rarity among medieval writers. Children of the
labouring and artisan classes were not mentioned in medieval chronicles; even royal children merit a word only at birth and death, or when
they appear at state occasions, or if unkind fate brought a prince to the
throne in childhood. For the most part, our knowledge of royal childhood in the Middle Ages derives from contemporary account books –
lists of payments to their servants, for their clothes and so on – rather
than from the formal chronicles which told the story of English history
of the period. It is possible to build up a picture of their life-style from
such documents, but only very rarely does an individual child emerge as
a character.

In the working classes of medieval England, children were valued
mainly for their labour potential, their assistance in a family farm or
business, their contribution to the family economy. In a royal family,
sons would be regarded primarily as safeguarding the royal succession,
then for the services they would render the monarch on the battlefield
and at the council-table, while daughters would be of use to the monarchy as brides for foreign rulers with whom their fathers needed an
alliance. Thus, the birth of a royal child was a matter of great importance, and many a queen was doomed to long years of pregnancy and
child-rearing to ensure an adequate supply of such useful commodities.

The pains of childbirth over, however, the royal or aristocratic
mother's work was done. At a time when children were suckled until
they were two or even three years old, a wet-nurse freed the lady to start
a new pregnancy as soon as possible (cows' and goats' milk never
figured in the medieval diet: it was considered fit only to feed back to
animals). The wet-nurse might be a woman who had lost her own baby
at birth, and so had milk to spare, or who, for the honour and tempting
wages, put her own child out to nurse, in order to take on a royal or
noble baby.

Bartholomew again:

> . . . *Of all things, it needeth to beware of evil milk and of corrupted nourishing and feeding, that the children be not fed therewith. For by uncleanness of nurses and sucking of clammy milk like glue, come full many sores and greves, as whelks, blains, pimples in the mouth, spewing, fevers, cramps, the flux and such other. And if the child be sick, medicines shall be given to the nurse and not to the child. And she shall be ruled according to good diet, so that the virtue of the nurse be in stead supplied and fulfil the default of the child. . . . For of good disposition of milk cometh good disposition of the child.*[2]

In more ways than this too, the nurse was a 'mother-substitute':

> *A nurse is glad if the child be glad, and heavy if the child be sorry, and taketh the child up if it falls, and giveth it suck: if it weep, she kisseth and lulleth it still, and gathereth the limbs and bindeth them together and doth cleanse and wash it when it is defiled. And for it cannot speak, the nurse lispeth and soundeth the same words to teach more easily the child that cannot speak. . . . And she cheweth meat in her mouth and maketh it ready to the toothless child that it may the easilier swallow that meat . . . and pleaseth the child with whisperings and songs when it shall sleep, and swatheth it in sweet clothes and righteth and stretcheth out its limbs and bindeth them together with cradlebands, to keep and save the child that it have no crooked limbs.*[3]

This binding of the limbs – 'swaddling' – was an ancient precaution: the infant Jesus had been 'wrapped in swaddling clothes' after birth. It must have been an uncomfortable start to life, with no way for the baby to move and so strengthen its limbs – and most unhygienic, with the small body sore from its own excrement and urine. And yet babies were wrapped in layer upon layer of cloth, tightly bound with tapes, right through the first months of their lives, seemingly without harm– and the practice continued until the early eighteenth century.

In the Middle Ages, the peasants were bound by law to the manor on which they were born, and from infancy their children would be put to work on the lord's demesne and the home plot, scaring birds, clearing stones, weeding and following the harvesters. The aristocracy were more mobile, and the practice early grew up on sending noble children into the households of relations or friends for their 'nurture', the boys to act as pages, the girls as 'waiting gentlewomen', and so to learn by example the manners and duties of their caste. It was a custom which endured in England into the sixteenth century, strange to the foreigners who observed it and deplored by one, an Italian ambassador, who wrote:

> *The want of affection in the English is strongly manifested towards their children; for after having kept them at home till they arrive at the age of seven or nine years at the utmost, they put them out, both males and females, to hard service in the houses of other people. . . . And few are born who are exempted from this fate, for every one, however rich he may be, sends his children into the houses of others, whilst he in return receives those of strangers into his own. And on enquiring their reason for this severity, they answered that they did it in order that their children might learn better manners. But I, for my part, believe that they do it because they like to enjoy all their comforts themselves, and that they are better served by strangers than they would be by their own children.*[4]

The Italian was too cynical. English parents did have their children's best interests at heart: the aim was to place a child in a household of superior rank, where the boy or girl's own career would be advanced by association, where there would be opportunities for 'bettering' their own family's status.

For most of the population in the Middle Ages, there was no formal education. What use would learning be to a labourer or a housewife, even if any teaching were available to them? A little arithmetic – for counting bags of grain, heads of cattle, for ensuring fair dealing in the market – who would reasonably want more? Stories and songs were passed on by word of mouth, prayers learned by rote. Only in the Church (which provided clerks for civil administration as well as Mass-priests) could a man turn his mind to philosophy and theology, rudimentary science and medicine, history and literature – and even then, the majority of priests had only enough Latin to say the Mass, and clerks no more than was needed to frame legal documents. Even among the nobility in the early Middle Ages, there was little more than basic literacy: if a king could read his missal, he was more learned than most of his peers – King John did not sign but set his seal to Magna Carta in 1215, a plausible proof of his illiteracy. And before the invention of the printing-press in the late fifteenth century, it was only the very wealthy who could afford the handwritten books produced by leisured monks, so that any man's literacy was generally of a practical rather than a cultural nature.

There were 'grammar' schools in the major towns by the later Middle Ages, which catered for basic literacy, and to which many tradesmen's and prosperous artisans' sons were admitted, and in 1382 William of

Wykeham, Bishop of Winchester, founded a school where boys were to be grounded in English and Latin to prepare them for entry to his 'New College' at Oxford. Winchester College subsequently admitted children not destined for the priesthood, as did the later foundations at Eton, Shrewsbury, Harrow and Westminster.

Convents, contrary to modern opinion, were not the girls' equivalent of the grammar schools and clerical establishments. In the centuries before the Conquest, nuns had been famed for their learning, but as the Middle Ages continued, they took in few lay pupils, and those learned only a minimal Latin, French and some trifling accomplishments. It is not until the fifteenth century that we find middle-class women expressing themselves fluently on paper – among the famous 'Paston letters' are many by and to women who could read and write with ease.

Medieval life was not, of course, all work and warfare. Several children's games have been traced to this early period – it has even been suggested that hopscotch and marbles were first played when children had the convenience of flagstones in castle halls. Manuscript illuminations show children with hoops, shuttlecocks and balls (football was frowned on, as distracting boys from archery practice). There can have been little money to spare for toys in cottage homes, but an account book of Edward I's household lists expenditure on a toy cart, a painted crossbow, a model castle and a boat for his son Alfonso; Richard III paid out two pence to have his son Edward's whip mended – there are several medieval pictures of children whipping tops.

For the poor, there were the seasonal festivals of the countryside, and the travelling fairs at which they could buy gingerbread and tawdry trinkets. At Christmas a village might put on its own mummers' play, but throughout the year there was always the unexpected arrival of itinerant minstrels, jugglers, jesters and bear-leaders to enthral the community. Royal children had more opportunity than any others of seeing professional entertainments, for kings customarily kept their own minstrels and 'fools', and any touring 'showman' would certainly present himself at Court in hopes of finding a royal audience to boast of and capitalize on in his country-wide wanderings. Edward III's children had their own minstrel, named Gerard de Gay, who may also have taught them to play themselves, probably on the lute, the most popular instrument of the Middle Ages: they seem to have been fond of him – in November 1340 the young princesses gave Gerard a coat which they had made themselves.

However, privilege was paid for. While peasant children ran wild, unkempt and rough, those reared for higher things were disciplined into courtesy and elegance, though only from the fifteenth century did they have the advantage of books of advice on how to behave.

One of the earliest was *Stans puer ad mensam* – "The boy standing at the table" (a young page learning to serve his lord) – by John Lydgate (who died *c.* 1450). Here are some of its strictures on table manners:

> *With full mouth speak not, lest thou do offence;*
> *Drink not breathless for haste nor negligence;*
> *Keep thy lips from fat of flesh or fish;*
> *Wipe clean thy spoon, leave it not in thy dish.*

> *. . . Enbrew no napery for no recklessness;*
> *For to sup loud is against gentilesse*
> *Never at meat begin thou no strife;*
> *Thy teeth also thou pick not with no knife.*

> *Drop not thy breast with sauce nor with pottage;*
> *Bring no knives unscoured to the table;*
> *Fill not thy spoon, lest in the carriage,*
> *It went beside, which were not commendable. . . .*[5]

There were several other such books circulating noble and royal households in manuscript during the fifteenth century: *How the wise man taught his son* was matched with *How the good wife taught her daughter* (*c.* 1430) which included the telling couplet:

> *When thou sittest in church, o'er thy beads bend;*
> *Make thou no jangling with gossip or with friend.*[6]

There was John Russell's *Book of Nurture, c.* 1460, and the *Book of Courtesy*, of about the same date. *The Babees' Book* was written for the household of King Edward IV in the 1470s, probably for his own small sons and their companions. In the next decade came *The little children's book*, which gave so many rules for a child's behaviour that, if he kept them all,

> *Then will men hereafter say:*
> *"A gentleman was here today."*[7]

Rich and poor, noble and common, children were dressed in miniature replicas of their elders' clothes from the time they discarded the swaddling and smocks of babyhood. The boys in tunic, hose and cloaks, the girls in long gowns (though their hair was plaited and uncovered, unlike their mothers', which was concealed under veils and elaborate head-dresses). And to a large extent, their behaviour was expected to conform with adult standards, so that beating was a frequent resort when, naturally, they failed to come up to expectation. In the hierarchical society of the Middle Ages, respect for parents was exacted as sternly as obedience to one's lord, and even in maturity children knelt to their fathers and obeyed them without question.

It is one of the inevitable sorrows of the historian that detailed records were not kept of domestic life among the poor in the Middle Ages, that even accounts of noble and royal life at home are sparse. The customs of the age, and the living conditions of the people, are so far from our own that it is easy to forget the common humanity which we share through the centuries.

"Virtuous learning . . . honest disports"

The pains of childbirth link the experience of women from the first moments of the human race through to the introduction of anaesthetics in the nineteenth century. Nevertheless, pain may be better endured in comfort, and the queens of the Middle Ages were couched in far more luxury than peasant women on their beds of straw and rushes.

At the end of the medieval period, in the late fifteenth century, the mother of King Henry VII, Lady Margaret Beaufort, drew up a list of instructions for the lying-in of her daughter-in-law, Elizabeth of York. They included the provision that "Her Highness's pleasure being understood in what chamber she will be delivered, the same must be hanged with rich cloth of arras, sides, roof, windows and all, except one window must be hanged so that she may have light when it pleases her".[1] The instructions went on to detail the exact quality and dimensions of Elizabeth's bedding and the furniture of her chamber: besides her pallet-bed, with its embroidered canopy, there was to be an altar, so that she could hear Mass in her own room, and a cupboard filled with gold plate to be used at her meals.

Towards the end of her pregnancy, the Queen would 'take her chamber' attended by a great crowd of noblemen and ladies. They would hear Mass together, and Elizabeth would fortify herself with Holy Communion; then, after refreshments and the Lord Chamberlain's request for prayers for Elizabeth in her coming ordeal, she was to go into her chamber, accompanied only by her ladies, who, for the duration, would undertake duties usually allotted to men in the royal household, for the Queen was to see no man but her husband and her priests until the birth of her child.

More ceremonial would follow a royal birth. The Queen was first seen in her chamber, at the *relevailles*, a reception at which she showed off her child. Then came the 'churching', a solemn purification of the mother (still provided for in the Anglican Church to this day), then the christening, with its procession of nobles and clergy, the baptism of the child, the solemn oaths of the god-parents, the gifts and the inevitable banquet.

Nevertheless, though royal luxury and the importance of providing heirs cushioned many queens from the suffering borne by their humbler contemporaries, and though their safe delivery was hailed with far greater rejoicing than a new arrival — a new mouth to feed — in a cottage, there were those royal mothers whose very eminence added to their hazards: royal babies were born in stark fortresses in time of war, even in tents during royal campaigns and crusades. Eleanor of Castile, wife of the thirteenth-century King Edward I, gave birth to two daughters in the dangers and extreme climate of Palestine during a crusade — one died, the other survived, to be known as Joanna 'of Acre' from her unusual birthplace. Queen Eleanor, in fact set a record for royal childbearing with her thirteen children — and maybe more, whose names went unrecorded because they died at birth.

Despite the dangers of childbirth (and of the rough doctoring which queens received — perhaps adding to the hazards), not one medieval queen of England died during labour,* but many of their children failed to survive birth or to come safely through infancy. Eleanor of Castile lost six children before the age of seven, and one at ten; her mother-in-law, Eleanor of Provence, lost four babies and one child at the age of three. This was the Princess Catherine, born in 1253, who was deaf and dumb, though apparently not loved the less for that. Her parents sent her to live with her nurse at Swallowfield in Berkshire and provided a kid-goat from the royal forest to be her companion. When Catherine died, in 1257, her funeral cost the munificent £51. 12. 4, besides the cost of a brass effigy on her tomb, which was later recast in silver at further expense, while fifty marks were paid to the hermit of Charing for perpetual prayers for the child's soul.†

One of the most successful of royal mothers was Philippa of Hainault, who reared nine of her twelve children. But even she, and her husband Edward III, could grieve for a dead baby: when their second son, William, died only a few weeks old in 1336, the royal wardrobe book took account of payments for 393 pounds of wax candles to burn round the Prince's corpse at Hatfield and Pontefract, stopping-places along the

* Elizabeth of York died nine days after the birth of her seventh child, in February 1503.

† Edward I's kindness to children was also well illustrated some three decades later, when the King sent a ship to Norway to collect the six-year-old Queen Margaret of Scotland, his Norwegian-born great-niece, whom he intended to marry to his heir, thereby uniting the two crowns. On Edward's orders the ship that went out to Norway was provisioned with all sorts of sweet things dear to childish palates: gingerbread, sugar loaves, figs and raisins. The Norwegians, however, refused to send Margaret across the North Sea in any but their own vessel. In fact, the child sickened on the voyage, and she died soon after reaching the Orkney Islands.

road to York where he was buried, and for three cloths of gold in which to wrap him. These, with the cost of the hearse, came to £42. 11. 1½, and a further £99. 3. 5½ was expended for Masses to be said at churches along the route of the funeral cortège, and to pay the widows who watched over the baby's coffin overnight on his journey north.

In the Middle Ages, the royal household was generally itinerant: besides the many demands on the king, in supervising the government of his realm in the provinces, there was always the problem of provisioning the vast army of councillors, courtiers, clerks, soldiers and servants in attendance on the monarch, and only by moving from one castle, palace or manor to another could food be found to maintain them. Some royal parents kept their children with them for most of the year, others sent them off to country palaces with their own household. Edward III, for example, maintained a separate household for his children at Woodstock, where one baby after another was put into the care of the governess, Lady Elizabeth St. Omer. His grandfather, Edward I's choice had been Northampton, though that king's wife, Eleanor of Castile, gathered her children together as often as she was ensconced at Westminster for any length of time, and there was a good deal of building put in hand to provide an annex to the palace for the royal children and their staff. Part of it became known as 'maidenhall' from the many young princesses housed together there.

(It was Edward and Eleanor's daughter Eleanor who had one of the first known baby-carriages for her journeys between her homes: covered in green cloth, lined with crimson silk, it was a sort of carry-cot slung between two men on horseback.)

In this ever-moving world, without the 'natural' companionship of father and mother, it was inevitable that the nurse should play an important part in a royal child's life. That this was so is proved by the care princes took to provide for their old nurses: when Henry V came to the throne in 1413, he awarded an annuity of twenty pounds a year to his former nurse, Johanna Waring, and in 1474 Edward IV provided the same sum for his, Anne of Caux – proof of their enduring regard.

For their first few years, princes and princesses were often housed together, under the care of women, supervised by a 'governor' and 'governess', but at about the age of seven, princes were generally put in the charge of a nobleman in some separate establishment, where, with companions of their own age, they would begin their formal education. Two such boys were the future King Edward IV and his brother Edmund: in 1454 (when they were eleven and ten years old respectively), they wrote to their father from their own household at Ludlow:

. . . We thank your nobless and good fatherhood for our green gowns now late sent unto us to our great comfort. Beseeching your good lordship to remember our porteaux [prayer-books] and that we might have some fine bonnets sent unto us by the next sure messenger for necessity so requireth.

Our thus right noble lord and father, please it your Highness to wit that we have charged your servant William Smith, bearer of these, for to declare unto your nobility certain things on our behalf, namely concerning and touching the odious rule and demeaning of Richard Croft and his brother. Wherefore we beseech your gracious lordship and full noble fatherhood to hear him in exposition of the same and to his relation give full faith and credence.[2]

It was once thought that the Croft brothers were the governors or tutors of Edward and Edmund: now it is held more likely that they were fellow-pupils, in their late teens, so this complaint may be the familiar one of bullying. But this letter is the only evidence of the boys' problem, so perhaps it was soon resolved to their satisfaction. Often childhood companions became close friends of future kings: the seeds of King Edward II's problems were sown in his boyhood, when he came under the spell of one of his pages, Piers Gaveston, who initiated him into the illicit delights of homosexuality, to the horror of the virtuous Edward I, his father.

In the year 1474 King Edward IV laid down instructions for the education of his son Edward, which may well have been based on elements of his own education with his brother Edmund at Ludlow. The Prince's day was to begin with Matins, Mass and breakfast, followed by "such virtuous learning as his age shall now suffice to receive". His midday meal was to be enlivened by the reading aloud of "such noble stories as behoveth a prince to understand". Then came more study and "such convenient disports and exercises as behoveth his estate to have experience in", while after Evensong and supper, he was to be allowed "such honest disports as may be conveniently devised for his recreation".[3] But such phrases are sadly wanting in any real information as to the Prince's studies: most likely this future King Edward V was taught to read in French and English (in which his father had several books), with enough Latin to follow the Mass and state documents – but beyond that, even for this late date in the Middle Ages, there is no certainty. The boy may have been encouraged to start his own library, for his father was the patron of Caxton, who introduced printed books into England: Prince Edward would have enjoyed one of Caxton's first publications, the exciting adventures of the Knights of the Round Table in Malory's *Morte d'Arthur*.

The emphasis, especially in the early Middle Ages, was on training for war, in riding, sword-play, tilting with lances and so on. Every king was expected to be a war-leader, to show personal bravery and to plan strategy and direct battle tactics himself – and most of the English kings of the eleventh to fifteenth centuries were called upon to show their skills in wars at home and abroad. By the age of fourteen or so, a prince had to be ready to prove himself – Edward III's heir, the 'Black Prince', became a nationally-famed hero on the field of Crécy at fifteen.

A prince's appearance on the battlefield would usually be his first experience of royal duty. Occasionally chronicles of the Middle Ages reveal royal children joining their parents on state occasions, watching the reception of ambassadors, offering gifts at shrines, receiving loyal addresses in major towns which they visited, and so on, but responsibilities in statecraft came only with maturity. Sometimes an heir to the throne was awarded a nominal regency of the kingdom, when his father was out of the country (the pattern had been set in the early years of William the Conqueror's reign, when, in the King's absence in Normandy, his wife and eldest son, the fourteen-year-old Robert, were co-regents), but a regency would always be supported by an experienced council. Generally, introduction to government came in the years of the princes' mid-teens, when, just as they put their knightly skills into practice in war, so they followed the arguments for war or peace as members of their fathers' councils.

The training of princesses followed no such regular pattern as their brothers'. They remained with the nurses and governesses of their infancy, then took a place in the retinue of their mothers, to learn by example more than precept the lady-like arts. These included manners, fluency in elegant French, music and singing, embroidery – and very little else, for the role of princesses and queens was merely ornamental, apart from childbearing. Royal ladies of the Middle Ages were not even housekeepers – there were professional men, chamberlains and stewards, to provision, run and discipline the royal household.

Presumably most princesses were taught to read, for they, more than any of their contemporaries, would have access to the charming French romances of the Middle Ages, and to the delightfully illustrated missals and 'books of hours' which enlivened their frequent attendance at church services. The future King Henry IV, in 1398, generously laid out twenty pence for his daughters' books of 'ABC', and less than a hundred years later Edward IV's daughter Elizabeth could write on a fly-leaf in her own hand: "This book is mine, Elizabeth the King's daughter".

In *The most pleasant song of the Lady Bessy*, allegedly (but definitely not) written by Elizabeth herself, the Princess (later Henry VII's queen) says,

when an attendant offers to send for an amanuensis to write a letter for
her:

> *You shall not need none such to call*
> *. . . hearken to me,*
> *What my father King Edward, that king royal,*
> *Did for my sister my lady Wells and me:*
> *He sent for a scrivenor to lusty London,*
> *He was the best in that city;*
> *He taught us both to read and write full soon,*
> *If it please you, full soon you shall see;*
> *Lauded be God, I had such speed*
> *That I can write as well as he,*
> *And also indite and full well read . . .*
> *Both English and also French*
> *And also Spanish if you need.*[4]

Just as the names of royal nurses have come down to us in the records
of their wages and pensions, so we have the names of the select band of
royal governesses, forerunners of the famous Lehzen and 'Crawfie'.
The first known is of Anglo-Saxon England: Elgifu, a woman of rank,
who superintended the education of the daughters of King Edward 'the
Elder'. One of the most influential governesses of the Middle Ages was
Cecily de Sandford, who had charge of Henry III's sister Eleanor. The
Princess had married an English nobleman, William Marshall, when she
was only nine and was widowed at sixteen. Dame Cecily, herself a
widow, encouraged her charge to take a vow of celibacy with her, and
both dedicated themselves to a life of austere piety. But the younger
woman's resolve did not last long: in 1238 Eleanor married the attractive
Simon de Montfort at a secret ceremony – for which temerity the couple
had to pay a large fine to the King.

Most English princesses of the medieval period were married in their
early or middle teens to boys or men who were strangers to them, for the
sake of an alliance valued by their fathers. Few young brides rebelled:
after all, they had known from earliest consciousness that this was the
fate of a princess, to leave home and family and create her own far away.
Only very rarely were marriages made for love in noble and royal
families, so no princess would think herself particularly hard-done-by in
an arranged marriage, unless her husband proved unfaithful or unkind –
which he might, in any case, even after a 'true-love' match.

Though marriage was usually deferred until the onset of puberty
would allow consummation, betrothals might be made at any time from
early infancy. The youngest princess for whom a match was sought was

surely Edward I's daughter Eleanor, who was only four days old when her father opened negotiations with the Count of Burgundy for her future marriage with his son. (The match never transpired: Eleanor died before she was five years old.)

There was, in fact, a real advantage for a child betrothed young and sent to her adoptive country when still in her formative years, for not only would the wrench from home be more bitter later but in this way the princess could be educated in the language and customs of her future husband's people. King Henry I's daughter Matilda was only about seven years old when she was sent to meet the Holy Roman Emperor Henry V, with a magnificent dowry of ten thousand silver marks, and only ten when she was (nominally) married and crowned empress. However, when, widowed at twenty-two, she returned to England, she rather irritated her father's Court with the stiff, formal, Germanic manners which she had acquired.

Another seven-year-old bride was Edward II's daughter Joan, who was married in 1328 to the four-year-old David Bruce, who became King of Scotland a year later. This match is a fine example of the use to which kings put their children to make peace or to seal it, through a marriage between royal families, for Joan was England's pledge of peace to Scotland after years of war between the neighbouring kingdoms. In fact, she became known as 'Joan Makepeace'.

When King Edward IV was considering the future marriages of his children, between 1476 and his death in 1483, he made the most grandiose plans, intended as much to bolster and bulwark his own precarious place on the English throne as to aggrandize his family by alliance with foreign kings. His heir was offered, at various times in the first few years of his life, to the then heiress of Castile, the sister of the Holy Roman Emperor, the daughter of a fabulously wealthy Italian duke and the heiress of the duchy of Brittany. The King's elder daughters were intended as wives for the kings of France, Scotland and Denmark and for the Emperor's heir. However, when Edward IV died, he had not brought off one of these prestigious matches: international wars and changing patterns of diplomacy had brought his long years of negotiation to nothing. Nor were they ever revived: after the King's son had been dethroned and all the children branded illegitimate, only one of Edward IV's daughters made a royal marriage: this was Elizabeth, whose marriage to her cousin Henry VII was used to weld together the rival claims of the throne of the dynasties of York and Lancaster.

Of course the route of princesses was two-way. Of the twenty queens consort of England between 1066 and 1500, all but the last three were foreign-born, generally arriving for their weddings in early adolescence. The youngest was King Richard II's second wife, the seven-year-old Isabelle of France. But even this young lady had a fine appreciation of her position and dignity. When English ambassadors visited her father's Court and were presented to their future queen, she replied to their congratulations with the words: "An it please God and my lord my father that I shall be Queen of England, I shall be glad thereof for it is showed me that I shall be then a great lady."[5] She would also have known that her sacrifice of home and family was in the cause of ending intermittent Anglo-French wars of many decades' duration.

However, though Isabelle may have found grandeur in her new position, the child found little happiness in England. Her husband, in his thirties, was kind enough, visiting her in her own castles and bringing gifts, but there was no disguising the parlous state of England and the King's diminishing control over his lords. When Richard was at last, in 1399, forced to leave for Ireland to attempt to rally his supporters, he took leave of his child-wife with many kisses and embraces, while she wept piteously to see him go into danger. Husband and wife did not meet again. When Richard II returned, he was captured by his enemies and forced to abdicate in favour of his cousin Henry of Lancaster (King Henry IV). When Richard was murdered, soon after, Isabelle became a widow at the age of twelve: she could not have mourned him more if they had been a 'Darby and Joan' with a dozen children. But she was not allowed to return to France with her grief: the new King sought her father's agreement to the girl's marrying his own heir – her consent was not, of course, sought. When France refused the match, the young Queen was at last sent home to her family, in 1401. (A few years later, her situation was reversed: in her mid-teens Isabelle was married to her cousin Charles, future Duke of Orleans, several years her junior. She died in childbirth in 1409, aged twenty-two.)

One of the saddest of child-brides was Edward III's daughter Joan. In 1338, when she was aged only four, her father took her to Germany and at Koblenz handed her over to the Emperor and Empress (who was her maternal aunt). Joan was intended for the son of one of the Emperor's greatest fiefs, the Duke of Austria, but in 1339 her future father-in-law died and his brother, who was guardian of the heir, repudiated the English alliance: Joan was sent home. She was fourteen when she travelled south again, now towards Spain. This time her bridegroom was to be Prince Pedro, son and heir of King Alfonso of Castile. She carried with her a wedding-dress of cloth of gold, a Tripoli-silk bed-cover embroidered with fighting dragons, two tapestries – one flowered, one of popinjays sewn in worsted, besides numerous coffers full of clothes and jewels and plate and (incomprehensibly) twelve thousand pins.

The Princess arrived at Bordeaux on the last day of March 1348 and stayed to rest there before going on to her wedding, planned for November. But it was a fateful year: the dreadful plague known as 'the Black Death' was surging through Europe. Among many thousands of others, Joan succumbed to it. She died on the 2nd September.

In his letter of condolence to Prince Pedro, Edward III wrote:

> . . . *Whilst we, with parental affection, thought to have had an adopted son to our mutual comfort, behold! — with what sobbing sighs and a heavy heart, we sorrowfully relate — death, terrible to all the kings of the earth . . . has now by subversion of the wonted laws of mortality removed from your hoped-for embraces and ours, our aforesaid daughter; in whom all gifts of nature met; whom also, as due to the elegance of her manners, we sincerely loved beyond our other children. . . . Whereat none can wonder that we are pierced by the stings of the most intense sorrow.*[6]

The size and value of Joan's trousseau were not usual in an age when clothes and jewels were prized almost as highly as a cash dowry. Edward II's daughter Eleanor, aged fourteen at the time of her wedding to Reinald, Duke of Guelders, in 1332, took to her new home a wardrobe which included a mantle and hood of blue Brussels cloth fur-trimmed with ermine, two pelisses ornamented with green and gold beads, a sur-tunic of cloth of gold embroidered with a chase of hares and stags, a coronet of 260 large pearls and another made of 420 silver pieces, while her wedding-dress was of Spanish cloth of gold embroidered with coloured silks, to be worn under a tunic and mantle of crimson velvet embroidered with gold. She was also provided with a whole suite of furniture, including the marriage-bed of green, crimson and gold, and table-covers embroidered with the figures of the apostles, and a chariot lined with purple velvet embroidered with gold stars, each centring on a precious gem.

The famous London mercer and Lord Mayor Richard Whittington, provided the materials for the trousseau of Henry IV's daughter Blanche, when she, aged ten, went to Germany to marry Emperor Rupert's son Louis. Dozens of gowns and mantles were listed in her account book: her wedding-dress had a tunic and mantle with a long train of white satin and velvet, edged with miniver and ermine, but just as grand were her other gowns: one of cloth of gold of Cyprus worked with white flowers and edged with miniver, another of red velvet embroidered with pearls, a red cloth of gold of Cyprus embroidered with roses, one of green cloth of gold with a blue train, worked with golden eagles.

The gaily-dressed Blanche was happily received by her bridegroom, who acknowledged receipt of the Princess with a letter to her father, dated 22nd July 1402, very soon after the wedding-day:

Most illustrious and glorious prince and dread lord,
*   After my humble and devoted commendations of obedience, I signify*
to your serenity that no sooner did I understand that the illustrious and mag-
nificent Lady Blanche, Your Highness's daughter, then my betrothed bride
but now my sweetest wife, had crossed the sea with a splendid train than I
greatly rejoiced at the tidings; but when that countenance, lovely beyond the
daughters of men, presented itself before me, then indeed my very heart
exulted with joy; for not merely is her form English but it shines with such
angelic loveliness that all the nobles of the people would worship it. . . .
Thus, most serene prince, I know not how fully to thank you for so rich and
rare a gift. . . . Moreover, I will treat my aforesaid most beloved spouse
with all the kindness in my power, according to circumstances.[7]

Certainly this letter goes beyond the bounds of mere etiquette in its ex-pression, so it may well have been sincere. A frequent correspondence was kept up between Henry IV and his son-in-law, in the most compli-mentary vein, so perhaps the marriage was an outstanding success. Sadly, Princess Blanche died in childbirth, in 1409, at the age of seven-teen.

Not every princess was married abroad: some were given to English nobles, either to win loyalty for the monarchy or as a reward, or, in some cases, to bind a wealthy estate to the Crown. And there were other princesses who were not married at all – though of those who survived to maturity, these were very few. They did not, however, remain at home as daughters-in-residence, but were, for the most part, dedicated in infancy to a religious life. One of the Conqueror's daughters, Cecilia, was 'offered' at the altar of Holy Trinity at Caen in 1066, when she was about ten years of age. Holy Trinity was part of a huge double-complex of monastery and convent founded at Fontevrault by William and his wife Matilda, and by 1122 their daughter was ruling there as abbess. In fact, that dignity became something of a family legacy: Princess Cecilia was succeeded by her great-niece Isabelle. Another great-niece, King Stephen's daughter Mary, was brought up in the convent of St. Leonard's at Stratford-at-Bow before being, still in childhood, set up as prioress of her own convent, in Kent. At nineteen, she was abbess of Romsey in Hampshire, one of the most important convents in England. At twenty-four, however, she found herself the last survivor of her family, heiress of the county of Boulogne, and therefore forced to re-

nounce her vocation and marry. Nine years later, having provided a
new heir, she obtained a divorce from her husband, Matthew of Flanders, and took the veil again, this time in France.

In the following century, another Mary, daughter of King Edward I,
entered Amesbury convent (a cell of Fontevrault), where her grandmother, the widowed Queen Eleanor of Provence, had been living for
some time. Mary's parents, her brother and sisters were there to see her
professed, with thirteen young noblewomen her companions. The King
awarded her a pension of £100 a year – not all of which may have gone
into convent funds, for, as the years passed, the nun-princess made frequent visits to Court and went on pilgrimages to Walsingham and Bury
St. Edmunds, with a vast train of attendants, including minstrels –
though no one thought any the worse of her for that.

However, though princesses were dedicated to the religious life, none
of their brothers took holy orders: they were too valuable in the army
and council to be sacrificed to God.

It is hard to tell in most instances whether any generation of the royal
family was in any modern sense a happy family, but there are blatant
cases of discord on record: the sons of William I made war on each
other; the sons of Henry II made war on their father, abetted by their
mother, Eleanor of Aquitaine; during the reign of Richard II, some of
his uncles, sons of Edward III, were frequently embroiled in the dissen-
sion against the King's government. Most notably of all, of course, there
was the long-drawn-out feud between rival branches of the royal family
in the fifteenth century, the Wars of the Roses.

Nevertheless, from various sources for the reign of King Henry III, it
is possible to build up a picture of a king, his queen and their children together, often in each other's company and enjoying themselves –
although on one day, 19th May 1251, they may have huddled together
in fear, for comfort and reassurance, when a great storm hit the countryside around Windsor:

> . . . *A darkness sprang up very early in the morning* [recorded the
> chronicler Matthew Paris], *and all the world, as it seemed, both in the
> east and the west, and in the south and the north, became black, and thunder
> was heard as if a long way off with flashes going before. And about the first
> hour, the thunder coming nearer, with the lightnings, one stroke more
> dreadful than the rest, and as if the heaven were hurling itself upon the
> earth, transformed with fear the ears and hearts of those hearing it, with its
> sudden crash.*
>
> *Whereupon it fell with that stroke upon the bedchamber of the Queen,
> where she was then abiding with the children and her household, crumbled*

A royal lying-in chamber in
the Middle Ages.

Medieval children at school . . .

and at play.

The fourteen-year-old Richard II, surrounded by the peasant rebels of 1381, watches the murder of Wat Tyler.

Henry V's queen, Catherine of France, relaxes after the birth of her son, the future King Henry VI.

The young Edward, Prince of Wales, takes his place at Court with his parents, Edward IV and Elizabeth Woodville. His own reign would be tragically brief.

RICARDVS · III · ANG · REX ·

'The wicked uncle', Richard III, who ordered the murder of his nephews Edward V and Richard, Duke of York. Or did he?

The mid-sixteenth-century Cobham family at table – one of the
finest family pictures of the period (by Hans Eworth).

Two young Elizabethans: miniatures ascribed to Isaac Oliver, 1590.

The future King Henry VIII, sketched at the age of two or three.

Henry VIII and his daughter Mary (with the royal jester, Will Somers, in the background).

PARVVLE PATRISSA, PATRIÆ VIRTVTIS ET HÆRES
    ESTO, NIHIL MAIVS MAXIMVS ORBIS HABET.
GNATVM VIX POSSVNT COELVM ET NATVRA DEDISSE,
    HVIVS QVEM PATRIS, VICTVS HONORET HONOS,
ÆQVATO TANTVM, TANTI TV FACTA PARENTIS,
    VOTA HOMINVM, VIX QVO PROGREDIANTVR, HABENT
VINCITO, VICISTI. QVOT REGES PRISCVS ADORAT
    ORBIS, NEC TE QVI VINCERE POSSIT, ERIT.

The future King Edward VI as a baby – he was only nine years old when he
succeeded his father, Henry VIII. (Holbein)

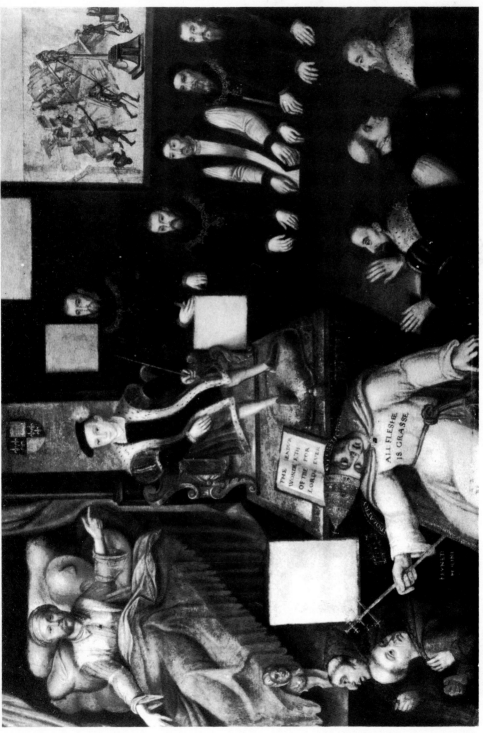

An allegory on the deathbed of Henry VIII. The King, in bed, indicates his heir, who is supported by the leaders of the royalCouncil (including his uncle Edward Seymour and Archbishop Cranmer). At the foot of the bed, the Pope is

*the chimney to powder, cast it to the ground and shook the whole house.
And in the adjoining forest, namely of Windsor, it overthrew or cleaving
tore them asunder, thirty-five oak trees. It destroyed besides certain mills
with their millers, and certain sheepcotes with their shepherds, with some
ploughers and wayfarers. And many damages that we who are describing
these things have not heard of or seen inflicted on mortals.*[8]

Apart from this terrifying experience, the children of Henry III had an
extremely pleasant life. They lived in comfortable and luxurious surroundings unparalleled in the kingdom: not only had the King beauti-
fied his palaces with painting, gilding and tapestries, sealed them from
drafts with expensive glazing and supervised the building of *garde-robes*
(latrines), so that they should not give off noxious fumes into living-
rooms – but he had also installed at Westminster a bath-house, with the
then unique appointment of hot and cold running water, drawn from
tanks filled from cauldrons heated in a furnace. Bathing was never a
favourite medieval occupation, but Henry III's family had fewer excuses
than most for 'going in their dirt'.

Besides the regular entertainments at Court, the royal children had
the pleasure of a family zoo, also an innovation of Henry III, which he
had built up round an elephant – probably the first ever seen in England,
which had been sent as a gift to the King by his wife's brother-in-law the
King of France in 1255. A special house was constructed for the animal
in the Tower of London. The elephant died three years later, but by then
the King had added to his menagerie a lion, a white bear, leopards and
other rarities, which must have been of never-ending fascination to his
children.

It was also Henry III who set the precedent for 'personalized' royal
charity. When, in 1244, his four-year-old daughter Margaret was
betrothed to the future King Alexander III of Scotland, the King cele-
brated the occasion by giving orders to his servants that "upon Friday
next after the Epiphany, they should cause to be fed in the Great Hall at
Windsor, at a good fire, all the poor and needy children that could be
found, and the King's children being weighed and measured, their
weight and measure to be distributed [in silver coins] for their good
estate".[9] In 1259 Henry instructed his almoner to pass out a hundred and
fifty pairs of shoes to the poor on behalf of himself and his queen, and
twenty-one tunics and pairs of shoes as their children's gift.

Such glimpses of royal parents and children may not be by any means
a full picture, but they, and the other slight evidences available, do
reveal a side of medieval life which brings the people of those centuries
closer to today.

The medieval boy-kings

"Woe unto thee, O land, when thy king is a child!": so reads an often-quoted text from the book of Ecclesiastes in the Old Testament. "Woe also to the child," might well be added.

If a child were to succeed to the throne of Great Britain in the modern age, the event would cause scarcely a ripple in the political pond: a Council of Regency would be set up according to instructions designed for such an eventuality, and the child-monarch would undergo no more strain of upbringing than any heir to the throne in normal times — apart from the fact that he or she would have to face coronation at eighteen and then take on the duties of monarchy, though even then government ministers and palace officials would smooth the way.

In the Middle Ages, however, a king wielded far more power than any sovereign of more recent times, and was essential to the smooth-running of government. If a king died while his heir was still a child, there was no constitutional machinery such as would operate today to ensure stability, and the kingdom would be left a prey to factional divisions between rival claimants to power.

In the 'dark ages' of English history, before the unification of the nation in the ninth century, the principle of primogeniture, the inevitable passing of the crown from father to eldest son, was not acceptable. A king was elected by his nobles, and they might choose between any of a number of candidates of the blood royal, though usually there was an obvious choice, especially when the late monarch's eldest son was already a seasoned warrior and statesman. Where a boy-king was chosen, it was usually to serve the interests of a group of lords who would seek to control him and his kingdom.

There was an interesting succession of young kings in the tenth century: the brother, sons and grandsons of Athelstan. The brother, Edmund, came to the throne in the year 940 at the age of eighteen (Athelstan's sons being all under ten at the time of their father's death), but he was killed in a brawl six years later, and the crown reverted to

Athelstan's line in the person of his eldest son, Eadred. When this king was killed in battle in 955, his brother Edwy, aged about fourteen, succeeded him but survived only four years, for the weakness of his government allowed a faction among the nobles to replace him with his younger brother Edgar. That latter survived more than fifteen years, and was, in fact, one of the best of Anglo-Saxon monarchs, strengthening the laws given by his great-grandfather Alfred. However, when Edgar died in 975, his eldest son, Edward, was only about twelve years old, and his accession to the throne was bitterly resented by his stepmother, Elfrida, who had a young son of her own whom she wanted to see king. Thus Elfrida invited Edward to visit her at Corfe in Dorset, and on his arrival set her servants to kill the boy even before he had dismounted from his horse. By this act the ten-year-old Ethelred was brought to reign – though scarcely to rule, for, even after he had reached manhood, his feebleness left his government open to manipulation, his kingdom wide open to the depredations of the Danish invaders, and it is as 'Ethelred the Unready', meaning 'Ethelred lacking council', that this unhappy man has found his place in history.

There was never again such a series of child-kings in English history: from the beginning of the thirteenth to the end of the fifteenth century, only five boys under eighteen were called to reign. In contrast, in Scotland, seven monarchs in succession were minors, in the years 1406 to 1567: all six Jameses and Mary Stuart, who became queen at about one week old. (She was not, however, the youngest European monarch to have reigned: in 1316 King Louis X of France died without a direct heir, but his wife, Clemence of Hungary, was pregnant at the time, and so a decision as to the succession was left until time would show if her child would be a boy – under France's 'Salic law', no female could reign. It was a boy, so from the moment of his birth he was a king, as Jean I. But he lived only five days and was succeeded by his father's brother.)

The series of minorities in Scotland in the fifteenth and early sixteenth centuries was a cause of irremediable damage to the unity of the kingdom. Factions of nobles vied for power, as regents and councillors of the young kings, and the feuds which their rivalries engendered continued even when the need for a regency had passed. Fortunately for Scotland, the neighbouring kingdom of England was too pre-occupied with its own civil war throughout the greater part of this period, to take advantage of the weakness of Scotland, or the British Isles might have been forcibly united by an English conqueror.

The English boy-kings were fortunate in that the rivalries for the regencies were not as bitter and vicious as those in Scotland. The worst that did happen was that their councils and, in the later period, their parliaments, became so accustomed to directing affairs that they were loath to give up all their powers once the king was old enough to take authority. Nevertheless, tragically, three of the boy-kings of England were affected by the malaise of child-rulers: the strains of such an un-natural childhood told on them in character and temperament, and all fell sadly short of contemporary standards of monarchy. Henry III survived his mistakes, but both Richard II and Henry VI were dethroned.

If ever any monarch succeeded to a throne in bad times, it was the nine-year-old Henry III. He was the son of that 'bad' King John who had lost Normandy in war – and the crown jewels in the Lincolnshire Wash, who yielded large-scale concessions to his barons and suffered a French invasion of his kingdom: John died while the French were marching north from the Channel coast. In fact, the accession of a child-king had an advantageous effect in this case, for the nobles who had formerly joined with the French against John, now remembered their natural allegiance and within a short time an almost united nobility forced the French to withdraw.

Henry III was crowned king ten days after his father's death, but in the most unusual circumstances: not in the traditional place, Westminster Abbey, but at Gloucester Cathedral (he had been sent west some time before, for fear of capture by the French); not by the Archbishop of Canterbury but by the Bishop of Winchester – the Primate was in Rome dealing with his own deposition by the Pope; and not with the royal crown, still lying on the bed of the Wash, but with a gold 'throat-collar' from his mother's jewel-case. Nevertheless, it was not a wholly inauspicious occasion: the barons present were overcome with emotion at the sight of the helpless child they were sworn to serve. Rough warriors that they were, they wept sentimentally. Old William Marshall, doyen of the barons, reluctantly but loyally allowed himself to be prevailed upon to take up the regency. He, and his successors over the next few years, proved themselves worthy of the trust.

A good mother might have eased the personal difficulties of a child-king, but Henry's mother, Isabelle of Angoulême, deserted her son before he had been on the throne a year, returning to her native part of France to marry the fiancé from whom King John had stolen her some sixteen years earlier. That her own daughter had since been betrothed to this man, Hugh le Brun, Count of la Marche, did not deter her: that engagement was repudiated and Isabelle married Hugh. She attempted to justify her act by informing her son that she had done so to keep the Count loyal to his English overlord, but subsequent events proved that Hugh was never to be wholly trustworthy.

Thus the boy was left largely to the care of priests, his tutors – he seems to have chafed under their rule. But he had not long to wait before his introduction to his career: when he was twelve he was crowned once more – this time at Westminster with full panoply, and soon after his sixteenth birthday he was given the Great Seal – though with some restrictions on his use of this the most authoritative impress on royal orders in the Middle Ages. At nineteen, in January 1227, Henry declared himself 'of age' and took up full power.

The years of waiting and observing had given Henry III a character full of contradictions: he could be secretive yet sometimes over-expansive; he sought affection but could often turn on his friends in blazing anger; he was wary of bestowing trust, but, where he did, he was frequently gullible; he was extremely intelligent and perceptive but remarkably poor in judgement. His career as collector and connoisseur proved his good taste in art, but that as king revealed his poor appreciation of men's characters.

As a contrast to his own 'deprived' childhood, the family life which Henry created with his consort, Eleanor of Provence (whom he married when he was nearly thirty, she about fourteen), was idyllic – apart from some natural friction with his eldest son, the future Edward I (a far wiser man than his father), who overstepped the powers the King had given him and was even rumoured at one point to be contemplating total usurpation of Henry's throne. However, in the wars which Henry III fought against his barony, Edward proved a loyal son.

The reign of Henry III was certainly not the total disaster which that of his grandson Edward II was to prove. This young man reacted strongly against the righteousness and severity of Edward I and from his teens showed himself prone to the political vagaries into which his homosexuality led him. As king, after 1307, Edward alienated his peers by his reliance on and generosity to his favourites, Gaveston and Despencer, and so humiliated his queen, Isabelle of France, that after nearly twenty years of marriage she not only deserted her husband but instigated an uprising designed to overthrow him.

The first sign of Isabelle's disaffection was her refusal to send home to England her son Edward, aged fifteen, whom she had chaperoned in France in 1325 while he was paying homage there to her brother the French king for England's estates across the Channel. King Edward wrote to Isabelle in the strongest terms, demanding her return home with her son, and when that failed, he wrote to the boy himself – though he must have been aware that the Prince had no power of independent action:

Very dear son [wrote the King, on the 2nd December 1325],

> *As you are young and of tender age, we remind you of that which we charged and commanded you at your departure from Dover, and you answered then, as we know with good will, "that you would not trespass or disobey any of our injunctions in any point for anyone". And since that your homage has been received by our dearest brother the King of France, your uncle, be pleased to take your leave of him and return to us with all speed in company with your mother, if so be that she will come quickly; and if she will not come, then come you without further delay, for we have great desire to see you and to speak with you — therefore stay not for your mother, nor for anyone else, on our blessing.*[1]

In the weeks that followed, while Isabelle and Prince Edward made no move towards home, fresh information warned the King that his wife was consorting with his known enemies, notably one Roger Mortimer, once a rebel against royal authority in the Welsh marches, who was now reputed to be the Queen's lover. Isabelle was still professing duty to her husband, even though she disobeyed his commands, but at the same time was working with English exiles in France, and through them with their confederates among dissidents in England. The King's letters to his son grew more urgent:

> *Edward, fair son* [he wrote in June 1326], *You are of tender age: take our commandments tenderly to heart and so rule your conduct with humility as you would escape our reproach, our grief and indignation, and advance your own interest and honour. Believe no counsel that is contrary to the will of your father. . . . Understand certainly, that if you now act contrary to our counsel, and continue in wilful disobedience, you will feel it all the days of your life, and all other sons will take example to be disobedient to their lords and fathers.*[2]

However, the most Edward II could do was to send copies of his letters (to Isabelle and his son) on to the Pope, who was persuaded to threaten the French king with excommunication if he did not send his sister and nephew home. Isabelle left France, but she did not immediately cross the Channel: with her son, Mortimer and other confederates, she travelled to the Netherlands, where she had found an ally in Count William of Hainault. It was not until the end of September that the Queen and her son landed at Harwich, and now they had an army behind them. Her propaganda of recent months had been so successful that hundreds of men flocked to join her, seeing in Isabelle the innocent victim of a deviant husband who was at the same time a most unpopular monarch.

By the end of the year, the Queen and her partisans had occupied key-points in southern England, captured and executed Despencer, the royal favourite, and taken the King into custody. A writ was sent out, in the King's name, for the meeting of a new parliament early in the new year, and here, after exposition of Edward II's shortcomings, he was deposed with some semblance of legality, and the young Edward hailed as his successor.

To his credit, the sixteen-year-old boy refused to accept the kingdom without an assurance by his father that this was his will. The two Edwards were not allowed to meet, but the elder was induced to yield up the regalia in token to his son that he had abdicated voluntarily. He may have been swayed by the feasible argument that, if he did not, Mortimer would be put on the throne instead of his son.

The boy was proclaimed King Edward III on the 20th January 1327; he was crowned on the 1st February.

The formal establishment of a council of regency, under the new King's uncle Henry of Lancaster, was by no means detrimental to the over-all control of Mortimer and Isabelle, for it was packed with their supporters. But Mortimer was never popular in England – his powers and his acquisition of money from the Crown reeked too much of those formerly attributed to Edward II's favourites, and he was loathed by the young King, who saw his mother and her lover as instigators of the murder of his father, that spring. Whatever sympathy Edward III had had for his mother's past sufferings was surely wiped away then. Nor could he approve Mortimer's rule in his name: when Mortimer's army was put to flight by the Scots in a border campaign in the summer of 1327, he and Isabelle were hard put to persuade Edward to submit to the humiliating peace which they were forced to conclude with the Scots.

Still, the Queen and Mortimer retained their control of government and policy for three years more. It was only in 1330 that Henry of Lancaster would suffer them no more and won Edward III's agreement to ridding themselves of Mortimer.

The King (now aged eighteen) staged his *coup* at Nottingham in October 1330, during a session of the Council there. Suspecting that some plot was afoot even before his enemies showed their hand, Mortimer barricaded himself into the castle with the Queen, but Edward's friends found a secret way in and joined up with him to force their way into Mortimer's chamber. He was taken prisoner and (despite Isabelle's entreaties to her son to have pity on him) taken to London, where he was put to death as a traitor. The King's mother was spared her share in the blame, and in fact was allowed to live out the rest of her life in peace and comfort.

If Edward III went through life scarred by his youthful experiences, there is no evidence for the fact. For forty-odd years he was a mighty king, capable of waging successful warfare abroad and of controlling his own subjects. Only in his late fifties (a good age in those times) did he suffer a physical and mental deterioration which marred his otherwise successful reign.

Edward III was succeeded, in 1377, by the third minor-king of post-Conquest England. This was his grandson Richard II, son of Edward, 'the Black Prince', who had died before his father.

Richard was the Black Prince's second son. The first had died, aged five, in 1370 – there is evidence that he was mentally retarded. Not so Richard, a bright if frail boy who was nine years old when his father died, ten when his grandfather's death brought him to the throne.

Richard's accession was well received by his subjects. "It was a day of gladness," wrote a contemporary chronicler, "the long-awaited day of the renewal of peace and of the laws of the land, long exiled by the weakness of an aged king. . . ."[3] The King's eldest uncle, John of Gaunt, Duke of Lancaster, did his best to foster such a spirit in the first days of Richard's reign. He staged a magnificent coronation, on the 16th July 1377, in which the boy comported himself well.

If later accounts are to be believed, however, there were two incidents during the day which were seen as ill-omens for Richard's future. First, one of his shoes slipped off – no ordinary shoe but one of those 'blessed' in the coronation ritual: it was never found. Then, tiring of the weight of the crown which he had worn throughout the ceremony and the banquet, the King took it off his head. Perhaps ashamed of his weakness, he offered it to his cousin Henry of Lancaster to test its weight. Two decades later, there were men who would recall these facts and believe them to be portents of the ease with which Richard lost his kingdom – and lost it to his cousin Henry.

Under the Will of the Black Prince, the boy had been put in the care of his mother, Joan of Kent, a former belle of Edward III's Court who was a widow with grown-up sons when she married the Prince. At a time when members of the royal family were treated with scant respect by contemporary chroniclers, Joan was always spoken of with admiration, even affection. Certainly, she devoted herself to her son's welfare and personally supervised his upbringing. His formal education was entrusted to former servants of the Black Prince, of whom the most important proved Simon Burley. This brave knight and able tutor was a formative influence on the boy's development and, perhaps even more than John of Gaunt, provided the father-figure of his adolescence – in later years, Richard would abase himself, even put his throne at risk, to attempt to save Burley's life when he was under attack by his political enemies.

Richard grew up under the shadow of his late father's fame, and under that of his half-brothers' prowess in knightly skills: himself naturally sedentary, neither fond of nor excelling in physical activities, he suffered badly in comparison. It has been well argued that the boy grew up with an 'inferiority complex' which ill accorded with his sense of superiority by reason of his unique rank. Certainly, he showed the 'classic' over-compensating arrogance in adult life.

There was no formal regency on Richard's behalf, only a 'continual council' of twelve magnates appointed annually to administer the kingdom. None of the three surviving sons of Edward III had a place in the council, though the eldest of them, the Duke of Lancaster, was repre-sented there by his friends and had, in fact, considerable influence on government. The system had been devised to prevent any one man from taking over-all power – in that it succeeded, but succeeded so well that no real element of leadership, no effective policy line, could emerge. The council's main success was in its ability to persuade Parliament to award large grants of taxes, ostensibly to keep England in war-readiness. During the first four years of Richard II's reign, the people of England were bled dry by the repeated 'poll-taxes' imposed upon them, and by the year 1381 there was open discontent.

The unease among the peasants had its origins, to a great extent, in the terrifying episode of the 'Black Death', the plague which had struck England in 1348 carrying off an estimated twenty per cent of the popula-tion. For some time past the old system of serfdom (by which a peasant owed his lord labour on the manor farm in return for a smallholding of land) had been breaking down, and wage-labour had become more widespread: now, with fewer men to do the work, peasants began to de-mand higher wages and forced landowners to pay them. In 1351 Parlia-ment attempted to control the situation by imposing wage-restraint, but prices kept rising, and in many parts of the country peasants and their families were living below subsistence level. Add to this the poll-taxes, and it is easy to see why peasants rebelled in 1381.

The revolt began in East Anglia: there was rioting and arson, looting of the local clergy and gentry's property, even murder. Kent heard the news and followed suit: men who had been imprisoned for their wage-demands were released by the rebels. Soon, peasants from all over south-eastern England (there were only minor outbreaks of revolt elsewhere) were marching on London, intent on putting their grievances to the King and forcing redress.

The Duke of Lancaster was not in the capital (he was away fighting the Scots), and there was no one to take command of the resistance to the rampaging peasants as they approached. King Richard was brought from Windsor to the safety of the Tower, where he met with his council and received the peasants' request to present their petitions. Some sixty thousand countrymen were encamped on Blackheath, south of the river, orderly at first but increasingly inflamed by the oratory of their leader, the Essex man Wat Tyler, and by the sermons of his colleague, the priest John Ball.

Without an army to put down the revolt by force, there was no other recourse than to send the fourteen-year-old King to confront the rebels, who had lost patience in waiting some days to see him and were rioting once more. The mob destroyed John of Gaunt's palace, the Savoy, in the Strand, and the Priory of St. John at Clerkenwell – the Master of the Order happened also to be the Treasurer of England. Even as the King made his way to the *rendezvous* at Mile End, the Tower was attacked: the Archbishop of Canterbury (who combined his office with that of Lord Chancellor) was seized and murdered.

"My friends, I am your king and your lord," Richard called to the great crowd which surrounded him at Mile End. "What do you want? And what do you wish to say?'

"We want you to set us free for ever, us and our descendants and our lands, and to grant that we should never again be called serfs, nor held in bondage," came the cry from the peasants.[4]

Not only did the King give his promise to put an end to serfdom (which he must have known he and his government would never honour) but he offered a free pardon to the rebels. However, if he expected this to disperse the peasants to their homes, he was to be disappointed. The next morning the rioting continued, and he was forced to grant another interview, this to be at Smithfield.

Wat Tyler was the spokesman that day – a bad choice, for he treated Richard in a manner exactly calculated to rouse his anger: he addressed him with familiarity when all his life the boy had received only the most humble reverence.

"Brother, be of good comfort and joyful," said Wat, "for you shall have, in the fortnight that is to come, praise from the commons even more than you have yet had, and we shall be good companions."[5]

Richard kept his temper and tried to soothe Wat Tyler, though he remained firm in his demand that the peasants should leave London. But the King's companions could not stomach the man's insolence. One of them called Tyler a robber and thief, and the rebel leader made to stab him with his dagger. William Walworth, the Lord Mayor of London, tried to intervene and was stabbed in the stomach – though, as he was wearing armour concealed under his robes, he was not seriously hurt. But that was the signal for the King's men to fall on Tyler, mortally wounding him. However, even as he was dying, he rode back to his friends calling for revenge.

It was the worst moment of the day. Many of the peasants were archers, experienced in the wars with France, and they now drew their bows on the King. If Richard's friends had attempted to resist, all would have been killed. But before they could do so, the King himself rode forward, shouting, "Gentlemen, what do you want? You have no other captain but me. I am your king. Keep the peace."[6] Suddenly the mob went quiet. They allowed Richard to lead them away, out onto Clerkenwell Fields. There the London militia surrounded them, herding the peasants into pens like their own sheep.

The revolt in London was over, though there was rioting still in East Anglia. In the capital and the counties courts were set up to try the rebels – the King's former promise of pardon was set aside in the case of the ring-leaders, though his justices were moderate in their treatment of the mass of the peasants. Needless to say, the Council revoked the charters of promises which had first been awarded to the rebels. Nevertheless, though the peasants' revolt had failed, the decline of serfdom continued – not from principle, but from the fact that hired labour proved more profitable than serfdom.

King Richard II, for all his broken promises, had come well out of the incident. He had proved beyond doubt his personal courage, as though he had faced an enemy army in battle.

It was the one great moment of his life. In the years that followed, he gradually gained power until, in May 1389, at twenty-two, he declared himself of age, to rule without restraint; but even before that date he had incurred the distrust of lords and commons by his reliance on a small circle of courtiers, to the disparagement of his 'natural' counsellors the great magnates: in 1388 the nobles had gained the upper hand, adamant in imposing humiliating restraints on the King's power, under the pretence of striking at his 'unworthy' advisers. After May 1389, Richard governed England ostensibly with the support of his lords, but in fact taking on the powers of a despot, using a complaisant Parliament to codify his 'rights'.

The attack on the royal tyrant came in 1399, and from within the royal family. Henry of Lancaster (son of the late John of Gaunt) had been stripped of his inheritance by Richard, and now swept through England at the head of an army with the avowed intention of regaining his dukedom. But once he had the King in his power, he forced him to abdicate in his, Henry's favour: like his grandfather Edward II, having abdicated, Richard was murdered.

Henry IV, as Lancaster became, could not pretend that he was

Richard's natural heir. Though the former King was childless, his cousin the Earl of March had a better claim to the throne than Henry – but March was a child, Henry a strong man with strong ambitions. Though there were many to say that the Lancastrian line had no right to the throne, Henry IV, and his son Henry V, reigned without any real opposition, and it was only the weakness of the person and rule of Henry VI which gave rise to the claim of Richard, Duke of York (March's eventual heir) that he, rather than the Lancastrian Henry VI, should be king.

Henry VI was only nine months old when he succeeded his father, Henry V, on the English throne in 1422; he was only eleven months old when the death of his French grandfather gave him the throne of France (under the terms imposed by Henry V's conquest of France some years earlier).

Like Richard II, Henry VI had uncles fit to rule in his place, the Dukes of Bedford and Gloucester, and they became his 'protectors', ruling in France and England respectively with the aid of Councils.

John of Bedford might have been a great ruler, for he was an able and wise man, but he had insufficient support from England, in financial resources and manpower, to hold in check the rising tide of French nationalism which, by 1453, had accomplished the overthrow of English rule across the Channel.

Humphrey of Gloucester was less able, more ambitious. He chafed at the restraints imposed on his powers by the Council, in law and in fact the real ruler of England, and he was always in contention with his cousin Henry Beaufort, Bishop of Winchester, for leadership of the Council.

The child-king's mother played no part in the power-struggle and apparently had little influence on her son's upbringing. She was the French Princess Catherine, who had been given to Henry V as his bride in token of French submission to English rule. Married some two years before her husband's death, she was still only twenty years old when arrangements were being made for her son's minority, and no one thought to give her any formal place in them. Catherine made a pretty picture with her infant when he was enthroned at the opening of the first Parliament of his reign, and she was seen with Henry several times on state occasions over the next few years, but soon, at some date unrecorded, she retired from public life, secretly marrying a young Welshman, Owen Tudor, and bearing him three sons. That she could do so and go several years without detection, must mean that the Queen lived sufficiently far from Westminster, where Henry was kept, to escape notice: mention of her in records and chronicles is slight over these years. Catherine died in 1437.

Though naturally the child King Henry was kept in palace nurseries for most of the time, he was brought out occasionally to give a focal point to ceremony, and, when he was seven years old, in November 1429, he was deemed old enough to behave fittingly in a coronation. He may also have been allowed to eat some of the delicacies prepared for the coronation banquet, which sound as if they had been designed especially to please a child's sweet-tooth: there was a boar's head ornamented with golden castles, a custard with the figure of a leopard sitting on it, holding a *fleur-de-lis*, and a 'subtlety' (a sugar-sculpture) depicting St. Edward and St. Louis in armour, holding between them a child-figure meant to be Henry VI himself; there was a jelly too, inscribed with the words of the prayer *Te Deum Laudamus*, a pork pie seasoned with sugar and cheese, also ornamented with leopards, and, as a *pièce de résistance*, a final subtlety of the Madonna and Child receiving Henry VI from the hands of St. George and St. Denis. Perhaps French cooks attempted to rival these feats when, two years later, Henry was crowned again in France.

Under the Will of Henry V, confirmed by Council and Parliament, the child was first consigned to the care of his kinsman (his great-half-uncle) Thomas Beaufort, Duke of Exeter, but, elderly and childless as the Duke was, he can have made little personal impression on his charge, who was only five years old when he died. More important to Henry's development was Exeter's successor, Richard Beauchamp, Earl of Warwick, who took his duties seriously and, under instruction from the Council on Henry's behalf, was to "teach us nurture [manners], literature and languages, and to chastise us from time to time according to his discretion".[7] Henry grew up with a reputation for sanctity, but Warwick must have found some faults in him for the boy was beaten so often that he began to complain. The Earl panicked then, fearing the King's revenge in after-years, and found it wise to obtain from the Council a document which authorized him, in Henry's name, "from time to time reasonably [to] chastise us, as the case may require, without being held accountable or molested for the same at any future time".[8] In the event, when the boy came of age (at fifteen), he took no revenge on Warwick (who was appointed Lieutenant of Normandy and died two years later).

More to the taste of Henry VI than the stalwart soldier Earl must have been his tutor John Somerset, who combined his teaching duties with those of royal physician. Somerset was a Cambridge man, and it may well have been he who prompted the King's patronage of the university. Henry also learned to be faithful in prayer and worship, to give generously to charity and to live, amid a notoriously licentious Court, as chastely as in a monastery. At a time when the disembowelling and burning of criminals was treated as a welcome public spectacle, the King was notably squeamish.

Henry came of age, without any formal ceremony to mark the occasion, in 1436, and seems to have done his best to rule, though he was not strong enough to stand above or to quell the power-struggle still dividing his Council. He was unfortunate, if not wholly unwise, in allying himself with the group which pressed for an end to war in France – and, in a truce of 1444, took a French bride, Margaret of Anjou. She was only sixteen years old (he was in his early twenties), but already Margaret was more worldly-wise than her husband, and where he was quiet and timid, she was energetic, extrovert and strong-willed. No one doubted, when the Queen failed to produce a son through eight years of marriage, that it was the King's fault, not hers; and when Margaret did give birth to a son, in October 1453, there were many to doubt royal paternity.

By then, only months after the final ignominious peace with France, after the impeachment of Henry's chief minister the Duke of Suffolk and the three-day occupation of London by another peasant horde, Henry VI had suffered a mental collapse. He had inherited the strain of madness which had shown, just as suddenly, in his French grandfather, breaking him under strain. For some years past, men had been calling him 'childish' – though some said his daze was a sign of sanctity; now he was known to be mad.

Until the birth of Henry's son, his heir had been his cousin Richard, Duke of York (representative of that senior line of Edward III's descendants who had a better theoretical claim to the throne than the House of Lancaster). During the months of the King's breakdown (July to December 1453), York ruled as Lord Protector, and though he formally recognized the baby Prince Edward as Henry's new heir, the fiercely maternal Margaret was sure that, in the event of the King's death, York would claim the throne for himself. She allied with the Duke of Somerset to undermine York's authority in Council, and so harried him that in May 1453 he turned on her, took arms and forced his way back to power. However, it was not until 1460 that he showed his real hand, demanding recognition as rightful heir to the throne.

For some eleven years the Red Rose of Lancaster and the White Rose of York did battle for the crown – but the royal forces were never more than nominally led by Henry VI. He sank into a stupor and suffered himself to be led about the country by his wife and her supporters, to be taken prisoner, then released and restored, then, a prisoner once more, to be murdered in the Tower of London, in May 1471.

Henry VI lived only a few days longer than his seventeen-year-old son Edward, who was killed in (or soon after) the Battle of Tewkesbury, the final Lancastrian defeat, of the 4th May. The Prince had spent almost the whole of his life in war-camps, and it was no wonder that an Italian ambassador who saw him when he was thirteen could only remark that "this boy . . . already talks of nothing but of cutting off heads or making war", while, probably encouraged by his mother, he behaved "as if he had everything in his hands, or was the god of battles, or was seated on the throne".⁹ Perhaps England had a happy escape when Edward of Lancaster died before he could be brought to reign.

The man who did succeed Henry VI was not Richard of York – he had been killed at the Battle of Wakefield in 1461, but Richard's son Edward. As King Edward IV, he stabilized England and gave her some measure of prosperity after the long years of civil war. But he died in 1483 and, once again, the work of a strong king was undone by his leaving a minor to succeed him.

When Edward IV died, on the 9th April 1483, his heir (and namesake) was only twelve years old. The King's death was unexpected: he had always been a strong man, but now, after a sudden seizure (possibly apoplexy or a heart-attack), he died within the week. There was no time to summon his heir from Ludlow, the Prince's residence on the border of Wales, and the boy heard the news of his accession five full days after Edward IV's death.

It took even longer for the news to arrive at Middleham Castle in Yorkshire, the home of the late King's only surviving brother, Richard, Duke of Gloucester. He was not informed officially but by a friend at Court, the Marquess of Hastings, who told him that he had been nominated Regent by Edward IV; this may or may not have been so – there is no concrete evidence, but it would have been an eminently reasonable decision. The alternative was to have the King's brothers-in-law, the Woodvilles, exercise control over their nephew's person and kingdom – though Edward IV, for all that he had allowed them great powers in his Court and government, must have been aware of their unpopularity and of the strength of their rivals. The Woodvilles knew their weakness: from the outset they urgently laid plans to take control; at a meeting of a hastily (but scarcely legally) gathered Council, they admitted Richard of Gloucester's title as Protector but at the same time suggested that it was intended to give him only leadership of a regency council, not sole authority. Even before the King was summoned to his capital, there was already a deep division in the Council as to who should rule on the boy's behalf.

Nevertheless, Richard of Gloucester was politely invited to meet Edward V when he, with his Ludlow guardian, Anthony Woodville,

Earl Rivers, should arrive at Northamptom *en route* for London. Richard reached the town on the afternoon of the 29th April, and it was early evening before Rivers joined him – only to announce that Edward had bypassed the town to spend the night at Stony Stratford. The two men, with Richard's friend the Duke of Buckingham, dined together at an inn that night in apparent amity, but no sooner had the Earl retired than the two Dukes began to lay their plans. When Rivers awoke the next morning, he found the inn surrounded: Gloucester and Buckingham made him a prisoner before riding forward to Stony Stratford, where they took possession of the King, respectfully but very firmly. When the news reached London, the Woodvilles' party collapsed. The Queen, her brother the Bishop of Salisbury, her son by her first marriage the Marquess of Dorset and her younger children by Edward IV, sought sanctuary at Westminster.

Whether Duke Richard had planned from the outset to usurp the crown, or whether it was an idea which came to him, or was suggested to him, only in the weeks after his arrival in London with Edward, must remain a mystery. Certainly, he proceeded circumspectly with arrangements for his nephew's coronation and the opening of Parliament, but he now struck not only at the Woodvilles but also at his former ally the Marquess of Hastings, who was summarily executed, ostensibly on suspicion of plotting against the Protector – though perhaps it was for refusing to help Richard to the crown. Then the Duke extracted Edward V's younger (and only) brother, his heir, Richard, Duke of York, from the Westminster sanctuary and sent him to join the King in the Tower.

Suddenly, out of the blue, on the 22nd June the citizens of London, who crowded to hear open-air sermons at key points in the City, found preachers declaring that the boy-King, his brother and sisters were all illegitimate, that Edward V was not in fact the legal successor to Edward IV. (The argument for this case which Richard of Gloucester's associates formulated, attempted to show that his late brother had been 'contracted' to one Lady Eleanor Butler years before he married Elizabeth Woodville, thereby invalidating the later marriage and making his children bastards.) Nor were the next heirs to the throne, the children of Richard's other brother, George, Duke of Clarence, eligible for the crown, for their father had forfeited his and their rights when he had been attainted of treason by Edward IV. These were the arguments which were used, on the 25th June, to win over the Lords and Commons in Parliament: they were effective, – Richard was hailed as king. On the 6th July he was crowned.

Over the next few weeks Edward V and his brother Richard were seen playing in the gardens of the Tower. Then, no more. There were rumours as to their fate, but it was not until nearly twenty years later that the confession was published of their supposed murderer, Sir James Tyrell, confirming that he had been ordered by Richard III to kill the boys, which he had done by smothering them in their bed. But by then both Tyrell and Richard III were themselves dead, unable to contradict it.

For centuries historians have argued for and against Richard III's having caused the death of his nephews. His supporters claim that the King was a man of integrity and piety, that, with the boys in his custody, he had no reason to kill them, that he was slandered by enemies who had every reason to defame his memory. Richard's detractors say that he had no choice *but* to kill them, just as Henry IV and Edward IV had had to order the deaths of the kings whose thrones they had usurped.

A case has been made out for the survival of the 'Princes in the Tower' through the reign of Richard III and into that of Henry VII (who, as the last Lancastrian claimant to the throne, ousted Richard by his victory at the Battle of Bosworth, in August 1485, in which the last Yorkist king died). Certainly, if Henry did find the princes alive when he took the throne, he would have every reason to kill them, to prevent their becoming a rallying-point for the Yorkists (in 1486 he married their eldest sister, Elizabeth of York, to prevent her taking their place as Yorkist figure-head). But then, there is no proof that Henry did find the boys alive.

The only certain thing that can be said is that, after the late summer of 1483, Edward V and his brother Richard, Duke of York, were never seen again.

The tragedy of these boys is one of the darkest spots in the history of the royal family of England. For decades past, rival claimants to the throne, of the Houses of York and Lancaster, had made war on each other, killed each other, but these were men fighting as much from ambition as from conviction of their rights, risking their lives advisedly. The Princes in the Tower were innocent of any ambition, any crime, feared and killed not for what they did but for who they were. In terms of political expediency, the reasons for their murder – whoever ordered it – are easy to understand, but even in their own day the crime was looked upon with horror.

Yet, supposedly more 'civilized' times have not been free of infanticide: in 1794 the son of the dethroned King Louis XVI of France disappeared in circumstances similar to those of the Princes in the Tower; in 1918 the four daughters and thirteen-year-old son of Tsar Nicholas II of Russia were murdered with their parents as a supposed threat to the Russian Revolution.

In today's climate of international terrorism, many children have been taken hostage in the cause of 'political expediency'. Royal children – in Britain as well as in the violent Middle East – are prime targets for threats of all sorts, as vulnerable to modern criminals and terrorists as any medieval prince ever was to the cruel ambition of usurper.

The Tudor Age
1485–1603

"*What, hast smutched thy nose?*"

"The cause of the world being so evil of living as it is, is for lack of virtue and godly upbringing of youth": so wrote a moralist of the Tudor age.[1] It had been said before; it is said today; doubtless it will be said in centuries to come.

The Tudor parent had less excuse than his forebears for bringing up children badly. Throughout the century books on child-rearing poured from the presses in vast numbers, cheap enough for any pocket, offering advice on everything from breast-feeding to burying (infant mortality was still cruelly high). The great number of these books, and their often conflicting advice, makes one presume that there must have been a running debate throughout the sixteenth century on the proper way to bring up a child, though there was universal agreement on the need for proper respect for parental authority and a general consensus on strict discipline.

One book even proposed that a child should beg for chastisement for its faults, saying at the end of each day:

If I lie, backbite or steal,
If I curse, scorn, mock or swear,
If I chide, fight, strive or threat,
Then am I worthy to be beat.
Good master or mistress mine,
If any of these nine
I trespass to your knowing,
With a new rod and a fine
Early, naked, before I dine,
Amend me with a scourging.[2]

There was, however, one camp firmly opposed to beating a child into learning his books. Two schoolmasters especially, Roger Ascham and Richard Mulcaster, fervently advocated the carrot rather than the stick, advising teachers to make lessons pleasant, and to take the tension out of them.

In the Middle Ages, learning had been rather sneered at by the aristocracy as fit only for clerks: now, under the influence of the Italian Renaissance, the gentry and nobility vied for the best tutors for their
children, and boys were put to years of study in Greek, Latin (and even
Hebrew), philosophy, mathematics, modern languages and history. In
many noble households, girls too took advantage of the services of resi-
dent tutor or learned chaplain, studying alongside their brothers and
often rivalling them for the laurels.

The country gentry did not aspire to such refinements for their daughters, but even so, they had a sound education from their governesses.
Grace, daughter of Sir Henry Sherrington of Laycock Abbey in Wilt-
shire, was a child in the 1560s, taught by a poor relation who took her
duties seriously: the governess could not bear to see the girl "idly dis-
posed", and, as Grace later recorded,

> *would set me to cipher with my pen, and to cast up and prove great sums and
> accounts, and sometimes set me to write a supposed letter to this or that body
> concerning such and such things, and other times let me read in Dr Turner's
> herbal . . . and other times set me to sing psalms and other times set me to
> some curious work, for she was an excellent workwoman in all kinds of
> needlework. . . .*[3]

Most girls never progressed much further than basic literacy, with
some small attainment in French and a wider knowledge of music
(foreigners were amazed that many English families could perform so
well together on a variety of instruments and sing difficult part-songs at
sight), but then female education was not then, as in Victorian days,
designed to 'catch' a husband by showy accomplishments but to fit
women for a lifetime in household management, which Tudor women
raised to an art: a good housewife would know how to brew and bake,
distill and preserve, to spin and weave, sew and embroider, and how to
make her own medicines and cosmetics, and would keep her own books
on those subjects, for reference.

Boys of the gentry class, and the sons of the new Protestant clergy,
merchants', tradesmen's and even artisans' sons were taking full advantage of the many grammar schools which fed the universities and the Inns
of Court – and here too the emphasis was on ancient literature, though
many of the schoolboys would have had little use for it in a career in
trade and commerce. There was a huge market for text-books: Thomas
Lilly's famous Latin grammar was a best-seller, but there were many
others, along with reading primers in modern languages, using
everyday situations in play-form to give a useful vocabulary learned by

the child at home,

Who with his busy mother now and then
May prattle of each point in phrases mild,
The witty boys of books, of sport, of play,
The pretty lasses of their work all day.[4]

In Tudor towns, Shakespeare's schoolboy with his "shining morning face, creeping like snail unwillingly to school" must have been a familiar sight. (Shakespeare's father was a glove-maker and -seller of Stratford-on-Avon, a small town in Warwickshire; it is only tradition that the future playwright attended Stratford's grammar school, but whatever teaching he had, he made the most of it: he could draw on a wide range of ancient and recent history and on foreign literature for the stories from which he made his plays.)

Further down the social scale, where there was no money to spare to keep a boy in grammar school for years, there were 'petty schools', teaching only basic literacy – though many infant graduates did go on to at least some years in the grammar schools.

The children for whom there was no teaching were those of the very poor and of the vagrants who teemed through the countryside and in the town slums. Here the infant mortality rate was highest, both at birth and in the first few years of life: often, parishes were put to the expense of burying the corpses of children found lying on their roads. Philanthropists established 'foundling hospitals' for abandoned and destitute children – sadly, these institutions could not accommodate all the waifs passed on by local authorities. In 1597 an Act for the Relief of the Poor put the responsibility for orphans and deserted children on parish and borough, whose officers had to find them places as apprentices. Overwhelmed by the flood of children, many authorities paid 'masters' to take them in, just to be rid of them, caring nothing that such children were frequently abused, often starved, rarely put to any trade to provide for their future.

The contrast between the miseries of these children and the comforts of the upper classes was great, not only in material terms but in the care and affection they received. While foundlings and waifs were scarred, physically and mentally, by negligence and cruelty, children with homes and families were more cherished than ever before. They were kept at home, taught at home or at a local grammar school – or, as boarding-school boys, came home for long holidays, and took a greater part in family life. Always allowing for due respect, there was greater familiarity between children and their parents. Shakespeare, who could always catch the speech and manners of his time, has several memorable child-parts, the best of them that of Mamillius, a six-year-old boy in *The Winter's Tale*. His father teases him:

> *. . . What, hast smutched thy nose?*
> *(They say it is a copy out of mine.) Come, Captain,*
> *We must be neat; not neat, but cleanly, Captain.*

And the boy himself is allowed to be saucy to one of his mother's ladies who offers to play with him:

> *. . . I'll none of you. . . .*
> *You'll kiss me hard and speak to me as if*
> *I were a baby still.*

Surviving letters from the Tudor age witness to the increased interest in and concern for children: husbands and wives correspond on their children's health and upbringing; fathers away from home write postscripts to their small sons and daughters; children pen letters of family news, only 'topped and tailed' by conventional polite formulae. And, significantly, from this period, children begin to figure in the family portraits commissioned by nobility and gentry, and not only in the formal sort but in 'conversation-pieces' too: there is one showing children seated round a dinner-table with their parents, another of a whole family at leisure, playing cards and chess.

There is one delightful portrait of Lady Arbella Stuart, aged twenty-three months in 1577. (She was a cousin of Queen Elizabeth I, at one time tipped to succeed her.) The child wears an embroidered dress and, on her curly hair, a jewelled cap, and clasps a tiny doll, fashionably gowned. A Scottish portrait, rather later, shows a small boy in long skirts (which were worn until the ceremony of 'breeching' at the age of five or six), carrying what may be a hockey-stick or primitive golf-club.

In the Tudor age, childhood still had its hazards of health and, for the poor, gross cruelties, physical and mental, but for children in settled homes, life was good, with time to play, a chance to study and sincerely affectionate parents.

Tudor see-saw

Once Henry Tudor had won his crown, he set himself – with characteristic thoroughness – to making sure that he kept it. By the end of the century, some fifteen years after he had defeated and killed Richard III at Bosworth Field, he could rest easy. Yorkist pretenders had been thwarted; the Yorkist nobles had been deprived of their private armies; the country's economy had been strengthened and foreign alliances made.

The Tudor king's marriage to Elizabeth of York, designed to win the loyalty of her family's supporters, was also to ensure that the future heir of England would have both Yorkist and Lancastrian blood, thus ending the long rivalry of the Houses.

This potential peace-maker, Henry and Elizabeth's first son, was born in September 1486 and christened Arthur – underlining the family's Welsh associations and also harking back to the glorious king of ancient legend. Four years later, the Tudor succession was further assured by the birth of another prince, named for his father. Two daughters, Margaret and Mary, grew up with the princes, but two more and another son, Edmund, died in infancy.

The Tudor children were carefully reared, more often at the country palaces, such as Greenwich, Richmond and Eltham, than in the oppressive Tower and Palace of Westminster. They were carefully educated too, under the supervision of their paternal grandmother, Lady Margaret Beaufort, a famed patron of scholars and divines, who had the pick of England's finest masters to teach her grandchildren: their chief tutor was the Poet Laureate, John Skelton.

In the summer of 1499, the most famous European scholar of the age, Desiderius Erasmus of Rotterdam, paid a visit to England, and among the many 'sights' he took in during his stay was that of Eltham Palace. His friend Thomas More (himself a genius of Renaissance learning) took him there to pay his respects to Princes Henry and Edmund and their sisters (Arthur, as Prince of Wales, was in residence at Ludlow on the Welsh marches). More went armed with a manuscript to present to the nine-year-old Henry, but he had neglected to warn Erasmus that a gift would be expected, and the visitor could only give a promise to the Prince to send something on. "I was angry with More," Erasmus recorded, "for not having warned me, especially as the boy [Henry] sent me a little note, while we were at dinner, to challenge something from my pen. I went home and . . . finished the poem within three days."[1] In fact, Erasmus's verses, the 'Prosopopoeia Britanniae', would be a disappointing gift to any modern child, only a daunting exercise in Latin translation, but Prince Henry's Latin was already fluent and his taste in literature mature.

We have for the present dedicated these verses [wrote the scholar in the accompanying letter], *like a gift of playthings, to your childhood, and shall be ready with more abundant offerings when your virtues, growing with your age, shall supply more abundant material for poetry. I would add my exhortation to that end, were it not that you are of your own accord already, as they say, underway with all sails set, and have with you Skelton, that incomparable light and ornament of British letters, who can not only kindle your studies but bring them to a happy conclusion. Farewell, and may good letters be illustrated by your splendour, protected by your authority and fostered by your liberality.*[2]

While the younger children of Henry VII were playing and studying in their palace by the Thames, their elder brother, at Ludlow, was already being introduced to the responsibilities of his position. He had his own Council of State, which conducted the main business of the principality, and he attended their meetings, thus combining a study of practical government with those lessons in political theory which he learned from his tutors. He was also useful to his father in foreign affairs — not by participation in policy-making but by marrying a princess with whose nation Henry VII sought alliance. Arthur was only a baby when his father began negotiations with the most prestigious monarchs in Europe, Ferdinand and Isabella of Spain, for his marriage with their youngest daughter, Catherine. The two children were given each other's portraits and corresponded in elegant Latin, but they met only a few days before their wedding in November 1501.

Catherine was nine months older than her bridegroom, tall and well-made, in notable contrast to Arthur, who was too slim and frail to be 'a picture of health'. In fact, only five months after the wedding, in April 1502, the Prince of Wales succumbed to the 'sweating sickness' (probably a type of influenza) which tore through Ludlow Castle leaving the Spanish princess a widow at sixteen.

The death of his elder brother brought Prince Henry into the limelight. He was now Prince of Wales, heir to the English throne.

It had been rumoured in past years that Henry VII intended his second son to become Archbishop of Canterbury. That office, the chief ecclesiastical appointment in the kingdom, had often in the Middle Ages been combined with high office in government – several archbishops had been chancellors. With Arthur as king, Henry as archbishop, Henry VII's policy of centralizing government would be confirmed. But now that plan could not be fulfilled: with Arthur dead, the younger Prince must take on his responsibilities.

Physically, the younger Henry was robust; mentally he was sharp and alert, quick to absorb the wide variety of lessons which his masters provided: ancient and modern languages, history, geography, mathematics and theology. In childhood he had had a stable home-life, a good grounding for maturity – his brother's death in 1502, and that of his mother the following year, may have affected Henry little emotionally, for neither of them was part of his everyday life; more devastating, probably, was the loss of his elder sister Margaret, his childhood companion, when she went north in 1502 to marry the King of Scotland.

After Arthur's death, young Henry was kept more under his father's eye, more often at Court – where he was not allowed many frivolities but always surrounded by "sober and discreet" old men, scholars and statesmen. Everyone agreed that the boy was a paragon, not only learned and pious but untouched by worldly temptations.

Henry VII had no intention of giving up the Spanish alliance which the marriage of Catherine and Arthur had forged. Only weeks after the Prince's death, he was in correspondence with the Spanish monarchs, requesting their agreement to the betrothal of their daughter to his new heir. In June 1503, the young couple (Henry was twelve, Catherine already eighteen) were promised to each other by their parents' contract, on the understanding that they were to marry when Henry reached the age of fourteen. But that birthday came and went, and there was no wedding; in the interim the Spanish match had lost its attraction for the King of England, in view of a changed international balance of power, and before his heir gained the contractual age, he had the boy repudiate the vows earlier made on his behalf. Nevertheless, the Spanish princess was too useful a pawn to be sent home, and for years Catherine of Aragon remained in England, a 'poor relation' at her father-in-law's Court.

Sentimental biographers of Henry and Catherine have liked to assert that the young people were fond of each other, that Henry had been loath to cast her off. Certainly, his prompt marriage to Catherine in the spring of 1509, only a few weeks after the death of his father and his own accession to the throne (aged seventeen), bears out the theory – but then, also, the new King Henry VIII had a fine appreciation of the potential importance of a Spanish alliance.

All Henry VII's schemes had been successful. His son came to the throne without one protest from the surviving Yorkists and, indeed, with his youth, good looks and high spirits, promised to be one of the most popular monarchs, with an elegant, cultured wife to support him.

Nevertheless, Henry VIII fully appreciated the fact that he was only one generation removed from a bitter dynastic struggle, that there were Plantagenets 'in the wings' who would take advantage of any weakness in the Tudor monarchy to bring England back to its former state of civil war. And, like his father before him, he saw the urgent need of providing an heir to ensure the continuance of the Tudor line.

Catherine of Aragon gave Henry a son in January 1512, but before the lavish celebrations were out of memory, the young Prince, another Henry, died, aged seven weeks. The Queen had already given birth to a still-born child in 1510, and in the years that followed, she suffered one disappointment after another. Of four more royal births, only one child, a daughter, born on the 18th February 1516, survived.

It was later said that, before 1516, Henry VIII had already considered divorcing Catherine, to marry a woman capable of giving him sons, and that only the birth of his daughter Mary prevented this, with his renewed hopes of a healthy male heir. But Henry was always to be disappointed, and the royal divorce was 'on the cards' before the end of the century's ~~teens?~~ tens.

The King was the fondest of parents, proudly displaying his only daughter to courtiers and foreign ambassadors. "This child never cries," he once boasted – not knowing how many tears the Princess would shed over his unkindness in later years.

At the age of two, Mary Tudor was already betrothed. In cloth of gold, with a jewelled cap on her head, the child was formally betrothed to the Dauphin of France, a diamond ring placed on her finger by the French envoy. At four, she entertained her fiancé's ambassadors with strawberries and wine in her apartments at Richmond Palace. But even then, her father had changed his plans; he had met with the Emperor Charles V (Queen Catherine's nephew) and promised Mary to him. Aged six, the Princess stood beside the twenty-two-year-old Emperor in another betrothal ceremony.

However, she was not destined to be empress. Charles was as fickle as Henry, and when a better prize, the heiress to the throne of Portugal, presented herself, he snapped her up. In the years that followed, one suitor after another sued for Mary's hand, but, without a male heir, the

King of England could not put his daughter, potential heiress of England, into the keeping of a foreign power. And with every year that passed without the birth of a Tudor prince, her marriage must be weighed ever more heavily.

Although Queen Catherine could not give Henry VIII a son, another woman did. In 1519, a young maid-of-honour, Elizabeth Blount, gave birth to a royal bastard, yet another Henry. With no shred of a claim to the throne, this child was yet brought up in regal surroundings, trained as if he were a prince and awarded the title of Duke of Richmond. It was even suggested at one time that his father might make him King of Ireland, or – though it is hard to see how even Henry VIII could have condoned such a thing – that he might be married to his half-sister, Princess Mary, and share her throne at the King's death.*

Apart from her probable bewilderment over fiancés, Mary's childhood was largely untroubled. At one time, it had been mooted that she be sent to Spain, to be educated as future consort to the half-Spanish Emperor, but even at the height of Henry VIII's enthusiasm for the match, he would not allow it: her mother, he said, was a fine example of Spanish manners and culture, and was surely the best person to supervise their child's education. It was at this time that the Queen commissioned a fellow-countryman, the scholar Juan Luis Vives (then lecturing in classical literature and law at Oxford University), to draw up a system of education for the Princess.

It was a full and somewhat dry programme: the New Testament and part of the Old were to make up the bulk of the girl's reading-matter, supplemented by approved Greek and Latin texts of the pre-Christian era. Lighter literature was represented by Erasmus's works and the *Utopia* of Henry VIII's friend and later Chancellor, Thomas More. The charming romances of the Middle Ages Vives scorned, as he did most stories without moral or historical content. However, it is hard to see how Mary could have avoided some reading of contemporary or medieval literature, for her curriculum included the study of French, Italian and Spanish, in which formal text-books were still scarce.

From infancy the Princess had been provided with her own establishment, a large staff of servants under her 'lady mistress', Lady Margaret Bryan, which travelled from one country palace to another, with occasional excursions to Richmond and Greenwich when the King and Queen were in residence there.

Royal children still did not figure largely in the annals of the time, but here and there in chronicles, letters and account books, Mary appears. For example, there remains a list of the gifts sent to the Princess at New

* Henry Fitzroy, Duke of Richmond, died in 1536.

Year (a more important occasion than Christmas in the sixteenth century): when she was four years old, dukes and earls added to her already appreciable store of plate, with their gifts of gold cups, silver flagons and so on – but perhaps more to the child's taste was the offering of "a poor woman of Greenwich": a rosemary bush with spangles of gold. That same season, Mary was entertained by a company of child-actors; a year later she had her own 'lord of misrule' to 'make mirth' for her, presiding over morris-dancers and mummers.

Queen Catherine was undoubtedly a fond mother, but her role as consort and her care for her husband did not leave her time for constant supervision of her daughter. However, she had a worthy substitute in one of the last surviving Plantagenets, Margaret of Clarence, Countess of Salisbury, who had been appointed Mary's state governess at her birth. It was the Countess of Salisbury who was given charge of Mary when she was sent to Ludlow in the autumn of 1525.

This was a well-considered and symbolic event, marking Henry VIII's recognition of his daughter as heiress to the crown. His elder brother, Arthur, had resided at Ludlow, as Prince of Wales (as had the late Edward V), and now Mary was to fulfil the same role, even occasionally named 'Princess of Wales' in her own right, though at nine years old she can have had no more than ceremonial responsibility as her father's vicereine on the marches.

Detailed instructions were issued to Lady Salisbury before she and Mary left for the west:

First, above all things, the Countess of Salisbury, being lady governess, shall, according to the singular confidence that the King's Highness hath in her, give most tender regard to all that concerns the person of the said Princess, her honourable education and training in virtuous demeanour; that is to say, to serve God, from whom all grace and goodness proceedeth. Likewise, at seasons convenient, to use moderate exercise, taking open air in gardens, sweet and wholesome places and walks (which may conduce to her health, solace and comfort), as by the said lady governess shall be thought most convenient.

And likewise to pass her time, most seasons, at her virginals or other musical instruments, so that the same be not too much and without fatigation or weariness, to attend to her learning of Latin tongue and French; at other seasons to dance, and among the rest to have good respect to her diet, which is meet to be pure, well-prepared, dressed and served with comfortable, joyous and merry communication, in all honourable and virtuous manner.

Likewise, the cleanliness and well-wearing of her garments and apparel, both of her chamber and person, so that everything about her be pure, sweet,

clean and wholesome, as to so great a princess doth appertain: all corrup-
tions, evil airs and things noisome and unpleasant to be eschewed.[3]

If Mary, at nine, among her books and music, had been unaware of her father's unrest, after her return from Wales in 1527 when she was eleven years old, she cannot have remained long in ignorance of the great changes that were afoot.

For some time past, Henry VIII had been wondering if some remedy might not be found for his dangerously sonless state. God had blighted his marriage, he believed, because he had committed the sin of marrying his own brother's wife. Rejecting the fact that Catherine had sworn that she and Arthur had never consummated their union, on which basis she had been awarded a papal dispensation to marry Henry, the King now believed that he had never been legally married to her. In the sixteenth century divorce was allowed only if it could be shown that a man and woman had broken Church law by marrying: one or the other might have a spouse living (which the frequency of infant betrothal made likely), they might be related within the 'prohibited degrees' of consanguinity, and so on. Indeed, King Henry could point to a biblical text which expressly forbade a man to marry his brother's widow, and he could easily persuade himself that no papal dispensation could be warranted to cancel that: "And if a man shall take his brother's wife, it is impurity: he hath uncovered his brother's nakedness; they shall be childless" (Leviticus, XX, xxi.). In fact, he might also have noticed, but chosen to disregard, a contradictory text in Deuteronomy, XXV, v: if a woman's husband dies and they are childless, "her husband's brother shall go in unto her, and take her to him to wife, and perform the duty of an husband's brother unto her".

At the same time, Henry had a future wife already in view, one whom, he could hope, God would bless with sons for England.

This was Anne Boleyn, a dark, somewhat inscrutable young woman who had been one of Queen Catherine's maids-of-honour since 1522. She was, in fact, the sister of one of the King's already discarded mistresses, a woman of less wit than Anne who had been no more of a threat to the Queen's position than any other of Henry's (admittedly infrequent) fancies. Anne was a stronger character, playing for high stakes. By the year 1526 she had totally ensnared the King and held his fickle interest by refusing to become his mistress. Anne Boleyn would surrender only in marriage, and this she made very clear to Henry, who, in any case, burned as much for the heir Anne could give him as for the woman herself.

On the 22nd June 1527 King Henry VIII had an uncomfortable

meeting with his wife. He told her that, on learned advice, he had discovered that they were not truly married, that they must part. The Queen was aghast – though she must have felt something in the wind long before, with her husband so openly courting Anne Boleyn. Catherine could not speak; she burst into tears. Henry was not an unkind man: he had loved Catherine once; now he tried to comfort her, but with no success.

Only that spring, on her return from Ludlow, Princess Mary had been placed at the centre of her father's Court: a few weeks later, she was regarded as no more than the King's bastard, child of his illegal marriage, sharing her mother's shame and despair.

Above Mary's head, proceedings went forward for a divorce trial. In May 1529 a papal envoy opened the case – even though, with the Pope a virtual prisoner of Queen Catherine's nephew the Emperor, there seemed little likelihood that a verdict would be given against her marriage. And so it transpired. Cardinal Campeggio procrastinated, and the trial dragged on for more than three years. King Henry had become panic-stricken, driven to desperate measures, and in the spring of 1533 he had his own Archbishop of Canterbury override papal authority and pronounce the divorce. Trusting in Archbishop Cranmer's obedience, he had already married Anne Boleyn, in January 1533, and by the time she was crowned Queen, that Whitsun, she was already in the mid-term of her pregnancy. The Pope's pronouncement, in July, that Henry and Catherine's marriage was and always had been valid, was ignored.

Catherine of Aragon's refusal to help her husband to an easy divorce had hardened Henry's attitude towards her. For the price of her statement that she had lied about the non-consummation of her marriage to Arthur, she could have bought a quiet life, generous financial support and dignity as a Dowager Princess of Wales. But Catherine would not perjure herself. She was parted from her daughter and sent into lonely captivity in the country, where she pined and prayed herself into ill-health.

Mary Tudor was sixteen years old when she saw her mother for the last time, in 1532. The Princess and her retinue were sent off on their customary round of country palaces, out of sight and mind of the King.

On the 9th September 1533, Queen Anne Boleyn gave birth to a living child. To Henry's disappointment, it was a girl.

Nevertheless, the fact that Anne could produce a healthy child gave the King hopes for a future son, and Henry had his daughter christened in princely magnificence, himself in high good humour. She was named Elizabeth, for his mother, and she was to be 'Princess' – a title which was now taken from Mary.

Within a month of her half-sister's birth, Mary Tudor found that she was also to lose her independent household. Royal commissioners visited her at New Hall in Essex and informed her that she was to be sent to live with the baby Princess, for whom an establishment was already being set up.

Until that time, Mary had had no voice in any of the business which had so summarily dealt with her mother and herself, no chance to protest against her father's cruelty. Now she made her stand. She wrote to the King's Privy Council:

> My lords, as touching my removal to Hatfield, I will obey His Grace, as my duty is, or go to any other place his Grace may appoint me; but I protest before you and all others present that my conscience will in no wise suffer me to take any other than myself for princess, or for the King's daughter born in lawful matrimony; and that I will never wittingly or willingly say or do aught whereby any person might take occasion to think that I agree to the contrary. Nor say I this out of any ambition or proud mind, as God is my judge. If I should do otherwise, I should slander the deed of our mother, the Holy Church, and the Pope, who is the judge in this matter, and none other, and should also dishonour the King my father, the Queen my mother, and falsely confess myself a bastard, which God defend I should do, since the Pope hath not so declared it by his sentence definitive, to whose final judgement I submit myself.[4]

It was probably at this time that Mary received a long letter from her mother (it is not dated but seems to refer to the removal of the title), a letter which must have strengthened the girl's resolve:

> Daughter,
>   I heard such tidings today that I do perceive (if it be true) the time is very near when Almighty God will provide for you, and I am very glad of it; for I trust that He doth handle you with a good love. I beseech you agree to His pleasure with a merry heart and be you sure that, without fail, He will not suffer you to perish if you beware to offend him. I pray God that you, good daughter, offer yourself to Him. If any pangs come over you, shrive yourself; first make you clean, take heed of His commandments and keep them as near as He will give you grace to do, for there are you sure armed.
>   And if this lady [probably referring to Lady Salisbury's replacement] do come to you, as it is spoken, if she do bring you a letter from the King, I am sure in the self-same letter you will be commanded what to do. Answer with very few words, obeying the King your father in everything – save only that you will not offend God and lose your soul, and go no further with learning and disputation in the matter. And wheresoever and

*in whatsoever company you shall come, obey the King's commandments,
speak few words and meddle nothing. . . .*[5]

Over the next three years, Mary's troubles multiplied. She was
deprived of the servants she had known and trusted over a period of
years; her rooms were frequently searched 'for signs of a secret correspondence with foreign powers – in fact, every scrap of paper in her
possession came under the closest scrutiny; sometimes she was refused
permission to leave the house, even to go to church. No wonder it was
widely reported that she kept to her own room much of the time, pray-
ing and weeping. But still, whenever she had the chance, Mary Tudor
fought back, and for every insult there was a further lifting of her courage to win through.

The worst blow came in January 1536, when she heard that her
mother had died.

Then, four months later, news came that Anne Boleyn was being tried
for adultery, and before May was out that she was dead, beheaded for
her treason. And, as a precaution, Henry had first divorced her, making
the Princess Elizabeth (the only child Anne had managed to give him) as
much a bastard as Mary.

Within a few days of Anne's death, Henry VIII took a new wife,
another maid-of-honour, Jane Seymour, but this time a woman of no
guile, of apparently few personal charms and some friendship for Mary.
Indeed, the two young women may have known each other in earlier
years, when Jane was a member of Catherine of Aragon's household. In
any event, Mary, who had scorned Anne Boleyn, now wrote politely to
her father, congratulating him on his marriage.

This overture of Mary's prompted Henry to make another attempt on
her resolve. He sent commissioners to her at Hunsdon (who, incidentally, informed her that she must no longer style her sister Elizabeth as
'princess' – an irrelevancy, as she never had), bearing a document which
Mary was to sign, renouncing her own place in the royal succession, as
being illegitimate, vowing obedience to Henry's laws, repudiating the
power of the Pope over the Church in England. It was only several days
after the paper was put into her hand that she could bring herself to pen
her name to it.

Mary had her reward. That autumn she was summoned to Court,
welcomed by her father and Queen Jane.

It was a see-saw life. Before 1536, Mary was down, Elizabeth up. For
some time after, Mary was up, Elizabeth down.

Henry VIII had married Anne Boleyn in love and passion, and when
he learned that she had betrayed him, he had her hounded and killed

she had not

with a vindictive malice rooted in jealousy and humiliation. It was no wonder that he found the thought of her child distasteful. This was reflected in Elizabeth's treatment: his stewards failed – probably lacking Henry's orders – to send her governess any money to replace outgrown clothes or to give clear instruction as to her upbringing:

> *My lord* [wrote the governess, Lady Bryan, to Thomas Cromwell, the King's chief minister],
>
> *. . . my lady Elizabeth is put from that degree she was afore, and what degree she is at now, I know not but by hearsay. Therefore I know not how to order her, nor myself, nor none of hers that I have the rule of, that is, her women and grooms. Beseeching you to be good lord to my lady, and to all hers, and that she may have some raiment, for she hath neither gown nor kirtle nor petticoat nor no manner of linen – nor forsmocks nor kerchiefs nor rails [nightdresses] nor body-stitchets [corsets] nor handkerchiefs nor sleeves nor mufflers nor biggens [nightcaps]. All these Her Grace must take. I have driven off as long as I can, that, by my troth, I can drive it off no longer. Beseeching you, my lord, that ye will see that Her Grace may have that which is needful for her, as my trust is that ye will do. . . .*
>
> *My lord, Mr Shelton* [the steward] *would have my lady Elizabeth to dine and sup every day at the board of estate. Alas, my lord, it is not meet for a child of her age to keep such rule yet. I promise you, my lord, I dare not take it upon me to keep Her Grace in health, as she keep that rule. For there she shall see diverse meats and fruits and wine, which it would be hard for me to restrain Her Grace therefrom. . . . God knoweth, my lady hath great pain with her teeth, and they come very slowly forth, which causeth me to suffer Her Grace to have her will more than I would. . . .*[6]

By the end of the year, Henry VIII's emotions were on a more even keel, and Mary and Elizabeth's joint household was running smoothly once more. And in the following year, the King could afford to look more kindly on his daughters, for once again he was expecting the arrival of a son.

This time there was no disappointment. Quiet, docile Queen Jane Seymour produced a son – but she died from the effort . . .

Inevitably the baby Prince Edward was hailed not only by the King but by the whole of England with the utmost joy. He was christened with great magnificence, then consigned to a safe and quiet nursery – often in the company of his half-sisters, who were as doting as their father. Mary, now in her twenties, was frustrated in her maidenhood and lavished her thwarted maternal affections on many godchildren: she responded warmly to her brother, despite his upbringing in the

Protestant faith which was abhorrent to her, and her presents to him were many and generous. The child Elizabeth, only four years Edward's senior, had less pocket-money than Mary, and she made her gifts herself, such as the fine cambric shirts which the baby wore.

Before the decade was out, the two younger Tudors were doing lessons together, vying for the more rapid progress, for each was a prodigy of learning in the Renaissance tradition, as fluent in Greek and Latin as in English and French. Despite Elizabeth's four-year seniority, the gap in their studies narrowed with the years, for Edward was a brilliant, and diligent, student. He was also an earnest disciple of the Reformed faith – the religious principles which in England almost as much as on the Continent were bringing men back to the 'biblical holiness' which they saw lacking in Catholicism. Henry VIII had retained his Catholic doctrines, even as he took his kingdom out of obedience to Rome and formed the Church into a national institution, but his son was educated in the most advanced Protestant thinking, as was his sister Elizabeth – though Mary could never be brought to give up her Mass.

The fourth and fifth wives of Henry VIII can have made little impact on Edward and Elizabeth Tudor, so brief were their reigns, but the last, Catherine Parr, was a motherly woman, herself a student of the new learning, who undertook their upbringing with as much devotion as she put into nursing the ailing King. What family life the children knew came mainly from Catherine's efforts.

But this happy time was brief. Prince Edward was only nine years old when his father died in January 1547.

The last boy-king

King Henry VIII died at two o'clock on the morning of the 28th January 1547. When the news was brought into the long gallery outside his bed-chamber, the crowd of waiting courtiers knelt in prayer, but as soon as he decently could, one of them slipped away, left the Palace of West-minster and spurred his horse northward, towards the manor of Ash-ridge in Hertfordshire, where the new king, Edward VI, was staying.

This man was the boy's maternal uncle, Edward Seymour, Lord Hert-ford.

Yet, once arrived, Seymour did not immediately inform Edward of his accession to the throne – nor did he tell anyone in the household. But that same day he rode with the boy the few miles to the manor of Enfield, where Edward's sister Elizabeth lived, and the next morning gave both the children the news of their father's death. They burst into tears and clung to each other, sobbing.

Lord Hertford had good reason for postponing his announcement. He wanted time for his friend Sir William Paget, in London, to prepare the overthrow of Henry VIII's Will in favour of his, Seymour's, becoming Lord Protector for Edward.

Henry had provided for a Council of Regency to be set up at his death, to comprise the sixteen foremost men of his own Council, who were to administer the realm between them without any formal leader. In the old King's lifetime, Edward Seymour had made no open move to have Henry change this plan, but in the last few years he had made him-self the head of a party in government which might smooth his way to a seizure of power when Henry died. Now, even before Seymour and the young King had reached London, Paget laid before his fellow-Councillors the proposal that Seymour should become Lord Protector: the Lord Chancellor's was the only major voice against the plan, and he was overborne by his colleagues, Seymour's partisans.

Over the next few weeks, the new Lord Protector buttressed his power by taking on the offices of Lord Treasurer and Earl Marshal, and having the King create him Duke of Somerset.

An important aspect of the establishment of the new regime was the declaration that Edward VI would rule immediately with as full a power as his father, subject only to advice from the Protector. In practice of course, this statement had little effect on the boy's powers, for Somerset had the real authority in government, but it was useful in cloaking his acts with a semblance of their coming direct from Edward himself. In fact, it also had an important influence on Edward's development, for he was sufficiently mature in political theory to grasp the implications of his prerogative and to understand that, in being Supreme Head of the Church of England, as well as King, he had a unique responsibility. He was a solemn, contemplative little boy, not daunted by his eminence; he had that characteristic Tudor self-confidence which allowed him to believe that he would be capable of fulfilling those duties which he regarded as a God-given trust.

He had always admired Edward Seymour, a prodigy of scholarship and paragon of Protestant piety, a gentle man, an idealist, but even in the first months of his reign, the King began to see his uncle in a new light, to deprecate the Duke's use of his powers without more than formal deference to himself. Somerset, of course, was too busy coping with the problems of the nation's economy, diplomacy and religious settlement to consider a child's sensibilities.

But another man, another uncle, was not. Thomas Seymour, Lord Sudeley, was Somerset's younger brother, but flamboyant and energetic where Edward Seymour was reserved and quiet – the Seymours were alike only in that Thomas was as greedy for power as his elder brother. But where Somerset had achieved it by slowly building up a party in Council, Thomas Seymour saw the boy Edward as a quick and easy means to power. He paid him all the attentions which his uncle Edward neglected, slipped him pocket-money when the Lord Protector proved niggardly. He flattered the boy by deferring to his opinions and began, cautiously at first, then more openly, to turn him against the Lord Protector. One of Thomas Seymour's ploys to gain royal favour was his marriage to the King's much-loved stepmother, Queen Catherine Parr: and again, he attached Edward more firmly to himself by drawing him into the conspiracy of his secret marriage, leaving the Duke of Somerset an outsider who must be reckoned an enemy to the match.

Thomas Seymour had been working on Edward's resentment of Somerset for some time before, in July 1547, he spoke to the boy frankly about the Lord Protector's overbearing attitude towards him. "You must take upon yourself to rule," he said, "for ye shall be able enough, as well as other kings." Then he added, "Your uncle is old, and I trust he will not live long." Even so, for all his own daring, Seymour must have been surprised when his nephew replied, with a *sang-froid* remarkable at his age: "It were better that he should die."[1]

It was soon after this conversation that Thomas Seymour took advantage of the King's indebtedness to him (he already owed his younger uncle more than £100) to press Edward to write a letter to the Council to demand that his uncle Thomas should replace his uncle Edward as Protector. But he had overplayed his hand. The King was a student of history, and he need look back no further than the end of the previous century to see what had happened to an earlier king in the hands of rival uncles. In fact, soon afterwards, Somerset came to hear of his brother's machinations – Thomas had spoken too frankly against the Protector in the hearing of one of the latter's friends – and he was hauled up before the Council. But Somerset was loath to believe the stories against his brother, and no formal charges were made.

Throughout the year 1548 Thomas Seymour continued to plot against the Protector, though he was rather more cautious now. He worked indirectly on Edward through Queen Catherine, and now added to his armoury by taking into his household the King's favourite cousin, Lady Jane Grey, promising her parents that he would contrive to marry her to the King. Another guest in the Seymours' house at Chelsea was the Lady Elizabeth, of whom Edward was still very fond – "my sweet sister Temperance", he called her. With Jane Grey, Thomas Seymour was all seriousness and sobriety, for she was a solemn child; with Elizabeth Tudor, he was flirtatious and playful, for, at fourteen, she was precociously sexed: he would go into her bedchamber before she had got up in the mornings and make as if to join her in bed, and there were slaps and tickles which shocked and alarmed the girl's governess. It was later said that Seymour would marry Elizabeth hastily if Queen Catherine, then pregnant and ailing, should die – though in fact, when his wife did die, in childbirth, that autumn of 1548, he did not accomplish it.

Thomas Seymour was an impatient man, and he did not wait for his 'old' brother to die naturally, nor to enhance his influence over the King by marrying him to his ward, Jane, but in January 1549 staged a daring *coup* designed to oust Somerset and set himself at the head of government.

On the night of the 16th January, Seymour and two accomplices broke into the King's outer chamber. The boy's dog sounded the alarm, and was shot. The noise brought guards in at the double, to see Seymour trying the door of Edward's room. He was at once taken into custody.

Over the next few weeks the evidence against Thomas Seymour was gathered: it was enough to have him condemned for treason. Both his brother and his nephew signed the death-warrant, and he went to the block.

During the investigation of Thomas Seymour's crimes, many people had been questioned as to their dealings with him and his self-incriminating words to them. Jane Grey's father, the Marquess of Dorset, was one of the deponents, but he managed to prove that he had had no part of Seymour's plots; others were members of Elizabeth's staff, her governess, Catherine Ashley, and her steward, Thomas Parry, who were forced to provide evidence of his attempts to win their mistress's affections. There is no clear proof that Elizabeth herself was ever taken in by Seymour's wiles, nor did she make any attempt to help him when he was brought to justice – though she did write urgently to the Council on behalf of her servants. However, even if she did not suffer the heart-break of losing a lover, Elizabeth did feel the effects of the rumours as to their relationship: that spring she found it necessary to write to Somerset to beg him to proclaim that she was *not* pregnant by his late brother, as popular gossip had it.

Elizabeth was only fifteen when Thomas Seymour died, and might well have been intimidated by her own – albeit slight, but still potentially dangerous – implication in his treason. But she was not. Elizabeth had seen her stepmothers come and go, she had seen statesmen and churchmen rise and fall, and she was prematurely wise in the ways of survival: for all her youth, she never lost her wits and went through the difficult days of 1549 outwardly as calmly as she would face the trials of 1588.

Her young brother viewed the destruction of his uncle Thomas as coolly as he had earlier envisaged the death of his uncle Edward. And when, before the year was out, Somerset himself was in danger of death, Edward VI was not overly perturbed on his behalf.

The Lord Protector had been meeting one set-back after another, enduring violent opposition to his economic measures and fervent resistance to his religious settlement – seen by the lords of the Council as a sign that he could not control the kingdom. John Dudley, Earl of Warwick, who had supported Edward Seymour in 1547, now began to assume leadership of his critics.

During the first week of October 1549, Somerset received word that there was to be another *coup* and sent out orders for the arming of the citizens of London. Five hundred men were quartered on Hampton Court to protect the King – and his uncle.

For some days past, Somerset had been priming Edward with tales as to what would happen to him, the King, if his Protector were overthrown. On the night of the 6th, preparing to leave Hampton Court for the strongly fortified Windsor Castle, the Duke presented the boy to his troops and cried: "I shall not fall alone. If I am destroyed, the King shall be destroyed. Kingdom, commonwealth – all will be destroyed to-gether." At those words, Edward VI drew his dagger and waved it in the air as if it had been a battle-sword: "Will ye help me against those who would kill me?" he shouted. "God save Your Grace!" roared the soldiers, "We will die for you!"[2] Then the boy was hustled off to Windsor, and deposited in the stronghold.

Of course, Warwick and his colleagues had no intention of dethron-ing the King: Somerset was their prey. They disregarded Edward's letter to them – written most likely at his uncle's dictation – in which he begged them to respect the Protector, and insisted that he submit to arrest. On the 10th, the lords of the Council entered Windsor Castle, cautioned Somerset and made their bows to the King. Three days later, Somerset rode away, to the Tower.

Edward asked the lords for his uncle's life, and it was granted, but the Duke remained in prison while the Earl of Warwick gathered the reins of power into his own hands, placing his own friends in key posts at Court and in the government. He ingratiated himself with the King by assuring him that the days of the Protectorship were over, that he ruled now with full and actual power. Edward had been greatly frightened by the events of early October; now he was exhilarated by his sudden accession to authority, and could only bless Warwick who had given it to him. The Earl asked for the boy's opinion on matters of state and seated him in the Council (where he was acclaimed for his politeness and deference), even though the King's chief councillor had his way in most things. At twelve years of age, Edward VI believed himself truly king.

His new duties in no way interfered with his education: the classics still figured large in the curriculum, but he enjoyed the added novelty of translating them into Italian and French (he was also learning Spanish). And his interest in matters ecclesiastical became paramount: he received into his household the most famous of Continental Protestants, who had been exiled by their Catholic sovereigns; he harangued his bishops on their duties and doctrine; he personally supervised the preparation of the Prayer Book which was published in 1552 as the standard form of Angli-can worship.

The strength of Warwick's power lay in his prudent avoidance of ad-vertising it. In Council he took no open lead, preferring to test men and their loyalty in private conversations; nor did he make any show of open influence over Edward: their discussions were conducted late at night, in the royal bedchamber, without witnesses.

Somerset had been released before long and was once again figuring in Court and Council early in 1550, undertaking all the duties allotted to him without any show of resentment at his relegation to a lower place: almost exactly two years after his overthrow he was to be seen, on the 11th October 1551, leading Warwick to his investiture as Duke of Northumberland. But only two days later, the new Duke was reporting to the King that he had uncovered a plot, already some six months old, by which Somerset sought to regain power. Edward's uncle had, said Northumberland, formed a conspiracy with several other lords, by which an armed insurrection was to lead to his reinstatement as Lord Protector; Northumberland and some of his friends were to be assassinated. On the 16th Somerset was arrested. Again he was sent to the Tower. On the 1st December he was tried on two charges of treason and three of felony: his condemnation was a foregone conclusion. He was pronounced innocent of treason but found guilty of the felonies, which also carried the death penalty. He was executed on the 22nd January 1552. The King had been reluctant, when it came to it, to sign the death-warrant, but Northumberland persuaded him.

It may have been the strain of these proceedings which weakened Edward in the spring of 1552, causing an attack of measles seriously to affect him. His life was not in danger, but the illness left him frail and feeble, easily tiring. Northumberland organized a summer tour of the southern counties to give the boy fresh air and exercise, but though he went bravely, even cheerfully, through the whole schedule, the King was noticeably weaker at the end of it. Early in the New Year, he suffered a serious attack of bronchitis, with heavy congestion on the lungs. Even then, he continued to work from his bed, reading and discussing state papers, receiving ambassadors. By April he thought himself fully recovered.

Northumberland was not so sure. Having attained such power, he had no wish to lose it, yet he could see just that eventuality if Edward were to die.

The Will of Henry VIII had provided for the succession. After Edward, his sister Mary would reign, then her heirs; in default of them, Elizabeth was to have the crown.

Northumberland dared not think what would happen if the Catholic Mary sat on the throne: certainly she would have no use for the man who had supervised the reform of the Church. Nor – though here his reasoning is less clear – did he wish Elizabeth to rule, even though she was a Protestant: perhaps he recognized her already strong character, which, if she were queen, would allow no one such as he to govern. In those weeks while everyone watched the King closely for signs of decline, Northumberland hatched an ingenious scheme, which would not only preserve him but actually enhance his power. Mary and Elizabeth were to be debarred from the throne as bastards; their two Catholic cousins Mary, Queen of Scots, and Margaret, Countess of Lennox (descendants of Henry VIII's elder sister Margaret), were to be excluded too – Mary as an alien and a Catholic, Margaret as of dubious legitimacy. That left the representative of Henry VIII's younger sister Mary: her elder daughter Frances, who in turn had three daughters. Northumberland persuaded Frances to give up her own claim to the throne in favour of her eldest daughter, Lady Jane Grey, who at that Whitsun of 1553, Northumberland married to his own son Guilford: Jane thus became the Duke's pawn in his bid to keep control of the kingdom.

However, the King himself was the key to Northumberland's future power, and over these months the Duke worked on Edward's natural fears for the future of his kingdom, persuading him to prepare a Will in Jane's favour. Edward knew that he was dying: he had no fear of death itself, only of the sin of leaving his subjects' souls in the hands of Mary, who would return them to papal obedience; Elizabeth he feared would marry a foreign prince, likely a Catholic, who would do the same. That June, he penned his 'device for the succession': like the rest of Edward's statecraft, it was neat and orderly, and in the final draft appeared the words, so gratifying to Northumberland, that Lady Jane Grey and her 'heirs male' should succeed him. It took all the boy's little strength to persuade his councillors to sign the device, but in the end they did so.

By then, Edward was in great pain and distress. His lungs were suppurating, his body was covered in ulcers, he ran a high fever intermittently (during which he was delirious), and he coughed continually.

In a lucid period, the fifteen-year-old boy composed a prayer:

Lord God, deliver me out of this miserable and wretched life, and take me amongst Thy chosen; howbeit, not my will but Thy will be done. Lord, I commit my spirit to Thee. O Lord, Thou knowest how happy it were for me to be with Thee; yet, for Thy chosen's sake, send me life and health, that I may truly serve Thee. O Lord God, bless Thy people and save Thine inheritance. O my Lord God, defend this realm from papistry and maintain Thy true religion, that I and my people may praise Thy holy name, for Thy son Jesus Christ's sake. Amen.[3]

His faith did not leave him at the end. The last words King Edward VI spoke, in the evening of the 6th July, were, "Lord have mercy on me – take my spirit."

Historians have not been kind to this last Tudor king. They have labelled him a prig, filled with self-importance and arrogance, untouched by sympathy for anyone. It is too harsh a judgement, over-coloured by modern attitudes to children. Edward certainly knew his own importance, but that was only reasonable when all about him paid so much reverence to his person – even his sisters knelt three times before taking a seat at his table. And his studies in political theory showed him the unique prerogatives and dignities of kings: he would have failed in his duty, as he saw it, by being casual and informal in his behaviour; and duty warranted, in contemporary terms, his ordering and advising men four and five times his age.

The young King was not entirely cold-hearted. In his own small circle he was openly affectionate: his stepmother, his sisters, his cousin Jane, his boy companions, his nurse Sybilla Penn – whom he called 'Mother Jack', his tutor John Cheke, his godfather Archbishop Cranmer – all knew Edward's love. Only with politicians, notably those in the highest places, was he cold and reserved: but then, he had good reason to mistrust those who so obviously sought to manipulate him for their own ends.

It was a tragedy, in both personal and national terms, that the King should have died so young. He would surely have become a great monarch. As Bishop Hooper wrote in 1550: "If he lives, he will be the wonder and terror of the world."[4]

The King's death was not immediately announced. Northumberland concentrated his troops in London, assured himself of the loyalty of the Council, sent messages to the King's sisters asking them to attend his death-bed and sent for his daughter-in-law Jane Grey. But even from the first his plans misfired. Elizabeth Tudor was too cautious to put herself into the hands of Northumberland and sent word that she was too ill to move from her home at Hatfield; Mary was less sagacious, but a friend warned her of the Duke's machinations – she rode swiftly and secretly into East Anglia, raised the royal standard at the great fortress of Framlingham and sent out couriers to proclaim her as queen in the major cities.

Nor, at first, would Jane Grey fall in with Northumberland's plans. The first she knew of her accession to the crown was when the lords of the Council, and her own parents, knelt to her on the 9th July, three days after her cousin's death. Only fifteen years old, totally unprepared for this news, she fainted when she heard it. Then, through a torrent of tears, she protested that she had no right to the crown, that it was her cousin Mary's. It took all Northumberland's persuasive powers to convince her that it had been Edward's will. More effectively, her parents, the Duke and Duchess of Suffolk, added their voices, reminding her of the obedience she owned to them. Jane saw that she must submit. The 'Queen' now knelt and prayed: "If what hath been given me is lawfully mine, may Thy Divine Majesty grant me such spirit and grace that I may govern to Thy glory and service, to the advantage of the realm."[5]

The next day she was put into the Tower of London for safe-keeping, while news of the King's death and her accession was broadcast through the kingdom.

It is unlikely that the Duke of Northumberland knew his daughter-in-law in any degree of intimacy, even though she had been his son's wife for several weeks. He would see that she was short in stature, with sandy hair and freckles; she was silent and reserved in company; everyone knew her great reputation for learning and piety: but most likely he had not been told that she had at first refused to marry Guilford Dudley, and that it was only when her father swore at her and her mother beat her that she could be induced to give her consent to the match. Over the next few days, he would find that he was dealing with a real Tudor in temperament and temper.

Sentimental Victorian biographers of Jane, impressed by her virtues, have shown the girl as the patient victim of parental harshness. Everyone quotes her words, aged thirteen, that,

> When I am in presence of either father or mother, whether I speak, keep silence, sit, stand or go, eat, drink be merry or sad, be sewing, playing, dancing or doing anything else, I must do it, as it were, in such weight, measure and number, even as perfectly as God made the world — or else I am so sharply taunted, so cruelly threatened, yea, presented sometimes with pinches, nips and bobs and other ways — which I will not name for the honour I bear them — so without measure misordered, that I think myself in hell.[6]

Less frequently quoted are Jane's words just prior to that outburst, which she made to a sympathetic and admiring tutor — telling him that her parents were out hunting in the park; she deplored their frivolity: "I wish all their sport is but a shadow to that pleasure I find in Plato. . . . Alas, good folk, they never felt what pleasure means."[7] In fact, though her mother was a thorough-going courtier, fond of dance and chase, Jane's father was a respected patron of scholars and divines: it must have been infinitely galling to them to find their daughter so arrogant and patronizing. When this incident occurred, the girl had not long since come home from her residence at Thomas Seymour's, where she had likely been praised and spoiled: her parents would think they were doing her no harm in criticizing her, bringing Jane 'down a peg or two'.

If Northumberland did not know of his 'Queen's' character before he put her on the throne, the next few days left him in no doubt as to her implacability. First, she refused to cohabit with his son (a mother's boy who tried to domineer his wife and sulked when she snubbed him); then she would not have her father sent off on the dangerous mission of capturing her cousin Mary – Northumberland himself had to go. In fact, it was his absence from the capital which finally undermined his power. The lords of the Council had never been easy in their minds about bypassing Mary Tudor's claims to the throne, and without Northumberland to chivvy them, they were not long in going over to Mary's side. On the morning of the 18th July they met and discussed events: unanimously they decided to support Mary. The next day they had her proclaimed in London and informed Suffolk that his daughter was no longer – in fact, had never been – queen. A weak man, already fearful at the scope of his pretensions, he gave in without resistance. When Jane heard the news, she said calmly that she was glad to put off her regality, adding balefully, "Out of obedience to you and my mother, I have grievously sinned." Then her dignity disappeared, and she was only a frightened child: "May I not go home?" she begged.[8]

Jane did not go home, then or ever. For months after Queen Mary I had arrived in her capital, after Mary had been crowned and had condemned Northumberland, the girl remained in the Tower. Mary knew what it was to be powerless in the hands of unscrupulous men, and she was loath to condemn Jane, who was so obviously only Northumberland's pawn, but while she would not agree to have her executed, she could not let her go free to be so used again. It was only after the Duke of Suffolk had made a foolhardy attempt to restore Jane, in 1554, that Mary submitted to her councillors' pressure and had the girl tried on a charge of treason. Inevitably, Jane was found guilty, inevitably she was sent to the block.

Lady Jane Grey may not be the most attractive member of the Tudor family, having that priggishness which Edward VI had escaped, but she certainly knew how to die with dignity. The sixteen-year-old girl cried for her father, and even for her husband, who died with her, but for herself she made no complaint. She refused Mary's offer of mercy conditional on her conversion to Catholicism, pardoned her father all his offences against her, put in some hours of prayer and meditation and wrote a characteristic message to the world: "If justice is done with my body, my soul will find mercy with God. Death will give pain to my body, for its sins, but the soul will be justified with God. If my faults deserve punishment, my youth at least, and my imprudence, were worthy of excuse; God and posterity will show me favour."[9] On the 12th February 1554, Lady Jane Grey walked calmly onto Tower Green, mounted the scaffold and offered her neck to the axe.

The pretension to the crown of Lady Jane Grey had come about because of the lack of an indisputable heir to the throne. Queen Mary hoped to remedy that deficiency by providing England with an heir of her own body and accordingly married her cousin Philip of Spain (son of her former fiancé the Emperor Charles V). But she was nearly forty when she married and never conceived. In her anxiety, Mary thought she was pregnant when her body began to swell, and there was national rejoicing when she announced that she was with child, but the tumour which gave rise to these hopes killed her just over five years after she had come to the throne.

Mary had done as she had always promised: she had offered England back to the Papacy; under pressure from Spain, she had persecuted Protestants – before her marriage she had been notably, and laudably, tolerant. Yet, despite the failure of her attempts to convert her sister Elizabeth to Catholicism, the Queen was resigned to the fact that the crown would pass to her at her death – anyway, Spain preferred that to having the Tudor women's cousin Mary Stuart, a Catholic but a French protégée, on the English throne.

When Elizabeth claimed her crown, in November 1558, she was twenty-five years old, and her subjects might reasonably expect her to give them royal children. She did not. In the years that followed, the Queen toyed with the idea of marriage – to her favourite, Robert Dudley (a son of the late Duke of Northumberland), to a French prince, to several other suitors of royal and noble blood, but she could never be brought to announce it. It may well be, as many biographers have argued, that Elizabeth's childhood experiences, the death of her mother, her father's matrimonial career, had given her a subconscious fear of marriage and of sexual submission; certainly, she could well see the dangers of putting herself and her crown into the hands of a husband, either one of her own subjects, who would bring his faction to rule her government, or a foreigner, whose own land would dominate hers, as Spain had dominated England in her sister's reign and as France influenced Scotland during the long minority of her cousin Mary Stuart.

So, for nearly forty-five years, there was no 'royal family' in England, only a Virgin Queen, the last of the Tudors.

The Tudor age had been an unhappy one for royal children. Mary and Elizabeth had grown up under the shadow of their mothers' disgrace, their characters warped by their experience; Edward VI had been deprived of the natural joys of boyhood by a regime which pushed him into a precocious maturity and which contributed to his early death; Lady Jane Grey had been killed before she knew more than the theory of living. In different ways, each was the victim of adult ambition.

The Stuart Age
1603–1714

"The thing is called Bridget"

A child born in, say, 1640, would live through a turbulent age. At the time of his birth, King and Parliament were in bitter conflict; when he was two, they clashed in a war which would continue, intermittently, into his adolescence; he would be eight years old when King Charles I was beheaded – a traumatic experience for his elders, reared in an age of respect and affection for royalty, personified by Elizabeth I. He would be in his teens under the strict rod of Puritan government, in a time of political experiment. He would be twenty when the nation recalled a Stuart king, Charles II, and in his early forties when Charles's brother James was dethroned and a constitutional monarchy established. If he exceeded his three score years and ten, he would have survived the Stuart dynasty and died a 'Georgian', firmly in the modern age of industry and capitalism.

The Victorian painting 'When did you last see your father?' is often derided today as a piece of crass sentimentalism – but it does illustrate the point that not even children were spared the effects of England's civil war. (It shows a small boy in 'Cavalier' finery being interrogated by dour Parliamentarians as to the whereabouts of his father, presumably a fugitive after one of the Royalist defeats, possibly concealed in his own house.) There were pitched battles in the old style during the civil war, but more common were the skirmishes which took place on country roads, in ploughed fields, in sight of cottagers – and their children; and the civilian population, besieged in garrison towns, came under the bombardment of cannon: the children of the civil war suffered fear, privation and risk of life along with their elders. Also, many Royalists fled abroad after the final defeat of Charles I, some taking their families with them, others leaving their children at home in the care of relatives and friends. It was an unsettling and unnerving period for children, comparable to that of aerial bombing and evacuation in the Second World War.

The republican Commonwealth, established in England through the 1650s, was more than a constitutional and political experiment: it was hailed by Puritans as 'the rule of the saints', supposedly men dedicated to Christian living and government – though to many it seemed a tyranny of 'kill-joys'. There had been Puritans ('left-wing' Protestants, biblical fundamentalists, plain livers and high thinkers) in England ever since the mid-sixteenth century, and it was from their ranks that the Parliamentarian dissidents of the 1630s, the 'Roundheads' of the 1640s, were largely drawn. Their triumph in the civil war meant their imposition on England of their forms of worship and way of life. They swept away not only priestly vestments, church adornments and ritual services but such 'signs of popery' as the merry-making customary at religious festivals – away went Christmas junketings, the maypole and midsummer frolics, along with masques and plays and secular music, with fine lace and jewellery and love-locks, dooming everyone to sober colours, long-faced piety, frequent fast days and two-hour sermons. It was not a gay time, least of all for the defeated Royalists.

There are fine examples of loving, joyful Puritan homes, but too often children over-reacted to the perpetual emphasis on godliness, on fear of God and the inevitability of hell-fire as punishment for bad-living. The diarist John Evelyn's son was one of these: his preferred reading, before he was five years old, was 'pathetic' psalms and the most melancholy portions of the Book of Job; he was in the habit of asking visitors to pray with him 'alone in some corner' and, on his death-bed, aged six, fretted lest God should be offended that he prayed with his hands under the covers, which he had been told not to throw off. This boy was the type eulogized in the moral tales written for children in the period, such as those by the then famous James Janeway: among the titles of his works was the daunting *Of a wicked child that was taken up for begging and admirably converted: his holy life and joyful death when he was nine years old*.

Perhaps one benefit of this emphasis on godliness, undoubtedly sincere if to us unpalatable, was the fortification of the small child against death. In an era of high infant mortality, many a four- and five-year-old had grasped enough of its parents' deep faith and confidence in God's mercy to face the prospect of death with equanimity.

In the seventeenth century women still endured many pregnancies, without knowledge of (without desire for knowledge of, usually) effective birth-control. There is a telling letter from a father to his son in 1659, informing him that "your mother was well delivered of her tenth daughter upon the thirtieth of March (the thing is called Bridget), so that now you have had three sisters born within the space of thirty-two months. You may well think that this is not the way to get rich."[1] This man, William Blundell, might have spared a few daughters with scarcely a sigh; other men were more tender-hearted: in the sixteenth century and earlier, the deaths of small children had gone unrecorded in family annals, so inevitable they were; now small effigies were usually raised, surely a sign of love and grief. (In Westminster Abbey may be seen a finely made, brightly painted cradle, in which a dead baby princess, Sophia, daughter of James I, lies as if asleep; nearby her slightly older sister Mary sits up quite cheerfully, raised on one elbow, as if ready to toddle away at the first blast of the last trump.)

Swaddling clothes were now removed when a baby was about three months old, and he or she was put into long gowns. At five or six, a girl left off her baby-caps and pinafore, while a boy stepped into his first breeches. A proud grandmother describes the breeching of 'Frank', aged six, in 1679:

> You cannot believe the great concern that was in the whole family here last Wednesday, it being the day that the tailor was to help to dress little Frank in his breeches in order to the making an everyday suit by it. Never had any bride that was to be dressed upon her wedding night more hands about her, some the legs and some the arms, the tailor buttoning, and others putting on the sword, and so many lookers-on that had I not had a finger amongst them I could not have seen him.
>
> When he was quite dressed, he acted the part as well as any of them, for he desired he might go down to enquire for the little gentleman that was here the day before in a black coat [the gown worn by children before 'breeching'], and speak to the men to tell the gentleman when he came from school that here was a gallant with very fine clothes and a sword to have waited upon him and would come again upon Sunday next. . . . Little Charles [Frank's brother] rejoiced as much as he did, for he jumped all the while about him and took notice of everything.[2]

The practice of sending children away to other families for their up-bringing had largely died out even before the mid-century. The nobility continued to have their children educated at home, by tutors, but the gentry and yeomen, professional men and prosperous merchants took full advantage of the many 'public' (boarding) schools for their sons and – an innovation of the century – of the proliferating boarding-schools for girls.

The classical curriculum was still favoured for boys, but the era of serious study for girls has passed with the Elizabethans. There were a few learned ladies in the seventeenth century but, for the most part, parents agreed with Richard Braithwaite's ideal of *The English Gentle-woman* (1631), who "desireth not to have the esteem of any she-clerk; she had rather be approved by her living than learning. . . . Some books she reads, and those powerful to stir up devotion and fervour to prayer;

others she reads, and those useful for the direction of her household affairs".[3] Even the tuition at girls' boarding-schools was not very testing: besides the ubiquitous French, dancing and deportment, pupils might learn the fashionable accomplishment of shorthand – widely approved as a means of taking down sermons verbatim, and some 'female academies' specialized in needlework and handicrafts, as enthusiastic as the Victorian seminaries in their crazes for the manufacture of useless bric-à-brac. One of the few 'blue-stockings' of the period, Bathsua Makin (governess to Charles I's daughter Elizabeth and later proprietress of her own school) was scathing on the subject of schoolgirl hours spent "making flowers of coloured straw and building houses of stained paper".[4]

A small girl remaining at home would read with her mother and, under supervision, prepare a colourful 'sampler', a linen square on which she would practise every type of embroidery stitch, forming a picture, often with a verse of pious invocation. She would follow her mother round the house, watching and helping her work and gaining practical knowledge of domestic economy. Or she might attend a local school, in the house of a working lady. Mrs Hannah Woolley was one such, a school-mistress from the age of fifteen, and in middle age, in 1675, she published her *Gentlewoman's Companion*, part of which was intended to prepare girls for school – her strictures strike a familiar note:

> *Hasten to school, having first taken leave of your parents with all reverence. Do not loiter on the way or play truant. . . . Leave not anything behind which you ought to carry with you, not only things you learn in or by but also gloves, pocket-handkerchiefs. . . .*
> *When you are called to read, come reverently to your mistress or any whom she appoints; . . . and if you are doubtful of a word, carefully spell it and mistake not one word for another; when you have done, return, showing your reverence, to your place. . . . Sit upright at your work and do not lean or loll. . . .*
> *Preserve your pens, spill not your ink, nor flirt it on your own or others' clothes, and keep your fingers from being polluted therewith.*[5]

There were still child-marriages at the end of the seventeenth century, but far fewer than ever before, and those mainly in royal circles and the high aristocracy, where advantageous alliance or the fortune of an heir or heiress was to be gained. Even at the beginning of the period, parents were starting to allow some latitude to their children in seeking life-partners, such as Lord Huntingdon, who admitted to his son in 1613 that "I myself was married when a child and could not have chosen so well myself nor been so happy in any woman I know, but because one proves well, it must not beget a conclusion."[6] In fact, even in the royal family, this was the last century of real child-marriages (Charles I's daughter Mary was nine at her wedding, her nieces Mary and Anne in their mid-teens, while the later, Hanoverian, princesses were generally in their late teens when they were brides).

Old and effective methods die hard, not least those on child-rearing, but at the end of the seventeenth century the philosopher John Locke published his book *Some Thoughts Concerning Education*, in which he examined the nature of childhood and came to some conclusions startling to the contemporary parent. The earliest impressions on infants, he wrote, were the most enduring, formative on the characters they would take through adult life: therefore childhood must be made pleasant. "Childishness" – that is, thoughtless, careless behaviour, a preference for play over work, wilfulness and stubbornness – was inevitable, and should be left for time to cure. Beating (and this was a revolutionary thought) must be left as a last resort when other methods of control failed. A kindly God, rather than the Puritans' ogre, should be presented to children, and they should not be frightened by thoughts of hell-fire.

Children, opined Locke, should be brought up to be hardy, not pampered by mothers and nurses: he advocates the use of cold baths and condemns soft beds.

Locke was in many ways in advance of his time, but in the years that followed, some parents adopted his precepts, or came to the same conclusions independently. But that is not to say that childhood became a utopian time for all – not by any means.

Intrigue and complicity

King James VI of Scotland, who became James I of England in 1603 on the death of his cousin Elizabeth Tudor, was the last of the seven infant monarchs of the House of Stuart. Born on the 19th June 1566, he was the son of Mary, Queen of Scots, and her second husband, her cousin Henry, Lord Darnley.

James was only seven months old when his father was killed – most likely (though the truth remains obscure) at the order of Queen Mary. He was just over a year old when his mother was forced to abdicate her throne in his favour: having lost the confidence of all but a small number of her nobles, having taken a third husband, Lord Bothwell, of obvious ambition to become ruler of Scotland, Mary had faced her enemies in battle, been defeated and forced to flee over the border into England, where (for once facing reality) she acceded to her lords' demand for her resignation of her crown. On the 29th July 1567 the infant James was crowned King of Scotland.

Years of faction and civil disturbances, intermittently breaking out into armed warfare, had left the country weak but resistant to strong rule. James's first regent, the Earl of Moray, was assassinated in January 1570; the next, his paternal grandfather, the Earl of Lennox, was killed by his enemies in August 1571; the third, James's guardian the Earl of Mar, may have died of natural causes – though it was rumoured at the time that he had been poisoned; the fourth, and last, of the King's regents, the Earl of Morton, was a strong man, who put an end to the worst of civil unrest and survived in power from 1572 until 1580, but he too came to a violent end, convicted of treason (for implication in the Darnley murder) and sent to the block.

James was not wholly shielded from these upheavals. From his earliest years he was forced to hear those closest to him vilify his mother (whom he could not remember, having parted from her before he was a year old) – effecting in him a sentimental devotion to her name, though, even in his early manhood, he sensibly did nothing to aid her schemes for regaining power and gave only a token protest to England when, in

1587, Elizabeth I had her troublesome cousin Mary executed. At the same time, he lived in constant tension, with his household's fears that he would be kidnapped by Mary's friends or by any of the rival factions of nobles: in fact, in 1578, James was kidnapped, by Morton's enemies the Earls of Atholl and Argyll; Morton staged a counter-*coup* and regained, albeit temporarily, control of King and kingdom, but the affair left the eleven-year-old boy with an obsessive terror of violence which dogged him even into old age.

For the most part, however, James was left in peace, passing most of his first twelve years at Stirling Castle, where he was put through an arduous education. The King responded well to teaching, applying himself as diligently as had Edward VI, though his studies left him more pedantic than wise. Also like Edward, James cultivated a deep interest in theology and the administration of his Church – the Presbyterian Church, as established in the reign of his mother. And again like his Tudor cousin, James's concept of his sovereignty was dominated by theology, so that he saw himself as God's elect, his prerogatives theoretically inviolable – which only made the attempts of his nobles on his power the harder to comprehend.

Understandably, from childhood, James tried to create some semblance of family life for himself. His governess, Lady Mar, was the most dour of Scotswomen, but he could find something lovable even in his 'Lady Minnie', and was devoted to her son, the young Earl of Mar, some eight years his senior (whom he dubbed 'Jock o' the Slaittis' from the boy's, to him, incomprehensible love of mathematics). But it was not until he was thirteen years old that the King found someone apparently eager to respond to his craving for real affection: his cousin Esmé Stuart, a young man come from France like a breath of spring from the warmer south. Used as James was to plain-speaking Scots war-lords and sober ministers of the Kirk, Esmé was an exotic, with his fine clothes, jewels and perfumes, his casual manners and ready laughter. From the outset, Stuart was viewed with mistrust and disfavour by the royal councillors, who realized better than the naïve James that here was a product of the depraved Court of the homosexual French King Henri III, as eager for power as any of his Scottish rivals. Soon rumours were circulating that the two young men were themselves deep in a homosexual relationship. Certainly, James fell completely under Esmé's sway, creating him Duke of Lennox, awarding him Court office and a generous income, and allowing him, in 1581, to succeed Morton at the head of his Council. The favourite's rule was short, however: in August 1582, the King was again kidnapped, this time by former adherents of the late Earl of Morton (who included his old friend 'Jock'). They forced James to send

Esmé into exile; he returned to France, where he died shortly afterwards.

James VI survived his unhappy childhood, gathered power into his
own hands, stabilized his kingdom and married. But even into the 1590s
he was made miserable by (wholly warrantable) fears of his nobles, and
even while he fathered children on his queen, Anne of Denmark, he still
enjoyed his entourage of bright and pretty young men.

James's accession to the throne of England in 1603 brought to that
kingdom the first royal children for half a century: Princes Henry and
Charles and Princess Elizabeth (their brother and sister, Robert and
Margaret, were left behind in Scottish graves; two princesses, Mary and
Sophia, would be born in England, to die in infancy).

The King loved children, and it was one of the many minor tragedies
of his life that none of his responded to his affection as warmly as he
would have liked. He succeeded so well in giving his heir, Prince
Henry, the stable, healthy childhood which he had lacked, that he
formed a character unlike and unsympathetic to his own in all but
devout respect for exalted principles of monarchy. Henry was all that
James was not: self-confident, extrovert, athletic, open-minded and precociously sophisticated in judging men's characters – including that of
his own father, whom he soon found wanting in the very virtues of
manliness and firm government which James so fervently advocated.
The Princess Elizabeth was always ready to follow the lead of her elder
brother, and gave him the devotion her father wanted for himself;
Prince Charles was too sickly a child to be often in his father's company.
So James had another reason for turning to fawning favourites for companionship and affection: he never grudged his young men their marriages and openly dandled their children.

Despite the care lavished on royal children, the younger of James I's
sons, Prince Charles, was a poor specimen. Bad nourishment had left
him with rickets, so weak in his legs that he was nearly four years old
before he could walk; he had a speech impediment too. The Prince was
the last of the royal children to leave Scotland, following his parents to
England when he was nearly four years old, for King James had been
hard put to find an English noblewoman willing to take on the responsibility of his son's health, despite the honour and obvious rewards of the
post. Lady Carey was at last appointed Charles's governess, and in her
the King met a woman of independent and forthright views on the
child's management:

Many a battle my wife had with the King [recorded Sir Robert Carey],
but she still prevailed. The King was desirous that the string under his

[Charles's] *tongue should be cut, for he was so long beginning to speak as he thought he would never have spoke. Then he would have him put in iron boots, to strengthen the sinews and joints, but my wife protested so much against them that she got the victory.*[1]

By the time Charles left the Careys, when he was eleven, he was notice-ably stronger, playing tennis and riding well, though he stammered till the end of his life and grew to be only five feet four inches tall (his brother was five feet eight).

The younger boy idolized the Prince of Wales – even though Henry could tease him cruelly in elder-brother fashion (he once advised him to become a bishop, to wear the episcopal long robes which would hide his spindly legs). In 1607 Charles wrote to Henry:

Sweet, sweet brother,
    I thank you for your letter. I will keep it better than all my graith [possessions] *and I will send my pistols by Master Hinton. I will give anything that I have to you, both my horses and my books, and my* [firing-] *pieces and my crossbows or anything that you would have.*
    Good brother, love me and I shall ever love and serve you.[2]

Of the royal children, only the Prince of Wales went often to Court; his brother and sister went there only occasionally, sometimes to take part in the masques (entertainments of music, dancing and poetry, lavishly costumed) staged by their mother. By 1610, Charles had suf-ficiently graceful a gait to represent 'Zephyr' in a masque, wearing a robe of green satin embroidered with golden flowers, a garland on his head surmounted by a fine lawn halo, two silver wings attached to his shoulders, dancing by an artificial waterfall, surrounded by twelve little girls in pale blue satin tunics. Princess Elizabeth had a role also: she was the 'Nymph of the Thames', one of several dryads who emerged from a scenery cavern to sing the glories of their water, before dancing in a ladies' quadrille with the Queen.

England had accepted the change of monarchy and dynasty remark-ably well in 1603, but there remained one dissident element – the Catholics - for the King to fear. He had good cause: in November 1605 their Gunpowder Plot was discovered. The seizure of Guy Fawkes in the cellars of the Houses of Parliament was followed by a penetrating enquiry as to his associates and their plans. It was revealed that, having killed the King, the Queen and their sons, their council-lors and Parliament-men, the conspirators aimed to put the only sur-viving member of the royal family, the nine-year-old Elizabeth, on the throne, to effect her conversion to Catholicism, marry her to a Catholic and manipulate their 'puppet' queen to their own advantage. Timed to coincide with the Westminster explosion was a plan to kidnap the child from her home at Combe Abbey in Warwickshire. But, just as the Parliament plan misfired, so did that for Elizabeth: her guardian, Lord Harrington, was warned of 'papist' movements in the neighbourhood and had the child put into safety in Coventry.

The Princess was appalled by the thought of the fate she had so narrowly escaped. As Harrington recorded the following summer: "Her Highness doth often say, 'What a queen should I have been by this means? I had rather have been with my royal father in the Parliament House than wear his crown on such condition.' This poor lady hath not yet recovered the surprise and is very ill and troubled."[3]

The death of Henry, Prince of Wales, in 1612, came as a shock to the two kingdoms he would one day have ruled. In the past couple of years he had emerged as a personality of some force, popular with statesmen and public alike. He quarrelled openly with his father's current – and most unpopular – favourite, Robert Carr, championed the ill-starred Sir Walter Raleigh and dogged the footsteps of the Master Shipwright of the royal dockyard, Phineas Pett, who taught him how he might one day manage the increasingly important royal navy. The Prince's disapproval of his father's lifestyle was accentuated by the decorum in his own apartments at St James's, while his criticism of the King's methods of government (which fell far short of his theory) left no one in doubt that the future 'King Henry IX' would be more firmly in control of Council and Parliament than King James I.

But then Henry died, aged eighteen, and hopes were dashed.

He was first taken ill at the end of October 1612, during celebrations for the forthcoming wedding of his sister Elizabeth (now sixteen) to the German Prince Frederick, Elector Palatine. When Henry missed the Guildhall banquet in honour of his future brother-in-law's arrival, it was given out that he had a fever, which was put down to his having taken a swim after over-eating of fruit and sea-foods; in fact he had been stricken by typhoid.

The royal physicians administered their most valued remedies to the Prince: unicorn's horn, crushed pearls and stags' bones dissolved in wine; they tried cupping him and bleeding him, and even applied an opened pigeon to his shaved head. Of course, in vain.

Princess Elizabeth was devoted to her brother. Several times she begged to be allowed to go to him, but was refused. She disguised herself and reached the door of his bedchamber, only to be turned away. The King and Queen, however, allowed themselves to be persuaded of the risks of infection in visiting their son.

Then, after only eight days of illness, on the 6th November 1612, the Prince of Wales died. It is said that his last words were, "Where is my dear sister?"[4]

Elizabeth's grief was not allowed to interfere with arrangements for her wedding, nor to abate its festivities. The Princess married the Elector on St. Valentine's Day 1613 and two months later set sail for the Continent, never to see father, mother or brother again, and not to return to her native land for nearly half a century.

Prince Charles had now to take his brother's place. He was twelve years old, still rather frail, with the promise of a delicate handsomeness but little of Henry's strength of character. These were troubled times for the monarchy, with the Crown deep in debt, Parliament fuming at King James's high-handedness and, as they saw it, ruinous policies – after his wrath with the 'Addled' Parliament, James managed without one for seven years, yet another cause for national discontent. At Court, the scandal of the royal favourite, Robert Carr's involvement in a notorious murder case was followed by the rise of the even more unpopular George Villiers, who soon came to dominate the King's life. For the first time, Prince Charles dared show some of his late brother's independence, taunting Villiers and sneering at him. The quarrel between the Prince and the favourite reached a dangerous level of tension – but then Villiers's famed charm won Charles over, and the two young men became as mutually devoted as even the doting King could wish. His "Baby Charles" and his "Steenie" were the props of his last years and by the early 1620s effectively ruled the nation through him. It is obvious that the Prince of Wales had transferred his hero-worship of his brother to Villiers – there was no hint of a homosexual relationship between them.

Nevertheless, George Villiers, who was created Duke of Buckingham at the end of James I's reign, did prove an obstacle to Charles's marriage, as well as to his good relations with Parliament.

James I died, largely unregretted, in 1625, and a few months later his son, now King Charles I, married the fifteen-year-old French Princess Henrietta Maria. But Buckingham, who feared to lose his influence to the new Queen, so effectively interfered between the royal couple that he alienated Henrietta Maria from Charles from the outset. It was only after Buckingham's death in 1628 (at the hand of an assassin – the one brave man who did what many wanted to do) that relations between the King and Queen improved, and Charles became a model and devoted husband. It is a noteworthy fact that Henrietta Maria went childless through the first three years of marriage, then conceived very shortly after Buckingham's death.

The royal couple's first child was born on the 15th May 1629, but he died the same day. Over the next few years, however, the Queen filled her nursery to everyone's satisfaction and lost only one of her later eight children in infancy. For the first time in many years, the royal family presented a picture of exemplary domestic contentment.

The eldest of the royal children, the future King Charles II, was an intriguing personality from infancy. Before he was a year old, his mother was writing to her sister, "He is so ugly I am ashamed of him, but his size and fatness supply the want of beauty. I wish you could see the gentleman for he has no ordinary mien; he is so serious in all that he does that I cannot help fancying him wiser than myself."[5] The wisdom that the child showed from his early years (and which would endear him to his subjects in later life) lay to a great extent in his dry humour, his penetration of absurdities: once, having been rebuked by his mother for refusing to take his medicine, he countered saucily by writing to his absent 'governor', the Earl of Newcastle, that "My lord, I would not have you take too much physic for it doth always make me worse, and I think it will do the like with you."[6] Equally endearingly, the boy disdained most of the fine toys in his nursery (though he did show an interest in pretty dolls – a foretaste of his later proclivities) and every night for some years took to bed with him what modern psychologists would call a 'security symbol' – a plain block of wood.

In 1637 the Court painter van Dyck produced a charming group-study of the royal children, centred on the Prince of Wales (by then plump and pretty), leaning on the head of a huge mastiff, with his brother James, still in the girlish gown of infancy, the already dignified Mary, Princess Royal, and the two little Princesses Elizabeth and Anne. The latter appears a sturdy, healthy child, squirming out of her wrappings, and she was to prove bright and intelligent – but she contracted tuberculosis when scarcely out of the cradle and died shortly before her third birthday.

By that time public approval of the royal family had been strained by the Queen's blatant attempts to bring up her children in the Catholic Church. When the King forbade her to take them to Mass in her own chapel, she surreptitiously wooed their interest by rewarding their efforts in family games with rosaries, statuettes and relics. It was no wonder, in an age of violent anti-Catholic feeling in England, that the Queen's domestic virtues were ignored by her husband's subjects who, now lacking a Buckingham to revile, accredited to Henrietta Maria the King's shortcomings in government.

In fact, it was his need to prove to Parliament his loyalty to Prot-
estantism that drove Charles I to give up his plans for mating his
elder daughter, Mary, with a prestigious Catholic monarch and give
her to a Protestant prince, William of Orange, son of the mere Stad-
holder of the United Provinces (the Netherlands). Charles had formerly sneered at such a match and had only reluctantly agreed that
William should have the younger princess, Elizabeth, but now, to pla-
cate his fiercely Protestant (Puritan) Parliament, Mary, the elder, was to
be sacrificed. Contemporary opinion had come some way from the
medieval as regards child marriage, but for these reasons of state, Mary
was to be a bride at the age of nine.

Nevertheless, the royal wedding could not stave off Parliament's
attacks on the King's ministers, its impeachment of the Earl of Strafford,
architect of his more arbitrary measures in government. The King and
Queen and their two elder children sat for hours in a room adjoining
Westminster Hall listening to the trial, hearing the Earl – and thus, by
implication, Charles himself – charged with all manner of crimes against
the state. When, inevitably, Strafford was sentenced to death, Charles I
still thought that he could save him: in desperation he sent the ten-year-
old Prince of Wales to the House of Commons, with a letter in
which the King begged Members to commute the sentence to that of
imprisonment. But the boy was turned away, to take the petition – un-
opened – back to his father.

Princess Mary's wedding took place during the tense days between
Strafford's trial and his execution, in May 1641. Fair-haired, with a
roses-and-cream complexion, she was a pretty, bright child, already
with sufficient dignity to go through the ceremony with her fifteen-year-old bridegroom and to undergo the embarrassment of a
public 'bedding' with him – though the couple were all the time supervised by the royal family and courtiers and were separated, after
exchanging a few kisses, to go to their own beds.

After Strafford's death, Charles I's relations with his Parliament saw
no improvement. By the end of the year, the Common's complaints of
grievances had reached fever pitch, and the King was in a passion of
anger and fear. In the first days of January 1642, he tensed himself for
action, making his famous attempt to arrest the five ring-leaders of dis-
sent – he failed: "the birds had flown". Parliament's subsequent demand
for control of the national army confirmed the King's resolve to take
arms against his enemies.

For some time past, Queen Henrietta Maria had gone in fear of her
life, with mobs surrounding the palace roaring against her; the King
even dreaded that she, like Strafford, would be impeached. His first act,

therefore, was to send his wife to safety, despatching her to Holland with Princess Mary, ostensibly to settle her daughter into her new home, in fact to raise money on her jewels with which to buy arms. Then Charles went north, taking the Prince of Wales with him. (The younger children were left in the presumed safety of Oatlands Palace.)

On the 22nd August, the King raised his standard over Nottingham Castle. The civil war began.

Before the year was out, Prince Charles and his brother James, some three years his junior, had become accustomed to life in army camps and had even viewed their first battle, at Edgehill, on the 23rd October, where Royalist and Parliamentarian forces met in a costly but inconclusive engagement. At one point in the battle, Charles became separated from his guards, with the enemy's troop of horses bearing down on him. "I fear them not," he shouted, brandishing his pistol, but before they — or he — could do any harm, his attendants spurred up and removed the boy from danger.

An exhilarating period followed. After Edgehill the King made his headquarters at Oxford (where his wife joined him in November 1643, on her return from the Continent), but he and his two elder sons made frequent forays into the countryside, and the Prince of Wales, nominal commander of his own troops, played his part in councils of war and sieges and battles under the protection of seasoned warriors his guardians. Lessons, of course, gave place to more urgent concerns.

Early in 1645, when he was fourteen years old, Prince Charles was named 'Captain-General of the West', again a nominal command but one which entailed his setting up his own headquarters at Bristol. On the 4th March he rode out of Oxford: father and son never met again.

Queen Henrietta Maria had already parted from her husband. Pregnant again, she had been sent west in the spring of 1644, to bear her (as it proved, last) child in the safety of Exeter, away from the war-area. However, even as the Queen nursed the baby to whom she had given birth on the 16th June, the Roundheads made an advance into the west, and only two weeks after her confinement, she put the baby Princess Henrietta into the care of one of her attendants, Lady Dalkeith, and fled in disguise from the city. Narrowly escaping capture, Henrietta Maria reached Falmouth and took ship for France. Shortly afterwards, Exeter fell to the forces of Parliament, and Lady Dalkeith and her charge were despatched to Oatlands Palace, to the 'protective custody' of the King's enemies.

Some two years later, in July 1646, a small family group might have been observed trudging southward away from Oatlands: a Frenchman, his deformed wife and their little son, whom they called Pierre. It was

King Edward VI in about 1550: a portrait attributed to Guillim Stretes.

Lady Jane Grey, the teenaged 'nine-days queen' of 1553, beheaded in 1554.

The family of Sir Richard Saltonstall, *c.*1660, by David des Granges.
Strangely, Lady Saltonstall is depicted not only in child-bed but also, at the
right of the picture, fully recovered and holding her baby.

Opposite: James VI of Scotland (the future James I of England), aged eight.

IACOBVS DEI GRATIA REX
SCOTORVM AETATIS SVAE 8
1574

The tomb effigies of two of the children of James VI and I who died in infancy. *Above:* Mary. *Left:* Sophia.

The three surviving children of James VI and I. *Left to right:* Henry Frederick, Prince of Wales, Charles Duke of York (the future King Charles I) and Princess Elizabeth.

Henry Frederick, Prince of Wales, on the hunting field. His early death robbed the nation of a promising future king.

The five eldest children of Charles I, painted by van Dyck in 1637. *Left to right:* Mary, James, Charles, Elizabeth and Anne (who died in 1641).

Two future queens – *left:* Mary of York (the future Queen Mary II); *right:* her sister Anne – both painted by Lely.

Prince William, Duke of Gloucester, the only survivor of Queen Anne's many pregnancies – but he did not live beyond childhood.

The children of James II's second marriage: James Francis Edward, 'Prince of Wales', and Princess Louise Marie. (Largillière)

Lady Dalkeith, her tall figure mis-shapen by a padding of rags in her clothes, with a royal valet and the now two-year-old Princess Henrietta. They had escaped from Oatlands, and made their way to the coast without detection – though the child several times hazarded their adventure by protesting loudly that she was "not Pierre, *Princess*". The refugees landed at Calais and made their way to the English Queen, now established at the Court of her French relations. Charles, Prince of Wales, was there too, having arrived a month earlier, coming from England via the Scillies and Channel Islands (where the precocious sixteen-year-old is said to have taken the first in his long line of mistresses). Miserable in exile, he was charmed by the blonde and already beautiful little sister, whom he named 'Minette'.

By then, too, the city of Oxford had fallen. The King had not been taken – he had earlier gone north to beg aid and shelter from the Scots, only to be made their prisoner and subsequently sold to the English Parliament; but Prince James had fallen into the Roundheads' hands, and he had been sent to join Elizabeth and Henry, who had long since been removed from Oatlands and placed in custody at St. James's Palace, hostages and bargaining-counters with the Royalists. Still, they were kindly treated by their guardians, former courtiers, and indeed Elizabeth and Henry could almost remember no other life, for they had been six and two years old respectively when separated from their parents in the crisis year of 1642.

In April 1648, however, the fourteen-year-old James suddenly appeared at his sister Mary's Court at The Hague. The royal children had not been held in very close confinement, and friends had managed to smuggle messages into their apartments with details of an escape plan for the older prince. The boy was to start a 'craze' for games of hide-and-seek among the royal children and their companions; he was to hide so effectively in the maze of deserted chambers that his guardians would become accustomed to his being missing for long periods of time; then, when all was prepared, he was to slip out of the palace. All went according to plan. On the night of the 20th April, James met his courier, the Royalist Colonel Bampfield, in St. James's Park and, in wig and cloak, drove in a hackney coach to a 'safe house' near London Bridge. There Bampfield's young fiancée, Anne Murray, was looking out for them. She takes up the story:

> The first that came in was the Duke, who with much joy I took in my arms.
> His Highness called, "Quickly, quickly, dress me," and, putting off his clothes, I dressed him in the woman's habit that was prepared, which fitted His Highness very well, and [he] was very pretty in it.

> *After he had eaten something I had made while I was idle lest His High-*
> *ness should be hungry, and having sent for a Woodstreet cake (which I*
> *knew he loved) to take in the barge, with as much haste as could be, His*
> *Highness went across the bridge to the stairs where the barge lay.*[7]

Bampfield and James, under the aliases of 'Mr. Andrews' and his 'sister',
embarked at Tilbury and safely reached Holland.

While the Prince had still been with his brother and sister at St.
James's, the three children had been allowed several times to visit their
father, in Parliament's custody at Hampton Court, and both James and
Henry had been solemnly impressed by the King's warning against their
being offered the crown by Parliament, as puppet-monarchs in place of
himself or their elder brother. Elizabeth and Henry also saw their father
in the last months of his life, before the trial at which Parliament-men
condemned him to death.

Princess Elizabeth was thirteen years old then, a pious, serious, schol-
arly girl, passionately attached to her father. She went through agonies
as Parliament planned his end. Then, on the 29th January, the day before
the scheduled execution, Elizabeth and Henry were brought to bid him
farewell. The Princess recorded the last meeting:

> *He told me he was glad I was come, and although he had not time to say*
> *much, yet somewhat he would say to me, which he had not to another, or*
> *have in writing, because he feared their cruelty was such as that they would*
> *not have permitted him to write to me.*
>
> *He wished me not to grieve and torment myself for him, for that would be*
> *a glorious death that he would die, it being for the laws and liberties of this*
> *land and for maintaining the true Protestant religion. . . .*
>
> *He told me he had forgiven all his enemies and hoped God would forgive*
> *him also, and commanded us and all the rest of my brothers and sisters to for-*
> *give them.*
>
> *He bid me tell my mother that his thoughts never strayed from her, and*
> *that his love should be the same to the last. Withal he commanded me and*
> *my brother to be obedient to her and bid me send his blessing to my brothers*
> *and sisters, with commendation to all his friends.*
>
> *Furthermore, he commanded us to forgive these people but never to trust*
> *them, for they had been most false to him and to those that gave them*
> *power, and he feared also to their own souls; and desired me not to grieve for*
> *him, for he said he should die a martyr and that he doubted not but the Lord*
> *would settle his throne upon his son and that we should all be happier than*
> *we could have expected to have been if he had lived.*[8]

So affected was the King by the parting with his children that, before
they were fairly out of the door, he stumbled into his bedroom.

Elizabeth's sobs drew him back for one last kiss.

On the morning of the 30th January 1649, in the courtyard in front of the Banqueting Hall of Whitehall Palace, King Charles I was beheaded.

That spring, rumours circulated England that 'Bessy and Harry Stuart' had been sent to a charity school: in fact, their humiliation lay in the removal of their titles and the former tokens of respect paid to them, and the dismissal of all but a few of their personal servants. But Elizabeth was visibly weakening: her physician first noted 'spleen' and scurvy, then a speeding pulse, her stomach's refusal of food and signs of a tumour there. The girl's petition to Parliament that she and her brother be sent to their sister Mary in the Netherlands (made a few months before and refused) was now given serious consideration, but Parliament's agreement came too late. On the 22nd August the Princess played her brother at bowls on the green at Carisbrooke Castle and was caught in a heavy shower of rain: the next day she came down with a fever.

On the afternoon of the 8th September, she was found lying dead in her bed, her cheek resting on the Bible which had been her father's. She had been reading the words "Come unto me all ye that travail and are heavy laden and I will give ye peace."

The Duke of Gloucester was not immediately despatched to his family. His brother Charles's alliance with the Scots and attempted invasion of England from the north made him still a valuable hostage, and it was not until February 1653 that the Prince, now twelve years old, was allowed to join his family abroad.

Henry had last seen his brother James in 1648, but he would not remember the mother who had parted from him in 1642 or his sister Mary, or his brother the new King Charles II, and he had never seen Princess Henrietta.

Queen Henrietta Maria had been aged by her troubles. Having fled the English civil war, she found herself in the midst of another, in France, before the 1640s were out – though this was short-lived and far less detrimental to the monarchy; at first she had lived in high style, but the French civil war and the demands on her purse to finance English exiles had plunged her into real poverty – at one point in 1648, the Queen had been hard put to it to heat her apartments and feed her daughter and herself; French relations and friends were charitable to the unhappy woman but compounded their generosity by an unpalatable measure of patronage which her pride found hard to bear. The death of her husband, in 1649, had shattered the Queen's nerves for a time, but with characteristic resilience she rallied and threw herself into plans for her son's restoration.

In fact, Charles II would have been better off without his mother's well-meant but impractical advice, and he let her see that he resented her interference. Throughout the 1650s, Henrietta Maria was intermittently at loggerheads with her eldest son, railing against his chosen ministers and criticizing his projects for a return to England.

The young King let his mother have her way with his sister Henrietta Anne, whom she was bringing up as a Catholic, but when Prince Henry went to live with her, Charles demanded a promise from her that she would not attempt to convert his brother, who was a potential heir to the English crown. However, the Queen was too much of a zealot in her religion not to take the chance of 'turning' Henry while Charles was far away on his own business. She sent him off to the abbey at Pontoise in the charge of an English priest (putting his Anglican tutor in a very difficult position), effectively isolating the boy from his English friends. Inevitably, the news was reported to the King, along with rumours that Henry was subsequently to enter the Jesuit College at Clermont, where he would be subjected to Catholic propaganda which the English, with their inbred fear of 'popery', looked upon with horror.

King Charles wrote to his brother in the strongest possible terms – a cruel letter, one would think, to a fourteen-year-old boy – threatening to disown him, never to see him again, if he gave in to his mother's threats and persuasions. At the same time, the King had his brother brought back to Paris.

Even so, Henrietta Maria would not give up. In an emotional interview with her youngest son, the Queen abused him for his 'disobedience' to her and sent him off for yet another session with his priest – to no avail: Henry remembered his father's words to him about not abandoning his religion, and had the more recent warning of his brother to fortify his resolution. Henrietta Maria refused to see Henry again, refused him even a parting blessing.

The next day was a Sunday, when the Queen would drive out to her favourite convent, at Chaillot, and knowing this the Duke of Gloucester placed himself by the roadside in wait for her carriage. When it drove up, he fell to his knees, but his mother would not even look at him. The boy then made his way back into Paris and attended an Anglican service there. Soon afterwards, Henry was removed from the Queen's care.

The heart-break of 1649, the bitter disappointment of 1651 (when Charles's attempt on his kingdoms with Scottish help failed) and the long despair of the 1650s were forgotten in the spring of 1660 when news at last came from England that the Commonwealth was breaking up. After the death of Oliver Cromwell, Parliament and the Army had vied strenuously for power, with the result that they only weakened the nation and created conditions ripe for a return of the monarchy. Thus

Charles II was summoned home.

Tactfully, the King embarked for England not from France or the Catholic Netherlands but from Protestant Holland, and his Catholic mother waited some five months before joining him, bringing the now sixteen-year-old Henrietta Anne with her. James, Duke of York, and Henry, Duke of Gloucester, had accompanied the King, however, and they were soon joined by their sister Mary (who had been widowed ten years earlier).

Nevertheless, though the nation continued to fête the King and his family and though the joy of restoration was slow to wear off, the Stuarts' troubles were not over. Before the Queen's arrival in England – and before Charles could effect her reconciliation with her youngest son – Prince Henry had taken smallpox and died of it, that September. During that autumn, Henrietta Maria set herself against her family by refusing to countenance her son James's marriage with his former mistress, Anne Hyde (daughter of one of the King's ministers whom she openly detested), and battle raged in the royal household through Christmas. It was only lulled by the sudden death of Princess Mary, also from smallpox, in the last week of the year. Even so, no one was sorry when the Queen returned to France, taking Henrietta Anne with her, to be married to the French king's brother (with whom the pretty and vivacious Princess, King Charles's beloved 'Minette', was to be supremely unhappy and who, it was rumoured, had her poisoned in 1670).

Charles and James now represented the Stuart family in England, and despite the great difference in their characters (Charles had learned, in his troubles, to be devious and canny, to present a bland face and keep his own counsels; James was open and straightforward, painfully honest about his political and religious principles so out of tune with current opinion), the two brothers remained loyal to each other. Time and again, Charles would risk Parliament's disapproval and national mistrust to keep James close to him and to safeguard his claim to the throne.

The Stuarts had suffered a good deal together, and if there was little real family life in the royal palaces, this vestige of family feeling at least remained.

The dynasty dwindles

On his restoration to the monarchy, King Charles II did his duty to his dynasty and his kingdom by taking a wife, planning to fill a royal nursery and safeguard the succession. It was his great misfortune that the bride he chose, the Princess Catherine of Braganza, proved incapable of fulfilling his hopes.

She, poor woman, had a good deal to bear in her married life. Charles was always kind and respectful to her, but he had long since begun a career of amorous self-indulgence which he would not renounce when he took a wife. One mistress after another (and often several at a time) made their appearance at Queen Catherine's Court, well-endowed by their royal lover and repaying him by giving him a host of children. Her jealousy of other women's fecundity, as much as her husband's infidelity, blighted the life of the lonely Portuguese Queen.

At one point, lying in a deep fever, Catherine rambled in her speech, giving vent to her cherished delusion that she was the mother of children. The King sat beside her, soothing her, but even this insight into his wife's misery did not make him forsake his paramours when she recovered.

During the reign of King Charles II (1660–85), the younger generation of the royal family was represented (apart from the King's bastards) by the children of his brother James in England, Princess Mary's only son, William, over in Holland, the two small daughters of Henrietta Anne, in France, and the numerous family of their aunt Elizabeth, the widowed Electress Palatine – also abroad, in the Netherlands and the German states. James, Duke of York, was his brother's heir, and thus his children were the first in line to succeed to the throne after him.

In fact, the first of his children had been conceived outside wedlock – or so it was said by many. Duchess Anne herself firmly denied it, asserting that she and James had been secretly married in Holland long before their union was recognized by the King. She had been the Duke's mistress for some time before that, while she was still maid-of-honour to his sister Mary, and it was only when the royal family returned to England in the summer of 1660 that she had asserted her rights as his wife. Anne was pregnant; James was shame-faced and none too sure that he wanted to marry a commoner; King Charles was amused – but irritated; Queen Henrietta Maria, when she learned that her second son was being trapped into marriage by a scheming girl, was furious; Princess Mary, in the few months of life left to her, was scornful and refused to accept as sister-in-law one who had formerly been her own attendant. Nevertheless, James had a conscience, and Charles had no wish to mar his return home with an unseemly family wrangle – especially as he relied on Anne's father, Chancellor Hyde, to represent his interests in government. Thus the couple were privately married ('again', Anne would have said) shortly before the birth of her child, a son, in October 1660. Fortunately, since his legitimacy would always be in question, the little Prince Charles died the following February. In the years that followed, Duchess Anne had no trouble in becoming pregnant, only in producing healthy children: at her death in 1671 she left four, Mary, Anne, Catherine and Edgar, but the latter two died a few months after her. Like Queen Catherine, Anne had to reconcile herself to her husband's amours, but at least she had the satisfaction of succeeding, where even his own mother had failed, in converting James to the Catholic faith – a step which, years later, would cost him a throne.

It was Anne Hyde who gave the Princesses Mary and Anne of York their unique asset: they were 'real English' in their maternal ancestry, the first such royal children since Edward and Elizabeth Tudor. The two English grandparents, the Hydes, both came of good country stock, of the yeoman and gentry class, and had none of the courtiers' sophisticated but fawning attitude towards royalty. Indeed, courtiers were amused to see the rotund Grandfather Hyde openly asking his stately son-in-law after the children's health with a fine show of familiarity. But then, even the Duke of York was once seen (by the diarist Pepys) to dandle his eldest daughter on his knee when he thought no one was looking.

Of course the care of the Princesses customarily devolved on a host of servants, and Mary and Anne were only rarely in the company of their parents, even before their mother's death in 1671. And Anne had suffered a break in routine and removal from the close circle of her intimates when she was only three or four, when she was sent to France to consult an eminent oculist for 'defluxion' (watering) of the eyes. Unfortunately, the treatment was not wholly successful, and she was left with weak eyes, and myopia, for the rest of her life. A childhood friend of the Princesses later recorded a characteristic incident:

When they were children and walking in the park together, they started a dispute between them whether something at a great distance was a man or a

*tree, her sister [Mary] being of the former opinion and she of the latter.
And when they came so near that both must be convinced it was a man,
[Mary] said, "Now, sister, are you satisfied what it is?" But Lady Anne
turned away after she saw what it was, persisting still in what she had once
declared, and cried, "No, sister, 'tis a tree!"*[1]

The incident was characteristic in more ways than one: Anne had a
streak of stubbornness in her character which would never, even in
maturity, be broken by reasoned argument; nor would she ever give
way to her elder sister where her pride was concerned. Still, Anne was a
good-natured child, fond of her sister and always on the look-out for the
affection which their position denied them. Even when their father married again, in 1673, Mary and Anne did not find the mother-figure
which they needed, for the new Duchess of York was only a few years
their senior. She was an Italian princess, Maria Beatrice of Modena, fifteen years old when she came to her forty-year-old bridegroom. However, there was a strong mutual attraction between the couple, which
later blossomed into love (though it did not cure James of his predilec-
tion for amorous Court ladies), and in January 1675 the Duchess gave
birth to her first child. It was a girl, named Catherine Laura, who lived
only nine months; of the three more living children produced by Maria
Beatrice over the next seven years, a boy, named Charles, died when
only a month old, and the Princesses Isabella and Catherine Mary at four
and a half years and two months respectively. After 1682 it seemed to
royal doctors that the Duchess of York would bear no more children.
This, of course, confirmed Mary and Anne as their father's heirs, and
King Charles exercised considerable vigilance to ensure that they were
brought up as Protestants, despite their father and stepmother's hopes of
their conversion.

At Court and at the 'nursery-palace' of Richmond, the two Princesses
were brought up in an almost exclusively feminine society. Their
governess, Lady Frances Villiers, was the mother of several daughters
and had also under her care several young girls of 'gentle' birth, so that
Mary and Anne, despite the due care which she gave them, could never
feel that they had any exclusive claim to their governess's attention.
Inevitably, too, the boarding-school atmosphere produced the usual
'crushes', as both girls sought friends who would reciprocate their
starved affections.

Princess Mary formed a devotion to one Frances Apsley, nine years
her senior, and her distress when the girl graduated from Richmond to
Court was profound. She poured out her love for Frances in one letter
after another, each couched in the 'poetic' and dramatic style which she

gleaned from the romances and plays which were her preferred read-ing-matter. Mary was, she once wrote, killing herself "with sighs, another time I kill myself with joy for her. All I know is so confounded together, the good with the ill, the ill with the good, I don't know what to make of it, but now a melancholy qualm comes over my stomach, and oh I tremble to think the ill will overcome the good".[2] Part of the 'ill' was Mary's jealousy, for once Anne had recovered from a passion for another Richmond friend, Cicely Cornwallis, she threw herself into an equally fervent infatuation for her sister's friend. Mary had to watch while the fickle Frances gave Anne a ring as token of their new attach-ment. And so Anne too began to write to Frances, in terms similar to her sister's, though even more randomly expressed. One 'conceit' which both sisters employed in their correspondence was the use of pseu-donyms culled from the plays which they enacted at Court with their friends: Anne was 'Ziphares', Frances 'Semandra' in Anne's letters to her; Mary 'Clorine' and Frances 'Aurelia' in theirs – though Mary often addressed Frances as her 'husband'.

It was all foolishness – rather pathetic – but it was unhealthy. Or so their elders thought. Anne's friendship with Cicely Cornwallis had been broken up on her stepmother's discovery of a 'passionate' letter, and Mary's attachment to Frances Apsley was frowned on by their govern-ess, so that the Princess had to resort to guile on at least one occasion to conceal a letter ready for posting. More important in the long term, however, was the bond forming between Anne (once she had allowed Mary to claim Frances's exclusive attention) and yet another member of their intimate circle, the fascinating, quicksilver, strong-willed Sarah Jennings, who was to keep Anne's devotion for years to come – to their mutual profit.

Still, at least the Stuart princesses were passing their formative years relatively harmlessly, away from the dissolute Court of their uncle Charles and the heavily Catholic atmosphere of their father's house-hold.

Mary was fifteen years old when she was told that a husband had been found for her. King Charles had decided on a Protestant match for her that would soothe the country (still watchful for signs of 'papistry' in the royal family) and forge a useful alliance with the Dutch. Her prospective husband was her cousin William, Prince of Orange, the son of her late aunt Mary. When she heard the news, the Princess wept all that day and the next; nor was she cheered by the sight of her bride-groom when he arrived a few days before their wedding.

William of Orange was then twenty-seven years old, but he had the gravity of an ancient, the solemnity of a man who had faced more problems than most – and overcome them. To the inexperienced girl, frivolous and shallow, he seemed only daunting and cold.

The Prince had good reason to be mature beyond his years. His life had never been easy.

He was a posthumous child, born in 1650 a fortnight after the death of his father. The latter, another William of Orange, had been fighting to keep control of Holland just prior to his death, and his removal from the political scene left the way clear for the 'left-wing' republicans who had long sought to break the hegemony of the House of Orange in Dutch government. They firmly put through legislation to bar the child William from ever taking up political power in the tradition of his immediate ancestors.

William's first years had been spent in the care of his mother, the English Princess Mary, but she was not the doting, over-protective mother suffered by so many only sons. Rather, Mary was fierce in championing her own and her child's rights – against the interference of the Orange family and the schemes of the republicans, and her battles for William left her no time – even if she had had the inclination – to cosset him. He was nine when she died, but there is no sign that he felt her passing unduly.

He was a self-contained child, intelligent and diligent in his studies, caring little for sport; he presented a dignified bearing in public but was endearingly humble among his boy-companions. With one of the latter, Willem Bentinck, he formed a strong attachment – some would say, in later years, a homosexual liaison, though that cannot now be proved or disproved. In fact, William was always at his best in wholly male company, as his future wife was with women: neither knew how to bridge the gulf between the sexes, to the detriment of their marriage.

Dutch reverses in their war with France cleared the political field of William's republican adversaries, who were swept from power by their unpopularity. By the time he reached his mid-twenties, he had gathered into his own hands as much power as his ancestors had wielded and was rapidly making a name for himself as a military commander. During a visit to his uncle King Charles in England in 1670, William had been confirmed in the royal succession, after his uncle York and York's children, but the possibility of actually inheriting the English crown seemed to have little appeal for him. It was only when he realized the usefulness of English arms and men in his war against France that a marriage with his cousin Mary, bringing him closer to the throne, began to interest William.

And so it was that the fifteen-year-old girl stood at the altar beside her cousin on the 4th November 1677 and became his wife.

Princess Anne was not present. She was suffering from smallpox at the time and was so ill that she did not find out that her sister had left until some days after Mary had embarked for her new home. An equal blow was the fact that her governess had taken the disease also, and had died of it. Lady Frances was replaced by a less sympathetic woman, Anne's aunt-by-marriage, Flower, Lady Clarendon, whom that lively wit Sarah Jennings characterized as one who "looked like a madwoman and talked like a scholar, which the Princess thought agreed very well together".[3]

There was, indeed, little reverence for female scholarship in royal circles in the second half of the seventeenth century. Mary and Anne had been taught to read and write (though, even in this age before the standardization of spelling, their orthography was, to say the least, 'individual'), and their reading matter was composed largely of romances, plays and poems, with a good deal of orthodox Protestant devotional literature. Both could chatter prettily in French, both were elegant dancers and enjoyed good music. Beyond that, they had no interest in learning more. Even when it became obvious that one or both of the girls would one day become queen, no attempt was made to instruct them in the necessary theory or practice of government.

Mary produced no heir to either the House of Orange or that of Stuart. Instead she had miscarriages. It was rumoured, of course, that William could not do his part, but Mary's continued hopes of one day giving him children belie the gossip. Anne, who was married at eighteen, in July 1683 (to a stolid, good-natured nonentity of a prince, George of Denmark), proved more fertile than her sister. She would go through seventeen pregnancies, averaging one a year – though once she was delivered of dead twins – but managed to produce only one child who survived infancy, a son, whom she named William, who was born in 1689.

King Charles II had died in February 1685 and, though one of his bastards, James, Duke of Monmouth, challenged for the crown, it was without success, and Charles's brother James, Duke of York, succeeded him on the throne, as King James II. England was prepared to overlook his Catholicism as long as the Anglican Church remained untouched, and as long as it could look forward to a Protestant monarch as his successor, but James had a conscience which always itched him, and he went too far, too soon, in attempting to achieve toleration for his co-religionists; at the same time, his Queen's pregnancy, after a long span of infertility, warranted fears that his Protestant daughters would be displaced in the royal succession by a new prince who would be raised as a Catholic.

Royal pregnancies were commonly a subject for inquisitiveness and gossip, but never more so than in the winter and spring of 1688. However, in her anxiety, Queen Maria Beatrice shied from allowing her ladies to examine her closely, and even her step-daughter Anne could not be certain that the Queen's bulk was genuine. Inevitably, it came to be said that James and his wife intended to produce a child, at the end of the nine months, that was not theirs but whom they would use to ensure a continuation of the Catholic line; others said that only the birth of a daughter would prove royal integrity. Understandably, Mary, William and Anne, who had the most to lose, were the most concerned that the baby should not be a boy, to displace them.

Prince James Francis Edward was born at St. James's Palace on the 10th June 1688 in the presence of sixty-seven witnesses — but that did not prevent his father's enemies from asserting that the child was a 'changeling' carried into the royal bedchamber, under the very noses of the spectators, in a warming-pan and put into the bed of his 'mother'. Despite the obvious impossibility of this procedure, and despite the fact that the Prince was strongly to resemble both his parents, the story gained wide credence.

However, before the year was out, the child's chances of ever wearing the crown began to recede. James II's religious policies and his mishandling of his Parliaments turned his subjects against him, and when a group of them summoned William of Orange to come and save 'ancient liberties', there was little support for the beleaguered King. William invaded and gathered an army but never unsheathed his sword: James was allowed to make an escape to France, whither his wife and son had preceded him. Parliament offered the crown to William and Mary (with the unprecedented notion of their being joint sovereigns, under certain limitations of power which they were induced to accept), and though Mary at least had qualms about her father's overthrow, they dedicated themselves to their destiny.

William was, of course, the dominant partner in the monarchy, but despite her intellectual inadequacies, Mary could perform creditably in Council during her husband's absence. Her religious upbringing made her valuable to him in Church affairs.

Themselves childless, they would not, of course, recognize Mary's half-brother, the Jacobite 'Prince of Wales' as their heir (though it was said at the time that, if the exiled King James would allow his son to be brought up an Anglican, something might be arranged), so Anne was recognized as heiress presumptive, and her one surviving son, the Duke of Gloucester, after her. His birth in 1689 was, in fact, a godsend to the new monarchy, though his health was always so precarious that Anne's continuing pregnancies (ten after his birth) were always the cause of much hopefulness.

In the first month of his life, the little William nearly died of convulsions. As he grew up, it became obvious that he would never be strong. He may, indeed, have suffered from hydrocephalus, for his head was too large for his body, and his legs were spindly and weak. He learned to walk upright, but he could not manage stairs, and if he fell could not pick himself up. In characteristic compensation, he developed into a lively child, eager for all sorts of martial sports and games and over-ambitious in what he could physically attain. He was always cheerful, however, and bore bravely the 'physicking' and constant supervision by his doctors.

Mary and Anne had been united in disapproval of their father's misgovernment, and Anne loyally received her sister and brother-in-law when they came to the throne. Thereafter, however, relations between them deteriorated. A chief cause of the sisters' quarrels was Anne's continuing devotion to her friend Sarah, now the wife of John Churchill, whose loyalty to the new regime was held in suspicion in the years immediately following that 'Glorious Revolution' of 1688. Anne stubbornly refused to give up her friend, and no plea or threat of Mary's could overcome her determination. Anne was notoriously indiscreet, and she did herself no good by openly referring to the King as 'the Dutch abortion'. Her husband, Prince George, was too dull-witted to advise his wife, and even Sarah could do little to temper Anne's resentment of her sister.

But the little Duke of Gloucester provided a point of sympathy within the royal family, and his visits to his aunt Mary were one of the last pleasures of her life. In 1694 the Queen left the world and the husband who had never cared for her deeply but who now sincerely mourned her death, and, the obstacle of her bitterness against Anne removed, King William entered on happier relations with his sister-in-law. He created her son a Knight of the Garter on his seventh birthday, occasionally visiting the boy at Kensington and admiring the troop of boy-soldiers his namesake so firmly drilled.

Then, on his eleventh birthday, William, Duke of Gloucester, over-exerted himself and took a fever. Smallpox was suspected, but in the end a battery of physicians diagnosed scarlet fever. After a week's illness, he died. His mother was stunned with grief.

Over in France the late Prince's half-uncle, James Francis Edward, less than two years his senior, was another delicate child: in 1704 he nearly died of a lung infection. But, to the discomfort of his relations in England, and of those Englishmen who feared a future challenge to the

Protestant throne, he survived. And his mother added further proof of his true birth by producing a healthy daughter in 1692: she was named Louise Marie.

Both James II and Maria Beatrice used the long days of their exile to pray for their restoration (of which chances became ever more remote with each year that passed) and in supervising the upbringing of their children. Both were fiercely possessive of and sentimental about the boy and girl who grew up in the sombre and formal atmosphere of their tiny Court at St. Germain, and the children were trained towards perfection in a strict but loving way. And both were, of course, firmly imbued with Catholic doctrine.

James Francis Edward was thirteen years old when his father died, in September 1701, and he was immediately proclaimed as 'King James III'. Always serious and reserved, the empty title seemed to weigh on him, and everyone who saw the boy was struck by his melancholy expression – in contrast to the careless gaiety of his young sister, whom everyone adored and pampered. (She became another victim of smallpox, in 1712; for days no one dared tell her brother of her death, for he was himself lying ill and it was feared that the shock would kill him. It did not, but his grief was acute.)

William of Orange had foreseen the possibility – the probability – of a Jacobite attempt on England, and after the death of his nephew, he had taken steps to ward it off. His sister-in-law was named as heiress-apparent, and provision was made for her to be succeeded by their German cousins, the descendants of James I's daughter Elizabeth. Several members of her family were Catholics, so they must be passed over; others were childless; and in the end the royal lottery fell to Elizabeth's youngest daughter, Sophia, who was married to the Elector of Hanover and who had had the good fortune to give birth to sons. William III died in 1702, and Anne struggled bravely through a twelve-year reign (fortified for much of that time by the good offices of her friend Sarah and her husband, the great Duke of Marlborough), and then, on the 1st August 1714, the last Stuart monarch died.

Sophia of Hanover, who would have loved to be queen, had predeceased her cousin by only a few weeks, and it was her eldest son George who came to England to claim his crown. He did so unopposed, despite general mistrust of him and his German entourage. It was only in 1715 that James III, 'the Pretender', mounted an army and made his bid for the crown – unsuccessfully as it transpired. Jacobite intrigues continued some three decades more, and in 1745 a final challenge to the Hanoverians came from James's son, 'the Young Pretender', 'Bonnie Prince Charlie', but though he managed to rally some support in Scotland, he made little headway and was turned back into exile. He was survived by a brother, who called himself 'Henry IX' and died in 1807, the last of the Stuart dynasty.

If Charles II had had legitimate children, James II would never have reigned. If James II had been willing to bring up his son as a Protestant, or if that son had never been born, he might have kept his throne. If William and Mary had had children . . . If Anne's children had lived . . . So much hung on the birth of royal children in the second half of the seventeenth century. It was the last tragedy of the generally tragic Stuart family that the right child was never born at the right time.

The Georgian Age
1714–1819

Idealists and philanthropists

Queen Anne's long career of child-bearing and her loss of all her children is an extreme case of the fate of many women of her time who became inured to pregnancy and bereavement many times over – though the Queen was more fortunate than many in surviving the hazards of frequent births and miscarriages. The infant mortality rate, in all classes of society, reached a peak at the turn of the seventeenth century, and those children who did survive birth and infancy had still to face the perils of disease.

It was only by the middle of the eighteenth century that the death-rate fell and the population began to increase, but from that time onwards the British population rose at a rate which amazed and puzzled pundits. Half a century after Queen Anne's death, George III's wife, Charlotte of Mecklenburg-Strelitz, was just beginning her twenty-year span of child-bearing, rearing thirteen of her fifteen children at least into late teens: many other women bid to rival her example.

One of the perils a Georgian baby had to face was 'artificial' feeding. Middle- and upper-class mothers still shied away from breast-feeding, and now not everyone sought a wet-nurse to take on the responsibility. Instead, many babies were fed on 'pap', a bread-and-milk or rice flour-and-arrowroot mixture often too heavy for their digestion. A contemporary gynaecologist's survey found that one child in two fed on pap died in infancy, compared with one in five breast-fed – still, the practice died hard.

Swaddling continued to fret small babies – and maybe even to contribute to their death-rate – into the eighteenth century, but that practice at least was on the wane. More pernicious was the refusal to feed small children on fresh fruit and vegetables, and scurvy was as rife as rickets. Smallpox, tuberculosis (the famous 'consumption') and typhus accounted for many more childhood deaths. The old remedies and 'cures' were still prevalent, usually administered without a thought for sending for a physician. Fried mice, boiled snails and other nauseous concoctions added to the suffering of the ill and dying, as did 'purging' and bleeding with leeches. One breakthrough in medical science was the practice of inoculation, brought from the Near East, which from the 1720s became extemely popular (until it was overtaken by vaccination at the end of the century) and certainly saved many a life. A mid-century mother, Mrs Boscawen, writes to her husband:

> *Pray Papa! Pray God to bless us, for we are inoculated. This day exactly at noon it was done; no fuss, no rout, no assistance. Nobody but me and the servants. I held the child myself and so effectually employed his eyes and attention (by a bit of gold lace which I was putting into forms to lace his waistcoat) that he never was sensible of the first aim. For the second, he pretended to wince a little, but I had a sugar plum ready, which stopped the whimper before it was well formed, and he is now (Mr Hawkins gone) tattling here by my bureau with some cards and papers etc, for the weather is so very hot that I reckon the chief service I can do him is to provide him such amusements as will keep him quiet and still.*[1]

For many of the children who survived, life would never be worth the living. In a dismal economic climate at the beginning of the century, poor families could not afford to provide for their children, and pathetic corpses could frequently be spotted in ditches and on city refuse-heaps. Other children were turned out of the house to fend for themselves. Child crime was rife, as was child prostitution; everywhere there were small beggars. The philanthropists who founded 'hospitals' and asylums for destitute children found themselves forced to turn away the droves who applied for shelter. The old Poor Law which catered for unsupported children could never cope with the demands made on it. Workhouses were full to overflowing, despite the horrors within. A theoretically worthy plan for apprenticing children to tradesmen and artisans was cruel in practice: many a 'master' would accept the few shillings paid out when he took a child, then so abuse and starve it that it was forced to run away, leaving him with a decent profit – the child, of course, took to crime or begging, or died. Those who were kept in service were generally used as drudges, rarely taught a useful trade which would give them a living in adulthood. Most piteous were the boy (and in some cases girl) sweeps, emaciated, begrimed animals forced up narrow chimneys often still hot from recent fires: some died in the chimneys, many perished from soot-clogged lungs. The squeamish did initiate legislation for the control of 'climbing boys'' conditions, even in the hard-hearted eighteenth century, but not till the nineteenth was any real attempt made to regulate the hours and conditions of children employed in the factories, the mines and the fields.

The Society for Promoting Christian Knowledge (founded in 1698) set up some two thousand schools for the poor at this period, but they were often empty in areas where children were employed in factories and on farms as vital contributors to the family economy. Sunday schools were the province of the various religious denominations, and they did much good work in 'taming' small savages and interesting them in Bible stories, but their contribution to literacy was minimal.

The gulf between the children of the poor, and abandoned, destitute children, and those of the rich and even moderately well-to-do was immense, perhaps more marked than at any time in history.

The great mansions of the rich were finely furnished, beautifully decorated, warm, quiet and elegant. The arts flourished; science became a fashionable cult. The huge, brightly flowered gowns of the early and mid-century gave way to the narrow, dainty frocks of the 1790s, when dandies cut a dash in tight white buckskins and elaborately knotted neckcloths. With children's fashions still imitating those of their elders, this was a liberation in terms of movement and comfort (gone were the torturing stays – though only for a couple of decades).

In many families, too, discipline was relaxing, and there was now no rule about children not sitting in their parents' presence or the nonsense of rigid etiquette which had lingered from past ages. Still, however, there were families in which children were kept in heavy subjection: the young John and Charles Wesley, in the early years of the eighteenth century, were brought up by a mother who believed in 'breaking the spirit' of her children, and did so with the rod and with long tirades and sermons. There still continued the old debate about the 'original sin' or natural innocence of the child, and the rivalry of precept and punishment was fierce. John Locke's strictures on the upbringing of children, from the previous century, had little currency now; but from the 1760s the tenets of another philosopher, the Frenchman Jean-Jacques Rousseau, won a good deal of interest in Britain. On the matter of discipline, he believed that a child should not be punished for its mistakes and faults but should profit by the effects of them. Thus, if a child wanted to overeat of some good thing, it should be allowed to – and make itself sick, an experience it would not wish to repeat; it should not be prevented from touching hot coals, but should burn itself. (Rousseau's ideas were still being presented, by the popular children's writer Enid Blyton, in the 1950s.)

Never before had the middle- and upper-class child been so well off for toys. The manufacture of dolls ('babies' they were still called, though they usually represented adults) was a fine art, and several outstandingly beautiful examples still survive in toy-museums; little girls

could also delight in elaborately furnished dolls' houses, which at
modern sales now command prices of thousands of pounds, so tastefully
were they built. Within the reach of even artisans' children were the
hoops and tops, marbles and balls which every pedlar had in his pack,
and for a few pence more there were hobby-horses and carts to please
any boy. Kaleidoscopes and jigsaws made their appearance in the eighteenth century, as did the intricate mechanical toys which came in from
the Continent – musical boxes and automata now prized by collectors.

Children's 'theatricals' were a popular form of family entertainment,
and outside the home there were 'curiosity shows' (two-headed calves
and dwarfs and 'mermaids' displayed like zoo animals today) and the
many circuses which rivalled that of the famous Astley from mid-
century. Thoughts of these delights must have filled the minds of many
children sitting stiffly in their pews through hours-long sermons of a
Sunday.

The eighteenth-century nursery would also contain several books
written especially for children. The charming fairy-stories of Charles
Perrault were translated into English in the 1720s, bringing Cinderella
and Puss-in-Boots into the childish vocabulary, and soon the presses
were turning out fables and fantasies by the thousand to rival them.
Nevertheless, the other side of the coin was the gloomy, moral-ridden
'improving' works of the religious, still full of early deaths and penitence for sins and childish dedication to improving the world.

One of the earliest books for children, the prototype of the boarding-
school saga, was written by Sarah Fielding, published in 1749: *The
Governess*. It is the story of a few days in the lives of nine little girls at
school, prim and prosy little women who address each other as 'Miss So-
and-so' – though some of them can be roused even to violence in the
desire to possess an unusually fine apple, an occasion used by their mistress, Mrs. Teachum, for some moralizing. It was an early attempt at realism in children's stories and was quickly followed by several others of
the same type, culminating in the 'classic' works of Maria Edgworth,
Mrs. Trimmer and other popular writers at the end of the century.

The boarding-school theme was one which was familiar to many a
small girl of the period. A few, in the nobility, were still educated by
governesses and tutors, and some mothers preferred to keep their daughters by them, but they were in a minority now. In every city and town,
even in some country villages, there were boarding-schools by the
score. Some were pricy and fashionable establishments, employing a
high proportion of staff to pupils and offering to turn out young ladies of
the most elegant manners and accomplishments; others were less osten-
tatious, in the style of 'Mrs. Goddard's' school in Jane Austen's *Emma*,

"where a reasonable quantity of accomplishments were sold at a reasonable price, and where girls might be sent to be out of the way and scramble themselves into a little education without any danger of coming back prodigies".[2] Between the two lay 'genteel seminaries' which admitted the daughters of the butcher, the baker and the candlestick-maker, and turned them out to inflict on their humble parents demands for drawing-rooms and pianofortes, to puzzle them with stock phrases in French and to despise their broad accents and 'vulgar' manners.

There were comparable academies for aspiring dandies, small, 'exclusive' academies at which boys were prepared for the world of fashion and idleness, frequently taken to the play and the opera, in frilled shirts, embroidered waistcoats and foppish cravats, armed for life with only the haziest ideas of arithmetic and literacy. The old public schools boasted a more arduous, classical curriculum and made no pretence to elegant living. At Eton, Westminster and the like, boys were herded into chilly dormitories, crammed into barn-like halls, with a minimal staff to superintend their studies and morals. The keen student could get an education; the careless or stupid could easily remain in ignorance. Bullying was rife and went largely unchecked. When sins were discovered, beating was the remedy and the punishment. But still the rich and titled continued to send their boys to such schools, despising the ancient grammar-schools where their offspring might be forced to rub shoulders with sons of the 'commercial classes' – though in fact the education there, which was veering away from the classics, was a much more realistic preparation for life than screeds of Greek and Latin poetry learned by rote.

To the modern eye there was obviously much room for improvement in the treatment and upbringing of children in the eighteenth century. So the Victorians thought too. Change came slowly but gradually, as the 'enlightened' legislated and planned to better the lot of the young. The pauper child and the poor child were to be liberated from 'sweated labour' and cruelty; even the humblest was to be taught the three Rs; girls were to be more rationally, boys more kindly, educated; religion and morality were to be induced not beaten into their heads. Much of the Victorian smugness – now so loudly deplored – was justified, by the Victorians' improvements in the treatment of children, as in so many other spheres of life.

Family feuds

The British public, viewing the arrival of their German king, George I, in 1714, was struck by the fact that now, for the first time since the 1640s, the kingdom was blessed with a royal family of 'normal' structure – a grandfather, father and mother and children. What few knew then, though many came to know in the years that followed, was that there were sad irregularities in the family's life: their king had divorced his wife and was keeping her locked up in a German castle – and he had no love for his son, even less for his daughter-in-law. 'German George' was a good enough king, but as a family man he left much to be desired.

More than thirty years before his accession to the British throne, George of Hanover had married his cousin Sophia Dorothea of Celle, an heiress whose lands he wished to bring back into the family. The couple had nothing in common and seem to have made little effort to make their marriage a success. Not even George's shrewd and perceptive mother, the Electress Sophia, could do anything to improve relations between her son and daughter-in-law, nor did the birth of their children, a son and daughter, bring them together.

The final break came with the Elector of Hanover's discovery, in 1694, of his wife's adultery. The fact that he had been consistently and blatantly unfaithful to her did not strike George as a mitigating circumstance: he had other standards for his wife, the mother of his children. The unhappy Sophia Dorothea was removed from the Hanoverian Court and from her husband's mind; he obtained a divorce – but, already having an heir for his electorate and future kingdom, made no move to remarry.

Sophia Dorothea must have been a good mother, for her children (who were twelve and seven years old when she 'went away', and who never saw her again) always cherished a fondness for her memory. The young Prince George managed to find a portrait of her, which he kept hidden, while Princess Sophia Dorothea the younger, once she was married and beyond her father's control, opened a correspondence with her mother. But neither of the children ever dared mention her name to their father.

The old Electress Sophia, their grandmother, was the formative influence on their upbringing and must have had a good stabilizing effect on Prince George at least, for his own marriage was to prove outstandingly successful (his sister's was not, but then she had no chance of happiness with such a husband as the notoriously choleric King Frederick William of Prussia).

Young George married Princess Caroline of Anspach in 1705 and found in her a woman not only of beauty and charm but of strong character and discretion, able to manipulate him without offending his *amour propre* and to bear with his infidelities with graceful *insouciance*. Their correspondence proves their real affection:

> *My very dear wife* [wrote the Prince to Caroline in November 1709],
> *I have just received the good news of the birth of a daughter* [their first, Anne], *at which I feel all imaginable pleasure, and I am delighted to learn . . . that you are well. I am only a little bit angry that it has caused you pain. You should know me well enough, my very dear Caroline, to believe that everything that concerns you is infinitely precious to me. This new token of your love attaches me the more deeply to you, and I assure you, dear heart, that I love the baby without having seen it.*[1]

Though the baby Princess Anne was the couple's first daughter, she was not their first child: Caroline had justified her marriage by producing a son and heir within eighteen months of her wedding. This was Prince Frederick Lewis, third in line to the British throne while old Queen Anne lived.

However, despite his potential eminence, the birth of the Prince was not conducted in a manner calculated to assure Hanover and Britain that he was a true-born son of his father. When Princess Caroline went into labour, it was behind locked doors, with only her own Anspach servants in attendance – not even a Hanoverian gained admittance, and the British envoy had the greatest difficulty in obtaining admission even several days after the baby's delivery. Why the couple, and the Elector George, permitted this strange negligence is hard to understand: it gave rise to all sorts of rumours, then and in later years, that Frederick Lewis was as much a 'changeling' as that 'warming-pan' baby of James II.

When the Hanoverians left their German home for England in 1714, Frederick Lewis was left behind, at the insistence of his grandfather, who on the one hand valued a German upbringing for the child and on the other had no wish to have two generations of heirs about him in his new kingdom. Already relations between him and his son were tense; they were to worsen considerably when he saw how British Tory politicians, in opposition to the Whig party then in government, wooed Prince George in hopes of future power when he came to reign.

The Hanoverians had been three years in Britain when the tension came to a head. It did so on the occasion of the christening of George and Caroline's second son, George William, in November 1717. There had been a dispute between father and grandfather about the child's godparents, and George I had insisted that one of them should be his Lord Chamberlain, the Duke of Newcastle. Coming after years of political sparring between King and Prince, this honouring of the Duke, the younger George's political adversary, was too much for him to bear. He gave in to his father's demand, but the insult gnawed at his mind.

The christening ceremony over, the Prince of Wales stalked up to Newcastle and thrust his fist in his face, rasping out, "You rascal, I will find you!" The Duke, already nervous and ill at ease, heard the words, uttered in George's thick German accent, as "You rascal, I will fight you!" and thought he had been challenged to a duel. The King was, of course, furious when he heard of the incident and had his son placed under arrest. In the difficult days that followed, with the scandal bruited about Court and capital, George I was persuaded not to send his son to the Tower, as he had originally threatened, but he could not be dissuaded from putting the offending Prince out of the palace. And he was adamant in his determination to take custody of his grandchildren. Princess Caroline, still frail after childbirth, was told that she might remain with her children under her father-in-law's roof until she recovered her strength, if she would promise to have no communication with her husband in that time – this she would not do and, hysterical and ill, she left St. James's with the Prince. Soon afterwards they established themselves at Leicester House, where 'opposition' politicians flocked to support them, despite the King's warning that he would himself receive no man who consorted with his son.

The three little princesses, Anne, Amelia and Caroline, and their baby brother, George William, were, of course, well attended by a large staff, but they pined for their parents. "We have a good father and a good mother," Princess Anne was heard to mourn, "and yet we are like charity children." And when asked if her grandfather did not visit them, she replied: "Oh no, he does not love us enough for that."[2] When her words were reported to the King, he did have the grace to feel ashamed and, after his first visit to the nursery, found that he actually enjoyed the company of his grandchildren. Not that this warmed him towards the Prince of Wales. Even when the baby Prince George William died, early in

1718, the tragedy did not soften the King's resolve to keep his son and his grandchildren apart.

The King had a further insult to deal out: having taken the children out of the Prince's charge, he insisted that his son pay him for their up-keep – to the tune of £40,000 a year. But for once George I did not have his own way: legal opinion backed the Prince of Wales's refusal to part with his money, on the grounds that the King had proclaimed himself the children's guardian. George I had already proved his authority by making new appointments to his grandchildren's staff – among them that of a new governess: their long-familiar Baroness von Gemmingen, a staunch supporter of the Prince and Princess of Wales, was ousted in favour of the King's nominee, the Dowager Lady Portland.

In fact, Lady Portland was to prove a great success in her post. The little girls, bewildered and frightened by recent events, were put to a soothing routine of work, play and prayer, with plenty of fresh air. As time passed, too, their mother took advantage of royal concessions to visit her daughters once a week (though she took good care to give the King warning of her coming, lest he should have the embarrassment of meeting her in the nursery), and she and the Princesses kept up a regular correspondence (the daughters' spelling in French and English very soon bettered that of their mother, who, albeit a respected patron of philosophers and men of letters, had taught herself to write in childhood with a degree of success satisfactory only to herself).

The Prince of Wales, unlike his wife, was not admitted to the palace, a matter for bitter resentment and no little heartache. When his three little girls sent him a loving message with a basket of cherries which they had picked themselves at Kensington, George broke down and sobbed. It was only when the King made one of his periodic visits to Hanover in 1719 that he allowed his son to see the children again – and even then, when he returned, he sourly rebuked Lady Portland for welcoming the Prince too frequently.

Throughout this period, various well-meaning third parties planned or even attempted to effect a reconciliation between George I and his heir. Their efforts came to nothing. It was only in the year 1720 that the rising politician Robert Walpole managed to drive in the thin end of the wedge. With the King, he used the lever of royal debts, which George wanted Parliament to liquidate; with the Prince, he worked through the Princess, to persuade him to write an apology to his father, for the sake of regaining his children – and, incidentally, of restoring royal prestige, which was at a low ebb.

Even while negotiations went on, there came a further blow for the Prince and Princess of Wales: Princess Anne contracted smallpox and lay seriously ill. The King allowed her mother to go to her, to stay with her for long hours – but only on condition that she took no physician with her and gave the child no medicine not prescribed by his own doctors. Fortunately Anne was to recover.

Then – at last – the Prince of Wales was summoned to a private interview with the King. The two men emergéd on no warmer terms than before, but at least, for the rest of George I's life, they would be on terms of outward politeness. Various honours, of which Prince George had been deprived in 1717, were restored to him, and he was again admitted to Court functions, but there was no domestic victory for the Waleses: their three daughters remained at St. James's Palace, under Lady Portland's charge, and though the parents had unlimited access to the Princesses, they had no real influence on their upbringing.

King George I reigned until 1727, respected but not loved by the British people, always eager for his visits to Hanover (where, to the chagrin of Prince George, he made much of his grandson Frederick Lewis). In fact, the King was on his way to Hanover when he died, on the 11th June 1727.

King George II and Queen Caroline, along with more public triumphs, were now reunited with their daughters. The three Princesses were aged between twelve and eighteen (there was a prince, William, aged six, and two princesses, five and three, still in the nursery – born since 'the reconciliation'), and they were quickly absorbed into the royal household. Their father they could neither understand nor wholly admire: he had a nervous energy which at home he employed in ceaseless chatter, and his temper had not been improved by the trials of past years. "When great points go as he would not have them," wrote Princess Anne, "he frets and is bad to himself; but when he is in his worst humours, and the devil to everybody . . . it is always because one of his pages has powdered his periwig ill, or a housemaid set a chair where it does not use to stand."[3] But the three girls, and especially Anne, became devoted to their mother.

One of the new King's first domestic plans was that of sending for his eldest son. British travellers to Hanover had reported well of the young Prince, but other stories had reached his parents' ears too: their 'Fritz' enjoyed 'low company', roistering about the streets and carousing in taverns with footmen and stable-boys.

When the Prince did arrive, in the last days of 1728, his parents were pleased with him at first, for he seemed eager to claim his place in family life and to play his part at Court. Then, inevitably, George II began to resent his son, seeing him courted by politicians just as he himself had been as Prince of Wales. As time passed, the whole dreary, unsavoury course of recent years was repeated, with a king again at loggerheads with his heir, disapproving of his activities in politics and refusing to train him for government. Caroline only urged her husband on in his spite against Frederick, and turned the young man's sisters against him.

There were some quiet passages in the royal family's life, in which the Prince of Wales and his sisters played music together, and George and Caroline smiled coldly when he made his bow to them on state occasions, but for the most part they kept their son at arm's length and reviled him even to their servants.

In 1736, a German princess, Augusta of Saxe-Gotha, was brought over to England to become Frederick's bride. At seventeen years old, she was immature (she brought a doll with her, with which she played until warned that she only drew servants' sneers), quiet and docile; she became devoted to her husband and never crossed him but at the same time had sufficient discretion never to offend his parents – though it was beyond her imagination to attempt to heal their breach.

Then, in the late autumn of 1736, the Princess of Wales became pregnant. From the outset, the King and Queen insisted that she should bear her child as publicly as possible, under their own eyes: the Prince of Wales had other ideas. Until the very last moment, he kept his plan secret, but then, with Augusta beginning her labour, he whisked her away from Hampton Court, where they had been staying with his parents, and under cover of darkness hustled her into St. James's Palace. Nothing was prepared: for want of bed-linen, Augusta lay down between two table-cloths.

Perhaps Frederick merely wished to annoy his parents, to retaliate for their interference. Perhaps, as modern biographers have suggested, Augusta begged her husband to get her away from the King and Queen, in fear that they would harm her baby: certainly George and Caroline made no secret of their wish to see Frederick Lewis without heirs of his own, to be succeeded by his brother William, whom they loved and admired as much as they loathed and despised the Prince of Wales.

The King and Queen, roused from their bed by news of the birth of their grandchild and coaching post-haste into London, are said to have conjectured as to the child's true-birth, for Caroline at least had long been convinced that her son could not play a husband's part.

As the Queen herself said later, if she had found a fine plump boy in the cradle, she could never have believed in his being her grandson, but as it was, her daughter-in-law had given birth to a girl – a 'poor ugly little she-mouse', Caroline declared.[4]

Queen Caroline was dead before the birth of a new prince, a new

George, in June 1738 – another birth without benefit of royal surroundings, for the family quarrel brought about by the Prince of
Wales's churlish conduct at the birth of his first child had so far angered
his father as to make George II emulate George I and drive his son out of
his house. Later the parallel came even closer, for the Prince and Princess
of Wales moved into that very Leicester House which George and
Caroline had occupied two decades earlier. Again it became a magnet
drawing politicians hopeful of future power under a new king.

If Frederick Lewis, Prince of Wales, was an undutiful son, as George
II had been, then also like his father he was a doting parent to his young
children. (Eight were born to the Princess Augusta in her husband's lifetime, the ninth was a posthumous child.)

In London, his eldest son, George, and Prince Edward (born in 1739)
had their own household at Savile House, across the square from their
parents' Leicester House, but in the country, at Kew, the family spent a
good deal of time together. The Prince of Wales was a man of refined
tastes (unlike his father and grandfather), a collector of splendid paint-
ings and a respected connoisseur; he also liked to indulge in amateur
theatricals and would spend hours coaching his children and rehearsing
them for a family performance. (A French nobleman, used to the sophisticated pursuits of the Court of King Louis XV, was amused to find that
he was offered a choice between a reading from Addison's works or a
game of baseball when he visited the Prince of Wales's *ménage*.)

Frederick Lewis also took a personal interest in his children's education and himself worked out a curriculum for his elder sons. They
were to rise at seven in the morning, study until twelve-thirty, play until
three, then dine and study again until their supper at eight, and to be in
bed by ten o'clock. They were to learn Latin, history, mathematics and
religion – but also music (the Prince of Wales was himself an accomplished 'cellist), dancing and fencing, and they played cricket with their
father at Kew.

There was no tension between the Prince and his eldest son, the future
George III, such as had existed in previous generations of Hanoverian
fathers and sons, but neither did he or his wife over-praise the boy. In
fact, they preferred his younger brother Edward and let George know it
– "George is a good boy," agreed Frederick Lewis on an occasion when
a foreign visitor praised him, "but Edward has something in him, I
assure you. Edward will be somebody. You will hear of him one of these
days."[5] (In this the fond father would be proved wrong: Edward, Duke
of York, distinguished himself for nothing more than his addiction to
strong drink and willing women.) And while Prince Edward was
always smiled on by his parents when, as he often did, he interrupted

adult conversation with a ready word, his elder brother, far more diffident and reserved, was put down with a "Do hold your tongue,
George; don't talk like a fool"⁶ whenever he offered an opinion. Fortunately, Prince George was not one to take offence, and relations between him and his parents were always peaceful.

On the 20th March 1751, Frederick Lewis, Prince of Wales died, after
a short illness: a post-mortem showed that he had had an abscess in his
chest which had burst and suffocated him. So now the ageing King
George II was to be succeeded by his grandson and namesake and need
not suffer the bitter prospect of having his own despised son follow him
to Britain's throne.

The late Prince of Wales had provided for the eventuality of his death
by writing for his eldest son a thousand-word political testament:

> *To my son George* [he wrote]
>   *As I always have had the tenderest paternal affection for you, I cannot
> give you a stronger proof of it than in leaving this paper for you in your
> mother's hands, who will read it to you from time to time and will give it to
> you when you come of age or when you get the crown.*

The Prince went on to recommend to his son that he should always live
within his means (preaching what he could not practise himself), that he
should never trust the flattery of courtiers and politicians or, when he
came to the throne, enter an international war before the national debt
had been greatly reduced. Above all, wrote the Prince, George should
"convince this nation that you are not only an Englishman born and
bred but that you are also this by inclination"⁷ – advice which the future
George III very wisely acted on in later years: with Frederick Lewis died
the last of the Hanoverian born, German-accented dynasty which had
taken so long to root itself in Britain and the affections of the British
people.

The death of her husband left Princess Augusta at the mercy of her
father-in-law. Fortunately, her own prudence and the King's surprising
but obviously genuine grief smoothed the way to a period of family
harmony in which she could gain personal control of her children's
upbringing without an unseemly new quarrel. But, inevitably, that
harmony was only brief, for the Princess could not resist privately
reviling George II to his heir, and indeed the King's own conduct later
reinforced the future George III's prejudice against his grandfather.

The root of the trouble was the widow's increasing reliance on one
John Stuart, Earl of Bute, a friend of her late husband. But where Frederick Lewis had a poor opinion of Bute's political abilities, Augusta raised

the Earl as a mentor to her son. (It seems in fact that he was a man of great ambition and average ability, which he used discriminatingly and with good principles.) The new Prince of Wales (aged twelve at his father's death) readily ceded to Bute the dignity of a 'father-figure' and refused to believe the (probably ill-founded) rumours that the Earl was his mother's lover. When George came of age and his grandfather offered him an independent establishment, hoping to sever the boy from the influence of Augusta and Bute, the Prince politely refused, declaring that his happiness depended on his remaining with his mother. Fortunately for the younger George, his grandfather did not live to re-enact the battles he had waged against Frederick Lewis but died when his heir was aged twenty-two – if he had not, the influence of Bute and Augusta might well have taken the young man into just such political and personal conflict with the King as his father had entered.

Until devastating illness overtook him in middle life, King George III was outstandingly happy in his marriage and fatherhood. Not every member of the Hanoverian dynasty, with their upsets and trials in childhood and adolescence, had emerged so unscathed and achieved such contentment as the King, however. His uncle William, Duke of Cumberland, who had been petted and praised by George II and Queen Caroline, while they reviled their elder son the Prince of Wales, had proved a cool-headed politician but a hot-headed military commander, loathed and feared in Scotland after his cruel repression of the Jacobites after 1745. Of the daughters of George II, the eldest, Anne, Princess Royal, had been a charming and vivacious girl, but so unhappy at home that when even her father warned her against the suit of William IV of Orange, she determinedly accepted him: she would marry a baboon rather than no one, she declared at the time. Later, she was to regret the decision and to live unhappily with the man she could neither love nor respect. Amelia and Caroline never married: the first was a shrew, the second a 'martyr' to ill-health; both soon lost the glossy good looks of their youth and put on too much weight. Princess Mary was gentle and timid, rather dull; Louisa, the youngest, was the most attractive, but she died young, after an unhappy marriage to the King of Denmark.

Two of George III's sisters and one of his brothers died in their teens. Of the rest, the Dukes of York, Gloucester and Cumberland all succumbed to female charms, with attendant scandals; the latter two married commoners, to the embarrassment of their brother the King. Princess Augusta married a German, the Duke of Brunswick – to find him brutal and unfaithful; Caroline Matilda's husband, Christian VII, was an oaf, and perhaps mentally defective – though that, at least in George III's eyes, did not excuse her flagrant adultery and her attempt to

'Farmer Giles and his wife showing off their daughter Betty to their neighbours on her return from school.' Gillray's satire of 1809 on the rising pretensions of the Georgian yeomanry through their children.

The future King George I's children, George (the future George II) and Sophia Dorothea (future Queen of Prussia), with their ill-fated mother, Sophia Dorothea of Celle, in 1691.

The children of Frederick Lewis, Prince of Wales.

George III's children: a detail from Zoffany's portrait of their mother, Queen Charlotte.

Queen Charlotte, George III's wife, with her two eldest sons, George, Prince of Wales (the future King George IV), and Frederick, future Duke of York, in fancy dress – Zoffany's portrait of September 1764.

The three youngest daughters of George III, painted by J. S. Copley in 1785.
Left to right: Mary, Amelia (in perambulator) and Sophia.

Opposite: Princess Charlotte of Wales, daughter of the future King George IV,
with her mother, Caroline of Brunswick.

A harrowing picture of life in the Victorian slums – no sentimentality about childhood there!

Opposite: Many happy returns! (1856), Frith's famous painting of an infant's birthday party, epitomizing the Victorian cults of childhood and family life.

The future Queen Victoria, painted by Beechey in 1824.

take over his kingdom, which led to her disgrace and imprisonment.

Thus, in contrast to the careers of so many of his relations – but also on his own merits – King George III was a paragon of respectability and regularity. At twenty-three he went a virgin to a virgin bride, the seventeen-year-old Charlotte of Mecklenburg-Strelitz, and lived happily with her and their fifteen children in virtuous ('dull' said the livelier courtiers) domesticity. The political failings of the monarchy and the King's serious illness from his middle years marred his reign and put unbearable strain on his marriage, but nothing could wholly mar the reputation of this king who made himself so thoroughly English – having learned well in childhood the lesson prescribed by his father's testament.

Happy families

Since the 'invention' of psychology in the nineteenth century and the popularization of psycho-analysis in recent years, a new dimension has been added to historical research. Psychologists who are amateur historians and historians who fancy themselves as psychologists have delved into the characters of historical personages and, along lines advocated by Sigmund Freud, examined their childhood to find out the causes of individuals' virtues and vices, achievements and failures. At best, such analysis provides valuable new insights into famous lives and their role in world-shaping events; at worst, every evil of every era is put down to the childhood misfortunes of individual rulers. Louis XVI's inability to come to terms with his politicians – resulting in the French Revolution, George III's loss of the American colonies, the fatal bellicosity of Kaiser Wilhelm II and so on – all have been accounted for by the failure of their parents to provide them with a stable or happy or healthy start to life.

In one instance, however, historian-psychologists have had a hard time in making out a case for childhood deprivation as the cause of adult vice and aberration – thus leaving a possible triumph to those who claim the importance of genetic heredity over childhood environment. They look at the wayward lives (political and sexual) of the children of George III and expect to find in their childhood some clue to their failings. They search in vain.

Compared with other royal children of their time – notably those in France and Spain – the children of George III were endowed with many blessings, not the least of which was their parents' mutual love. George and Charlotte had married after only the slightest of acquaintances, but there was something in them which attracted each other initially and which provided a basis for a lifetime of mutual devotion.

Their behaviour to each other speaks the most cordial confidence and happiness [wrote a courtier]. *The King seems to admire as much as he enjoys her* [Charlotte's] *conversation, and to covet her participation in everything he either sees or hears. The Queen appears to feel the most grateful regard for him and to make it her chief study to raise his consequence with others, by always marking that she considers herself, though queen to the nation, only, to him, the first and most obedient of subjects.*[1]

Court etiquette was still a blight on the lives of those who served George and Charlotte, whose public acts were governed by age-old ritual (though it was by no means as restricting as the Court etiquette prevailing on the Continent), but in their private lives the King and Queen had no taste for ceremonial and ostentation. George rose at five each morning, laid his own fire, made his own cup of tea and said his prayers before joining his wife (who had risen at six) for their breakfast; private evenings would be marked by nothing more lively than card-games and readings from 'improving' literature, and the royal family kept early hours. The great aristocrats might sneer at their bourgeois monarchs, but the rising middle-class, conscious of the gulf between their own respectability and the vices of most of their 'betters', could only admire and approve.

The King's affection for his children was amply rewarded by their love – while they *were* children. Political and financial considerations soon alienated the eldest son, the future King George IV, from his father (inevitably, it was in the Hanoverian tradition), and the careers of the younger princes separated them from the family circle, but even so, there was a residue of family piety and affection which kept the royal brothers and sisters together – often bickering, sometimes intriguing against each other, but never wholly estranged – into their old age.

Queen Charlotte was less out-going and demonstrative than her husband, and her devotion to George left less room for intimacy with the children. Still, while her children were in nursery and schoolroom, Charlotte was wise in her strictures for their upbringing, and there was no lack of effort on her part in creating a family unity.

The Queen produced the largest royal family to bless England since that of Eleanor of Castile in the thirteenth century. Over twenty-two years she gave birth to fifteen children, and it was to her credit that she lost only two of them – her two youngest sons – in infancy. After the first dozen births, the strain was undeniably weakened (the youngest princess, Amelia, died in her late twenties), but the elder princes and princesses survived to an average age of nearly seventy. Which also, of course, says a good deal for their early diet and the habit of taking exercise in the fresh air which all acquired from their earliest years: not even George IV's gourmandizing, and his and his brothers' addiction to the bottle, could counteract that good start. Whether or not any of them suffered from porphyria, the hereditary blood disease which is now thought to have been the illness which so marred George III's life, is debatable: but then even George himself lived to be more than eighty, and that despite the barbaric treatment he received, which contributed to his mental debility.

George and Charlotte began their married life at St. James's Palace, but it was not long before they were on the look-out for a less grand and formal (and less expensive) residence. Their first choice was the mansion of the former Dukes of Buckingham, which they called 'the Queen's house' but which (much altered and expanded) eventually became known as Buckingham Palace. However, even this *bijou* palace, with its large garden, set at the end of a tree-lined mall, overlooking St. James's Park, was not sufficiently rural for George and Charlotte's taste, nor, with the frequent additions to their family in the 1760s and 1770s, was it large enough to accommodate their household. Thus, on the death of King George's mother in 1772, he acquired her house at Kew, and in the years that followed, the family took root there, with the children and their own staff placed in various houses nearby, round Kew Green. In fact, Kew and nearby Richmond became a considerable community under royal auspices, with servants and courtiers (and the courtiers' servants) housed over a broad radius around the royal centre. And the spectacle of the King and Queen and their children at their leisure in the park drew hundreds of visitors – as it would later at Windsor, which George increasingly favoured by the end of the decade. There, the royal family would spend hours 'terracing' on summer evenings, with bands playing and sightseers promenading on the slopes below.

It was not want of affection or interest but genuine concern for their well-being that made George and Charlotte follow the old tradition of divorcing their sons from their own household when they reached a suitable age, forming separate establishments for them under the rule of governors and tutors. The King was assiduous in mapping out his sons' days and their curriculum of study; the Queen was equally watchful over their health, wardrobe and diet. There was to be no pampering: breakfast consisted of toast and milk or weak tea ('moderately' sweetened), dinner (between three and five in the afternoon) only of soup, lean meat and greens, or fish if they chose it – but that without any rich sauce; then, to follow, a fruit tart, though on Sundays and Thursdays the boys might each choose an ice-cream of the flavour they liked best. Coffee-drinking was limited to two days a week, but a glass of wine was to be provided every day. (Some parents today argue that it is best to accustom children to moderate amounts of alcoholic drinks, to prevent later temptations to excess; in this case at least that argument seems to be invalid – most of the princes became drunks, if not alcoholics.)

If the royal diet was spartan, so were living conditions. The King saw no need for carpeting in his own bedroom and thought it no hardship for his children to go without what even his middle-class subjects thought of as the necessary comforts of life.

When the whole royal family was at Kew together in the 1770s, the elder princes would be shepherded from their own houses to their parents' to bid them good-morning at 8 am, then join them and their elder sisters at breakfast, after which the younger children were brought in for inspection. Lessons followed until lunchtime (superintended by the King and Queen), then there were games in the garden – usually cricket or rounders – or work on the children's own plots of land. At five they went into their parents' sitting-room, where they remained until six-thirty, when they were taken off to bed. In later years the boys' curriculum of lessons was intensified, but not so much that healthy exercise was neglected.

The King had broad interests in science and the arts, was a student of history and music, could speak several foreign languages and was an avid collector of books; the Queen's favourite study was botany, but she too was fond of literature, drama and music. Both were determined that their sons should become cultured as well as informed, and a whole regiment of tutors grounded them in mathematics, literature, foreign languages, ancient and modern history and religion and touched on the outlines of science, and though the Prince of Wales was kept in England (much to his own disgust), the younger princes were sent off to university on the Continent in their early teens.

The second boy, Frederick, later Duke of York, was destined for an army career and took his training at Hanover; William (Duke of Clarence, later King William IV) was put into the navy as a midshipman at the age of thirteen; Edward (Duke of Kent) was to serve for years in the army overseas, at Gibraltar and in the West Indies and Canada, while Ernest Augustus (Duke of Cumberland) became a cavalry officer in Hanover; Augustus (Duke of Sussex) suffered from asthma and never felt himself up to any strenuous activity, but the youngest surviving prince, Adolphus (Duke of Cambridge), also had a career in the army. However beneficial to the nation and to the princes themselves this activity might be, it did keep them from enjoying home life and put them beyond the control of their parents. George III's relations with his sons in their adolescence and manhood were never easy, even before the onset of his illness, and the good he had done them in their childhood was largely negated by their freedom from parental discipline in their teens. They took mistresses; they took to the bottle; they ran up vast debts. Even Frederick, the second and favourite son, was never wholly satisfactory to his father. But the heir to the throne, closest to home and closely watched by his father, was to prove the greatest disappointment, rebelling against parental control over his activities even before he came of age. At sixteen he dived headlong into fashionable society; soon he had taken his first mistress – and soon afterwards was costing his father several hundreds of pounds for the purchase of his indiscreet love-letters from the blackmailing lady to whom he had addressed them. In the years that followed, the Prince's 'weaknesses' became ever more pronounced, and his entry into the world of politics, in alliance with a coterie of brilliant but irresponsible young would-be statesmen, infuriated the King. Inevitably, George III's preaching and his appeals to his son's sense of duty were laughed off by the prematurely sophisticated young man.

The princesses were shielded from their scapegrace brothers – not even allowed to be in a room alone with them, but that did not stop their forming affectionate, even passionate, attachments to the princes and corresponding with them. But then the girls were generally denied healthier relationships with other young men, and it was only natural that they should seek masculine attention where they could most easily get it.

Like their brothers, the princesses had been carefully brought up, but unlike them they had never been removed from their parents' household. Queen Charlotte daily supervised the administration headed by the chief governess, Lady Charlotte Finch, and hers was the main voice in the appointment of the sub-governesses, English and Swiss, who taught literature, languages, needlework, and drawing and music, assisted by some specialist tutors (whose lessons were always closely chaperoned). The Queen kept herself *au fait* with her daughters' progress by attending their lessons occasionally, but her vigilance also extended into every other part of their lives, from their prayers to their purses, their manners to their *modes*; the girls were in their late twenties before she would allow them to choose their own reading-matter.

Individually the princesses were beauties, with fresh rosy complexions, fine figures and bright hair; *en masse*, swirling in their hooped skirts round their mother at Court functions, they were an impressive sight. And it was *en masse* that they usually lived, under their mother's eye – Charlotte the Princess Royal, Augusta, Elizabeth, Mary, Sophia and Amelia, their ages spanning some seventeen years. But they were individuals too: "Royal" bossy, Augusta lively and gossipy, Elizabeth emotional, Mary her mother's pet and reputed informant as to sisterly misdeeds, but practical and kind too, Sophia as hypochondriacal as she was genuinely delicate, and Amelia, the baby of the family, her father's favourite, tragically succumbing to tuberculosis and erysipelas at twenty-seven after a brief flowering of beauty and gaiety.

To none of the princesses did their mother's strict regime and dull household really appeal. Their delight was balls and hunting, outings (rarely far from the parental nest) and chat with ladies who could tell them of the great world. They resented their mother's strictness and her meagre doles of pocket-money, but most of all they resented their parents' thwarting of their healthy urge to marry. Queen Charlotte wanted her daughters with her as perpetual companions; the King could never understand anyone's wish to leave the home he enjoyed so much: so when the first proposals came in from Scandinavia and a couple of German states, they were so firmly refused by the King (without consulting his daughters) that more were not forthcoming. The Princess Royal was in her early thirties when, in 1797, she was at last allowed to marry the Duke (later King) of Württemberg (a widower nearly twenty years her senior), and it was only after the Prince of Wales, as Regent, took over the control of his sisters' destiny from their father, that Mary, at forty, was allowed to wed her cousin William, Duke of Gloucester; and Elizabeth was forty-eight before she was at last awarded to the Landgrave of Hesse-Homburg. At home, the royal spinsters were treated as children, which they bitterly resented, but there is no evidence of full-scale rebellion – apart from their relieving their sexual frustration by taking secret lovers among the equerries of the Court. There were rumours at the time of secret marriages and gossip about illegitimate babies, since substantiated by the opening of royal papers in the Windsor Archives.

In 1788 the even tenor – some would say 'tedium' – of royal life was disturbed by the first major outbreak of the King's serious illness. George had suffered from unaccountable fevers and pains since his youth, and there had long been signs of a 'nervous agitation' which bewildered his doctors and alarmed the Queen. But it was only in 1788 that there came the onslaught of that illness which was to lead to the King's ostensible madness, and for three months that winter George seemed to be quite out of his mind: Court and nation were depressed and fearful; only the Prince of Wales, long at loggerheads with his father and now hopeful of inheriting the crown, remained cheerful. But by the spring the King had recovered. Even so, the root cause of his suffering had not disappeared, and events in future years – political upheavals, war and the perpetual torment of his heir's disobedience – exacerbated his condition. His symptoms re-emerged early in the nineteenth century, and from 1811 the King had to be relieved of his powers, confined and continually superintended by doctors who treated him with what now seems a barbarous brutality.

The royal malady has been tentatively diagnosed in recent years as porphyria, a hereditary blood disorder affecting the whole metabolism, which in many cases gives rise to symptoms of mental derangement. However, George's innate strength of constitution did not allow him to succumb to his ills, and he eked out a miserable existence until 1820.

By that date, George III should have been a grandfather many times over. If his own offspring had been as fecund as he and Charlotte, there would have been a round gross of royal grandchildren in Britain and on the Continent. In fact, until 1819, there was only one — or rather, only one who was legitimate and eligible to inherit the crown.

George, Prince of Wales, had married his cousin Caroline of Bruns-wick-Wolfenbuttel in 1795, and nine months later the Princess pro-duced a child, who was named Charlotte Augusta for her two grandmothers. However, the fact that this eventual heir to the British throne was a 'mere' girl was not enough to induce the Prince to resume relations with his wife in hopes of a boy next time. By the time of Char-lotte's birth, the couple were on the worst possible terms — indeed, their one point of agreement by then was that they could only be happy living apart. When they came to the arrangement of a separation, George even promised Caroline that, should their daughter die, he would never ask her to replace Charlotte with a new heir.

The traits of both parents were strong in this newest member of the royal family. The Prince of Wales was bonhomous, exuberant, lavish with friendship but adamant in enmity; Princess Caroline was lively, noisy, wayward, tolerant of others' faults — except those of her husband, generous and cheerful through her many troubles. What their daughter did not inherit was their robust good health, their unreliability and their sexual licence.

In Charlotte's first years, her mother was much in evidence at Carlton House, the Prince of Wales's London residence which she left some months after the baby's birth. The Prince was loath to grant his wife fre-quent access to the child, but his father, who was fond of Caroline, insisted that the mother should not be wholly separated from the daugh-ter of that disastrous marriage.

Caroline was a strongly maternal woman, and in later years adopted several children to fill the void of separation from her own daughter. Indeed, numbered among her many indiscretions is her vaunting of a child (an unpleasant brat whom she called 'Willikin') whom she told one credulous lady was her own, thus prompting that 'delicate investi-gation' which scotched the rumours but did Caroline's reputation little good at a time when it was already being said that she was taking lovers indiscriminately.

Charlotte grew up loving her mother, unaware of the gossip about her in Court circles and increasingly resentful of her father's treatment of his wife. In the 'classic' style of the child of a broken home, the small Princess came to hear her mother reviling her father, and her father bitterly vilifying her mother. Though the Prince of Wales had a charm which even his daughter could not but admire, and though he was generous with expensive gifts, he was not lavish with affection or in bestowing much time on her personally. It was no wonder that Charlotte took sides with her mother against the man who seemed to resent them both.

King George III, in the last years of his lucidity, adored his granddaughter and more than once tried to obtain custody of her from his son – though without success. At first, the old Queen was delighted with her namesake too, and she always tried to be fair to the child, but there was such antipathy between the elder Charlotte and her daughter-in-law that the Queen was often too hard with the younger Charlotte in whom the mother's characteristics were so strongly pronounced. In turn, the granddaughter came to loath the grandmother, whom she saw as interfering and domineering – "the old Begum", she called the Queen, indiscreetly, in letters to a friend. And the royal aunts, cloying in their spinster 'mothering', she dubbed "the old girls", or, in conjunction with their brothers, "the cows and bulls". After the Princess had learned discrimination, the only members of the family she really cared for were her eldest uncle the Duke of York and his wife, who were themselves childless and informally separated.

The gap in Charlotte's emotional life was filled partly by her affection for her servants. Her dressers Mrs. Gagarin and Mrs. Louis were closest to her heart – perhaps because they were not in a position to dictate to her, and her first governess, Lady Elgin, was a firm favourite, far more so than the woman who replaced her in 1805, Lady de Clifford. One of the sub-governesses, Mrs. Udney, was the Princess's *bête noire*: when Charlotte (aged nine) drew up her Will, she divided her belongings between her friends, her servants and her governesses, but stated that nothing was to go to Mrs. Udney – "for reasons".

One of Charlotte's first friends was Lady de Clifford's grandson, George Keppel, her companion – and frequent abettor – in all sorts of mischief, though she could still turn on him with teasing and even blows when he annoyed her. Most children brought to play with Charlotte found her rough and dictatorial, while her elders sighed over her 'hoydenish' manners and boisterousness. Nor was her temper easily controlled, and her manners were never such as 'became' a royal princess.

"My dear Princess," chided Lady de Clifford on one occasion. "You should always shut a door after you when you come into a room."

"Not I indeed," came the rude reply. "If you want the door shut, ring the bell" – and out went Charlotte, leaving the door open behind her.[2]

In adolescence the Princess was ungainly and gauche, often shocking her governess with coarse language and bad manners. A bishop (whose wig she had once pulled off and thrown into the fire in a tantrum) noted the fact that "her nose requiring to be wiped, she did not apply her handkerchief but wiped her nose with her sleeve as vulgar people do".[3]

"My dear Princess Charlotte," said Lady de Clifford (that was perhaps always the introduction to a lecture), when the girl sat down and stuck out her legs in front of her, "You shew your drawers."

"I never do," Charlotte excused herself, "but where I can put myself at my ease."

"Yes, my dear, when you get in or out of a carriage."

"I don't care if I do."[4]

Nor was the Princess's education an unqualified success. She became an accomplished musician (playing the piano, harp and guitar), but that was because she enjoyed music; in other subjects her concentration was too erratic to allow of good progress. It was not that she was unintelligent, merely that she lacked the diligence to profit from her intelligence. And no one made the slightest effort to prepare her for the role of queen which she could expect to take on after the death of her grandfather and father.

In 1812 the Princess made her first débutante appearance in public, attending an opera at which she was acclaimed so enthusiastically that her father, characteristically, was jealous and limited future displays of his daughter. And now that he had become Regent, the Prince had more power over Charlotte's visits to her mother: inevitably they were curtailed considerably. Perhaps that was fortunate, for in this same year Princess Caroline, an inveterate mischief-maker, put her daughter in a most awkward and potentially hazardous position by encouraging her flirtation with one of her own band of *cavaliere servante*, a Captain Hesse. On one occasion she even locked the young people into a bedroom together, telling them to amuse themselves. Fortunately the Captain remembered his honour – and Charlotte's.

When the Princess confessed this incident to her father a year later, he forbade her ever to see or write to her mother again.

By that time, Charlotte had learned the details of the past indiscretions of the Princess of Wales. "I *never have* and *shall not ever* recover [from] it," she wrote sadly, "because it sinks her so very low in my opinion."[5]

Nevertheless, she retained a good deal of sympathy with her mother's plight, and her resentment against her father intensified as his demands on her increased in the years that followed.

Charlotte was to marry young, the Prince Regent had decided, in order to provide an heir to the throne. And she was to marry a foreign (inevitably Protestant) prince, in whose country she was to live, thus removing the popular Princess from the limelight which her father hated to share. A new William of Orange was available, and in 1813 he was duly imported to meet his intended bride. Charlotte, at seventeen, was ready (physically and emotionally) for marriage, and the prospect of independence and a husband at first blinded her to everything but William's obvious pleasure in her company. It was only after the betrothal had been announced that she began to see her fiancé's defects and to realize that her marriage to him would mean a long exile from home. Promptly the Princess declared that she would not marry him. Besides, there was a Prussian prince in view, far more alluring than the Dutchman, and for a time she cherished the hope that her father might allow her to marry him.

It was not to be. The Prince Regent was furious at his daughter's reneging on her promise. There were bitter words between them, threats on the father's side, tears on the daughter's. At one point, when the tension at home became too much for her, Charlotte even made an impetuous dash – alone, in a hackney cab – to her mother's house, to beg Caroline's help. It was only then that the girl came to realize how unreliable her mother really was. The Princess of Wales made no real effort to aid her daughter, and Charlotte was taken home in disgrace.

Finally she did succeed in persuading her father to accept a man of her own choice, the handsome and intelligent but singularly impecunious and insignificant Prince Leopold of Saxe-Coburg-Saalfeld, who had caught her eye at the London celebrations which marked Napoleon's exile to Elba after the long wars on the Continent. At the age of twenty, Charlotte was united with her Leopold, and under his influence she blossomed into a charming young woman. And, for the first time in her life, she found a stable home.

The consort of this prospective queen of Great Britain was a shrewd young man with strong ideas as to government and monarchical responsibility. His first ambition was to 'tame' his wife, and by shaming her into decent, quiet manners, he had quite a success. Whether he would ever have made a good queen of her must, however, always remain a matter for conjecture, for Charlotte died in November 1817, a few hours after producing a still-born child.

The royal family's natural grief at the death of the Princess was somewhat overshadowed by their debates as to her replacement. As matters then stood, the now aged and frail George III would be succeeded by his son the Regent, then by the royal brothers, then their sisters, then their Gloucester cousins, all childless, and there was the real chance that the crown would then pass out of the family to their Brunswick cousins – unless one of them could manage to beget a new heir.

After the old King's death in 1820, the new King George IV did take advantage of his wife's latest infidelities to attempt to divorce her – without success, but she died soon after and for some time there were rumours that George would seek a young bride. But in the ten years of his reign, the King remained unmarried, content with his mistresses. Of the three royal dukes already married at the time of Charlotte's death, York had given up hopes of becoming a father; Sussex was tethered to a commoner, who had given him two children – but whose inferior birth had, under the terms of the Royal Marriage Act of 1772, made her children ineligible to stand in the royal succession; only Ernest Augustus, Duke of Cumberland, married in 1815, had any real hopes at that time of providing the much-needed heir. (Of the two married Princesses, Charlotte and Mary, the former was already a widow and the latter beyond the age for giving birth to a child for the first time.)

There were financial inducements as well as duty to the Crown to urge the remaining princes to marry now and beget children. Edward, Duke of Kent, was up to his ears in debt, and only the expectation (never in fact fulfilled) of having his slate wiped clean could prompt him to give up his mistress of more than twenty years and take a bride. His elder brother William, Duke of Clarence, had debts too but no mistress at the time (though by an actress not long since discarded he had several children – not an attractive menage to offer a future wife), while Adolphus, Duke of Cambridge, was without encumbrances. The three brothers duly cast around for brides among the princesses of the German states and went to the altar within weeks of each other, in the summer of 1818 – as did their sister Elizabeth, though, at forty-eight, she must have realized that she was not in the running for producing a future monarch of Great Britain.

The three new duchesses became pregnant almost immediately, and the Duchess of Cumberland, encouraged by the rivalry, followed suit. The most junior of them (in terms of her husband's place in the royal succession), Augusta of Cambridge, was the first to give birth, producing a son on the 26th March 1819, and the next day the senior, Adelaide of Clarence, bore a daughter. Victoire of Kent gave her husband a daughter, to be named Victoria, on the 24th May, and three days later a boy was born to Frederica of Cumberland. Sadly, the Clarence baby (another Charlotte) died when she was only a few days old, and her replacement, born the following year, survived for only three months (had she lived, she would have become a nineteenth-century Queen Elizabeth II). So it was Victoria of Kent, the child of the second royal duke, who stood senior among the new generation and, after her three elder uncles and her father, prospective heiress to the British throne.*

A brother would have outranked her – but no brother for Victoria, no son for the Duke of Kent, was ever born, for Edward died before he could beget a second child. He went to his grave, in January 1820, only a few days before his father, George III, at last left his life of pain and torment.

* The 'Salic Law' pertaining in Germany forbade the inheritance of kingdoms, principalities etc, there by a woman. Thus, when Victoria succeeded to the British crown in 1837, Hanover (a kingdom since 1814) passed to her uncle Ernest Augustus and his descendants.

The Victorian Age
1819–1914

An adolescent Victoria, sketched by
Hayter, with her mother, the Duchess of
Kent.

Louise, Baroness Lehzen
(a miniature by Koepke) – the beloved
governess of Victoria's childhood, the
tyrant of her elder children's nursery.

Victoria and Albert with their nine children, photographed at Osborne in 1858.

The matriarch Victoria with just a few members of her large family, in the 1890s.

The three eldest children of the future King George V, with their mother, Mary of Teck.

Gas-mask parade at a Dr Barnardo's Home nursery during the Second World War.

Childhood 1970s-style: an exponent of the skate-board craze which swept Britain in the mid-seventies.

The future Queen Elizabeth II and her sister Margaret, with their parents and grandmother, receiving the cheers of the crowd on Coronation Day, 1937.

Princesses Elizabeth and Margaret photographed painting.

Christening Day, 1948: the then Duke and Duchess of Edinburgh with their first-born, Prince Charles.

Coronation Day, 1953: Prince Charles and Princess Anne appear with their parents on the Buckingham Palace balcony after the ceremony.

The modern royal family. With the Queen and Duke of Edinburgh, *from left to right:* Princess Anne, Prince Edward, Prince Andrew and Charles, Prince of Wales.

"The happiest days of your life"

It would be pleasant to present the Victorian age as one in which children came into their own, to paint a picture of warm nurseries and bright schoolrooms, of gentle mammas and kindly papas, of doting nurses and enthusiastic teachers, of good little children enjoying books and toys and games and holidays of which past centuries had only dreamed. It would be pleasant to dwell on the memories of happy Victorian childhood presented by those who look back from an era of confusion and change to one of security and stability. But to present the whole story of Victorian childhood, one must also paint the darker, colder aspects of the age: of bare, wet feet trudging through the dawn to mill and mine; of scarred backs under the overseer's flailing rod; of lice-infested heads and the distended bellies of malnutrition; of minds ignorant of culture and beauty, warped by the daily need to beg, inveigle or steal food and shelter.

But the mood of the nineteenth century was one of reform, reform of attitudes and of circumstances, and for all the horrors suffered by Victorian children (rich as well as poor), there was real progress towards sympathy for and understanding of children, overcoming their oppression and exploitation.

The philanthropists of the eighteenth century had begun the mammoth task of revealing and overcoming the drudgery and ignorance of the children of the poor; in the nineteenth century idealists and reformers achieved wonders. Literature was a powerful weapon: the plight of the pitiful little chimney-sweeps was brought to public notice by Charles Kingsley's searing allegory *The Water Babies*; Charles Dickens revealed the iniquities of workhouse masters in *Oliver Twist* and showed how the unprotected child could be dragged into a spiral of crime; Elizabeth Barrett Browning's poem 'The Cry of the Children' reminded fat industrialists of the hunger and exhaustion of their infant employees: one after another, the concerned and sensitive spirits of the age used their talents to excite and shame the comfortable classes on behalf of the children at their mercy. Private enterprises on behalf of children burgeoned into national organizations, beneficed and systematized, to take orphans, waifs and strays from the streets and give them, if not a real home, at least a shelter, a coat and daily bread. Parliamentary commissions researched, codified and presented information on the plight of the homeless, the over-worked and the ignorant child, resulting in statutes curtailing child exploitation in industry, child prostitution and child crime, and offering education and moral instruction to all.

At the end of the nineteenth century there remained town slums and country hovels; children were still taken from school to bring in the harvest or to earn a few pennies selling newspapers, holding horses, running errands; there was still a high incidence of scurvy and scabies and rickets and worms among the children of the poor; but progress had been made, and progress was hastening towards triumph.

There were other ills in the Victorians' treatment of children not resulting directly from poverty. Charles Dickens thrust before his readers the miseries of boys unwanted at home and sent into the hell of such private schools as his 'Dotheboys Hall', and Charlotte Brontë spoke up for small girls bought places at hypocritically philanthropic institutions where their spirits were broken while their bodies were starved, out of sight and out of mind of their uncaring 'friends' and 'guardians'; Thomas Hughes revealed that even in the highest classes of society boys sent to the great public schools were subject to bullying and torture to which their masters turned a blind eye.

These were situations which legislation and personal 'enlightenment' could remedy, but there were other miseries to which nineteenth-century children were subject which few thought to challenge. Though the death-rate was falling, there was still a high incidence of infant deaths, and not all among the poor: a mother of a large family, weakened by years of pregnancy and labour, would produce sickly children, staggering to early graves. Inoculation, immunization and hygiene worked towards the eradication of formerly fatal diseases, but there remained the perils of typhus, diphtheria and 'consumption' (tuberculosis). Child medicine became a profitable business, with home cures being supplemented by popular patent medicines, beloved of mothers and nannies but loathsome to the children to whom they were regularly administered: castor oil, cod-liver oil, senna pods and ipecacuanha. And it was not fashion alone which kept small girls in stays and numerous petticoats, babies in long gowns and stiff caps, with pilches and body-binders, but the fear of the dangers of chill air on the skin, while the 'dangers' of night air let children sleep stifling and sweating in unventilated rooms.

And yet the Victorians' concern for their children was sincere and well-meaning, their precautions for health designed to protect children from the all too prevalent chances of early death, and if Victorian parents' methods for bodily welfare seem less than wise, they raised to an art that aspect of parenthood which offers a child security and balanced emotion. Victorian religion may not have been the well-spring of virtue which contemporaries liked to imagine, but the faith of many Victorians was a major factor in their stability and fortitude. And it was in the Victorian age that the first appreciable efforts were made to make childhood 'the happiest time of one's life', with a rapid proliferation of aids to child amusement and enjoyment.

In the last decades of the century there were more children's books on the market than there are today, and though the bulk of children's literature was still heavily moralistic and pietistic, much of it was well-written and stimulated the imagination. There was no dearth of fantasy: Lear's *Book of Nonsense* appeared in 1846, Thackeray's *The Rose and the Ring* in 1855, while the popularity of Lewis Carroll's *Alice's Adventures in Wonderland*, published in 1865, drew forth a sequel, *Alice through the Looking-glass*, in the next decade. In the years that followed, the books of R. L. Stevenson, Captain Marryat and Jules Verne inspired small boys to go adventuring in the wider world, while American imports, the works of L. M. Alcott and Susan Coolidge, encouraged little girls to admire more spirited heroines than those of the prim Charlotte M. Yonge who were home-grown, long before E. Nesbit's lively girl-characters prepared them for liberation and independence. And the wide range of children's magazines which appeared in the second half of the century were of the highest quality in both matter and illustration, offering stories and educational articles, puzzles and competitions, from 'Little Folks' to the universally loved 'Boy's Own Paper', the most famous of the many.

By the end of the century cheap toys were flooding every nursery. It was the age of mechanics, in toy-making as in industry, and the ambition of every small boy was to own his own clockwork engine and a velocipede, the forerunner of the bicycle. There were toy theatres, forts, farms and dolls' houses for 'realism', parlour-games, jigsaws and puzzles to challenge inventiveness and ingenuity, and a multitude of educational aids, such as albums for pressed flowers and postage stamps, partitioned boxes for fossils and minerals, carpentry sets and box-gardens, besides the outlets for little girls' passions in fancy-work: 'decalcomanie', poker work, filigree work and berlin work, to supplement their plain sewing, embroidering, knitting and crochet tasks. For entertainment outside the home, there was Madame Tussaud's wax-works (and its lesser imitators), the many touring circuses, the panto-mime and the minstrel show, the magic lantern and, at the end of the century, the wonderful 'bioscope', forerunner of the modern cinema.

The Victorians discovered that their railways could be used to take them from town and city to coast and country, and while the rich continued to enjoy their 'Grand Tours' of the Continent, for the poor there were 'Cook's tours', day excursions from London to Southend and Brighton, from Manchester and the manufacturing towns of Lancashire and Yorkshire to the northern coastal resorts, where millhands and miners could disport themselves in cheery crowds on beach and pier – those aspiring to gentility took their week at 'homely' lodgings in quieter watering-places. And so the Victorian child, still clad in flannel petticoats, could wander and wade among rockpools and, in modest bathing-dress, brave the icy waves.

Between these coddled nursery children and the waifs of the workhouse there was a large band of working-class children who were the chief beneficiaries of the new educational opportunities, the improved standards of health and diet, of their century. Sturdily booted and warmly (if not beautifully) clad, it was they who filled the desks of the town and village schools which burgeoned from the 1870s, learning to write elegant copper-plate hands, to do complicated sums involving the 'rod, pole and perch' and to read (if not to appreciate) the finest works in English literature. Sadly, few of them took advantage of the cultural opportunities open to them; as one of their number, Flora Thompson, was to record in her account of life in rural Oxfordshire in the 1880s, "If the children, by the time they left school, could read well enough to read the newspaper and perhaps an occasional book for amusement, and write well enough to write their own letters, they had no wish to go farther. Their interest was not in books but in life, and especially in life that lay immediately about them."[1] Even for a bright child, such as Flora herself, success at the elementary school was no guarantee of higher education, and the universities remained the preserve of the upper classes until well into the twentieth century, fed by the public schools; but for ambitious boys, technically minded, there were the 'mechanics institutes', and for both sexes there were teachers' training colleges by the end of the century. Pioneers of higher education for women fought a hard battle with reactionary parents as well as with the authorities, and even while the first classes of 'sweet girl graduates' were still shocking the dons of Oxbridge, there were still few outlets for their talents.

Nevertheless, the elementary schools of the late Victorian age laid a firm basis for the 'elevation' of the labouring classes which came so fast as the twentieth century opened, and the British Empire was stocked with young men and women eager for the adventure and prosperity which they had learned to seek beyond their quiet villages.

By the end of the nineteenth century, there was a 'cult' of childhood, an undefined but tacitly accepted ideal of giving children years of play and fantasy before they faced the hard, materialistic world. Childhood was still to be a preparation for adult life, laying foundations of solid knowledge, morals and manners, but it was to be a time of indulgence too. If one may allowably condemn Victorian sentimentality about children, let it be remembered that it was that sentimentality which clothed, fed and taught children who would otherwise have drudged in cold and hunger through the years or perished in gutters.

"Poor Vicky"

In the last years of the nineteenth century, the printing-presses poured forth a stream of books on the life of Queen Victoria. By the time of her death, in January 1901, there was surely not a child in Britain who had not read of or heard stories of the Queen's own childhood, so happy, so well-ordered, so warmed by maternal affection, as it was unanimously presented by these early biographers.

And yet, even in the last quarter of the nineteenth century, the more sophisticated reader could pick up hints that this picture was not entirely accurate. The publication, between 1874 and 1887, of the memoirs of a courtier, Charles Greville, produced a sensation at the time in their portrayal of the royal childhood as hedged around by adult ambition and self-interest and of the royal home as a hotbed of intrigue and controversy. Even while one run-of-the-mill biographer could praise Victoria's mother, the Duchess of Kent, as "everything that a kind, wise and good mother ought to have been",[1] the late Duchess's reputation was being tarnished by Greville's speculation as to her moral fitness to have had charge of the young Victoria.

But it was only in 1921, with the 'definitive' life of the Queen, written by Lytton Strachey and based on until-then private documents in the royal archives, that the whole picture began to emerge, balancing the real happiness which Victoria did find in childhood with the real distress which she suffered in the same years.

Victoria was not entirely the product of the royal dukes' scramble of 1818 to provide a new heir to the British throne. Two years earlier, before the death of Princess Charlotte introduced that urgency, Edward, Duke of Kent, fourth son of George III, had been considering taking a wife and, urged by Charlotte herself and by her husband Leopold, had begun courting Leopold's sister, the widowed Princess of Leiningen. However, the Princess's refusal of his proposal then had not prompted him to look elsewhere, and for a year afterwards he continued happily with the French mistress who had graced his bed and board since the 1790s. When, in 1817, the need for a royal heir (and the chance of liquidating his debts) roused Edward to seek a bride again, he renewed his application to Victoire of Leiningen, and this time he was accepted.

The Duke of Kent was a man who liked his home comforts and who was at his best in a family circle. Sent from home early in adolescence to take up a military career, he had soon settled down into respectable domesticity with his mistress and remained faithful to her for some quarter of a century. He was sincerely distressed at being forced to abandon her but also sincerely enthusiastic at the prospect of making a regular union and founding a family. Princess Victoire had been married at seventeen to a man more than twenty years her senior – a man of 'uncertain temper' – who had died in 1814, leaving her with two children in comparative poverty and the obscurity of his infinitesimal German principality: so there was the alluring prospect of royal grandeur in Britain to sweeten her marriage to another middle-aged bridegroom. But Victoire was not wholly mercenary: during the first months of her marriage she came to appreciate Edward's good qualities and to make an affectionate companion for him. Nor was the Duke's delight at his wife's pregnancy entirely a result of his desire to produce an heir to the throne.

Edward was not disappointed that his child, born in May 1819, was a girl. "I feel it due to myself to declare that such sentiments are not in unison with my own," he wrote to a friend, "for I am decidedly of the opinion the the decrees of Providence are at all times the wisest and best."[2] And Victoire's mother reassured the Duchess that, if no son came to take precedence of the baby Princess, "the English like queens" and that the infant might be "again a Charlotte – destined, perhaps, to play a great part one day".[3]

There was some thought, at first, of having the child christened 'Charlotte', but it was soon discarded. Indeed, the problem of naming this potential queen was a difficult one to solve. 'Alexandrina' was generally agreed upon, since one of the godfathers was to be Tsar Alexander of Russia, to be followed by 'Elizabeth' or 'Augusta' or maybe 'Georgiana' for the other godfather, the Prince Regent. The latter, however, had neither love nor respect for his brother Edward and was seriously annoyed by the suggestion that a version of his own name should *follow* that of the Tsar. So it was not to be 'Alexandrina Georgiana'.

Even when the Kents brought their baby to the font, that June, the British godfather had still not approved any second name. Only at the very last moment did he grudgingly agree to have his niece named 'Alexandrina Victoria'.*

* The name Victoria was not known in Britain until that time, though it was in use in other forms ('Vittoria', 'Victoire') on the Continent. The baby was called 'Drina' in

The Prince Regent's antipathy to them was not allowed to mar the Kents' happiness. They spent their summer at Kensington, not too much inconvenienced by the Duke's still-mounting debts, and made the best of their need to retrench still further by moving into an inexpensive but charming cottage at Sidmouth in Devonshire in the last days of the year. In the first weeks of January 1820 they were to be seen parading their baby along the sea-front whenever the weather allowed.

However, the family had been in Devon only about three weeks when the Duke took a heavy cold, which turned feverish and then became pneumonia. After only a few days' illness, Edward – who had boasted of good health all his life – died, on Sunday, 23rd January.

While arrangements were being made for the removal of the Duke's body to Windsor, the Duchess was at her wits' end for means to take herself, her German daughter Feodora, aged thirteen, her baby and her household back to London. Her husband had left nothing but debts, and there was not even ready cash for immediate expenses. Fortunately, her brother Leopold, who had been summoned to Edward's deathbed, was on hand to settle everything and to conduct the widow back to Kensington. And it was to be Leopold who, over the months that followed, took charge of Victoire's affairs and made her an allowance out of his own income, and Leopold who reasoned her out of her desire to return home to Germany by persuading her that such a step would mar her child's popularity in Britain if ever Alexandrina Victoria should come to the throne. After all, with the death of King George III just a few days after that of the Duke of Kent, the baby now stood third in line to the throne.

Many years later Victoria gathered together her memories of her earliest childhood. There were dim images of a yellow carpet on which she had crawled, of a kindly bishop letting her play with his jewelled Garter badge and of the fearsome King George IV demanding to shake her "little paw"; and as she lay each night in her cot in her mother's bedroom, there was the tick, tick, tick of her father's tortoiseshell watch to lull her to sleep. Then came clearer memories: of a carriage-drive in Windsor Great Park sandwiched between fat Aunt Mary and the even fatter King, of a Punch and Judy show at a party of Uncle York's, of her own temper tantrums and her refusal to learn her letters until she was five years old.

"We lived in a very simple plain manner," the Queen recalled, "breakfast was at half past eight, luncheon at half past one, dinner at

---

the family in her first months but was calling herself 'Vicky' by the age of four and seems to have grown up as 'Victoria'. At her accession to the throne she was proclaimed as 'Queen Alexandrina Victoria' but at her own insistence the first name was soon dropped.

seven – to which I came generally (when it was no regular large dinner-party) – eating my bread and milk out of a small silver basin. Tea was only allowed as a great treat in later years.''[4]

Fortunately, the Queen's sparse memories are filled out by others' letters and memoirs of the early 1820s. The writer Leigh Hunt recorded seeing the child walking in Kensington Gardens, holding her half-sister's hand and attended by a footman like "a gigantic fairy";[5] Princess Charlotte's friend George Keppel, now Lord Albemarle, liked to watch Victoria playing gardener on summer mornings, amused to see "how impartially she divided the contents of the watering-pot between the flowers and her own little feet".[6]

In the summer of 1825, the Princess's maternal grandmother, Duchess Augusta of Saxe-Coburg-Saalfeld, paid a visit to Kensington.

> I recollect the excitement and anxiety I was in, at this event [Victoria wrote many years later] – going down the great flight of steps to meet her when she got out of the carriage, and hearing her say, when she sat down in her room and fixed her fine clear blue eyes on her little grand-daughter whom she called in her letters "the flower of May", "Ein schönes Kind" – "a fine child".[7]

The "Mayflower" proved a constant source of amusement to the Duchess during her stay in England:

> Since one is six years old with impunity [Augusta wrote], there is often bargaining whilst going to bed. Then she blames her Sarah, often accusing her of hurting her while washing her, preferring to tell all sorts of tales. Lehzen (the governess) takes her gently from the bed and sits her down on the thick carpet, where she has to put on her stockings.
> One has to contain oneself not to burst out laughing when she says in a tragic tone of voice, "Poor Vicky! She is an unhappy child! She doesn't know which is the right stocking and which is the left! I am an unhappy child."[8]

Victoria's childhood world was peopled mainly by adults. There was her half-sister Feodora, of course, her first companion and playmate, but the German princess was more than a dozen years her senior and in 1828 left Kensington with a German bridegroom. For the rest, there was the Duchess of Kent, who never spent even one night away from her daughter and who devoted all her energies to Victoria's well-being. There was kind Aunt Adelaide of Clarence who had lost her own babies, and bluff Uncle William, both regular visitors to Kensington in Victoria's early years. There was generous Uncle York, who delighted his niece with the gift of a donkey, peevish Uncle Sussex, who had apartments next door to the Kents' in Kensington Palace and who must never be disturbed by a child's cries, and fat Aunt Mary Gloucester and lively Aunt Sophia, another Kensington inmate. Best loved of the royal relations was, of course, Uncle Leopold, still in England, still vigilant over his sister's *ménage*, and whose mansion of Claremont in Surrey was Victoria's favourite holiday home. And there was good old Baroness Späth, the Duchess's German lady-in-waiting, kind Mr. Davys, the clergyman who gave Victoria her first formal lessons, and, above all, Baroness Lehzen, the governess, who was with Victoria almost every moment of the day, superintending her studies, teaching her to dress her many dolls in historical costume, leading her by the hand on the narrow, treacherous stairs, sitting by her bed at night until her mother was ready to retire. Victoria loved Lehzen.

But there was an ogre too. Not King George IV, who, for all his antipathy to the Duchess of Kent, was invariably kind to his niece. Not even Uncle Cumberland, whom the adults suspected of having designs on Victoria's very life, to put himself back into the running for the British throne – he was rarely allowed near the child. No, the ogre was closer to home, a daily visitor to Kensington Palace.

This was Sir John Conroy, the late Duke of Kent's aide who had become steward to the widowed Duchess. Conroy was an Irishman, with the Irishman's easy, shallow charm, and he knew every wile to make himself indispensable to Victoire of Kent, with an eye to future influence and power when Victoria should succeed to the throne. He fed the Duchess's fears and suspicions of the British royal family, fanned her resentment of George IV's coldness to her and impressed on her his own fidelity to her interests and those of her daughter. Victoire was still a young woman, still attractive, and not averse from male attention, which Conroy, of course, knew how to provide. Probably their relationship was no warmer than that of flirtation, though it was rumoured that Baroness Späth was dismissed and sent back to Germany for remonstrating with her mistress for being too familiar with Conroy, and Victoria herself was said to have witnessed an amorous passage which shocked and disturbed her. But the gossip which made the Duchess of Kent the mistress of Sir John Conroy was almost certainly untrue: Victoire had the firmest religious principles; Conroy's wife was her own friend; and, besides, while both counted on future power through Victoria, any discovery of such a relationship would have put in jeopardy their plans.

Conroy's designs were obvious to Victoria as she grew up, even before he showed his hand. She saw through his flattery of her mother, his deference to herself – which combined obsequiousness and snide sarcasm. As the Princess grew ever more hostile towards Sir John, even his harmless little daughters, Jane and Victoire, her playmates, came in for cold treatment as their father's pawns to win her favour.

Prince Leopold might have put a stop to Conroy's schemes in the 1820s, if he had been aware of them, but for all his interest in his niece and her future, he was too busy with his own concerns to pay close attention to what was going on at Kensington. He advised his sister on her conduct when George IV died in 1830, making Victoria heiress presumptive to her uncle William IV (the Duke of York had died in 1828), but by then Leopold was already immersed in plans for going to Belgium, whose newly-created throne he accepted in 1831, and in the years that followed, though he corresponded regularly with his niece, he went unaware of her daily struggles with Sir John.

The plan of 1830, as dear to Leopold as it was, privately, to Conroy, was for the Duchess of Kent to become her daughter's Regent should Victoria succeed to the throne before she attained her majority at eighteen. (She was eleven when George IV died, and, since William IV was then in his mid-sixties and ailing, it was feasible that she might be called on to reign before long.) The first step was to prove that the Duchess was a fit guardian for her daughter, and this was demonstrated by the success of the Princess in an examination put to her by a specially invited panel of bishops, which showed that the Duchess's plan for her education was both apt and well carried through. The bishops' glowing recommendations were then, of course, used to make out a case for the regency, which was put to Parliament in the months that followed and which won the Duchess a promise of future power.

In fact, Victoria's education was excellent, neither too superficial nor too deep. She learned Latin (albeit unwillingly), mathematics (at which she shone), history (which she loved), French and German (which she was never allowed to speak informally with her German mother and German governess lest it mar her pure English), and as she entered her teens, her reading was broad and, to modern tastes, exceedingly heavy.

I am reading Russell's Modern Europe, *which is very interesting* [wrote Victoria, aged fifteen, to King Leopold], *and Clarendon's* History of the Rebellion. *It is drily written but is full of instruction. I like reading different authors, of different opinions, by which means I learn not to lean on one particular side. Besides my lessons, I read Jones' account of the wars in Spain, Portugal and the south of France, from the year 1808 till 1814. It is well done, I think, and amuses me very much. In French I am now in* La Rivalité de France et de l'Espagne, *par Gaillard.*[9]

Victoria's studies of history, government and international affairs were supplemented by discussions of political theory in her correspondence with King Leopold and her observations on politics of the day. "Pray, dear Uncle, have you read Lord Palmerston's speech concerning the Spanish affair, which he delivered the night of the division of Sir Henry Hardinge's motion? . . . The Irish Tithes question came on last night in the House of Commons, and I am very anxious for the morning papers."[10]

Much has been made by various biographers of Victoria's musical passions and of the hours she passed with Lehzen in 'fancy-work', but there can be no doubt but that she was far better prepared for her career than any earlier queen had been.

The story of Victoria's realization of her destiny has often been told, and as often dismissed as legend, but the account set down years later by Baroness Lehzen was read by the Queen herself and, on the whole, approved by her. The incident occurred just after the bishops' examination, before the introduction of the Regency Bill, on the 11th March 1830, when the governess presented the Princess with a family tree, showing herself as next in line to the throne. When Victoria took in the significance of it, she did say the memorable and often-quoted line "I will be good"; then she burst into tears.

With the Princess's elevation in the line of succession and her mother's (and Conroy's) success in their plan for the regency, Victoria began to take a place in public life. That was not to say that she was seen frequently at Court, for Conroy had primed the Duchess of Kent to fear a rival influence on Victoria from King William which would outweigh their own and that the girl's association with the King's bastards, the fitzClarences, who led the Court, would tarnish her own reputation in the eyes of the respectable bourgeoisie. The King would have been delighted to have his niece near him and to smooth her way into her future career; he resented his sister-in-law's efforts to keep Victoria away from Court for all but the most formal ceremonies, while kind Queen Adelaide, who had once befriended Victoire, was hurt that she was now cold-shouldered by the Duchess, who refused to bring Victoria to her private apartments. Victoria herself was not slow to understand who it was who was erecting barriers between Kensington and Windsor: it was Conroy, she knew, who feared a diminution of his influence over the Duchess and the thwarting of his designs.

Now, in 1831, when Victoria was twelve years old, there began the first of a series of annual tours through the provinces intended to introduce the Princess to the nation, with the Duchess to be much in evidence – all stage-managed by Conroy, of course. To the intense annoyance of

King William, who was becoming increasingly unpopular in the country for his opposition to parliamentary reform, Victoire and Victoria began to cream off the people's affection, which he felt was his own due. Everywhere they were received with loyal demonstrations and flattering addresses, and, as time passed, the Duchess of Kent began to expect ever more royal honours paid to herself and her daughter at each stopping-place. The King was furious when he heard that she demanded, as of right, gun-salutes from naval vessels and garrisons when her boat crossed to the Isle of Wight: with understandable spite, he insisted on the curtailment of the "continual poppings". Tension mounted as the 1830s passed.

Victoria herself was not, of course, unaware of the King's disapproval, but she thoroughly enjoyed her first excursions into the towns and countryside of England and Wales. On the first day of her first 'progress' in 1831, she began a journal, so enthralled by the inviting white pages and by the sights she saw *en route* that at first she made entries every few minutes. Later, her efforts, though never 'literary', flowed smoothly, displaying her lively intelligence and enthusiastic interest in new experiences. By the end of her long life, Victoria had penned hundreds of thousands of words, a fascinating unfolding picture of her life and times.

However, in those first years Victoria's journal came under the scrutiny of her mother, and she never wrote a word of the battles with the Duchess and with Conroy which were beginning to mar her years of preparation for the crown.

In the summer of 1835, the Princess was feeling unwell and begged to be let off the arduous tour which was planned. But everything was arranged, and so, that September, with aching head, often too sick to eat, she was taken through the Midland counties up to Yorkshire, then back through East Anglia. Victoria was given a chance to recuperate at Ramsgate, where for a few days she was invigorated by a visit from Uncle Leopold and his new wife, the French Princess Louise, but no sooner had the Belgian King and Queen departed than the girl contracted typhoid. It was a severe attack, and for weeks afterwards Victoria was too weak even to walk across the room.

Conroy chose this moment to attack. He had come to realize the extent of Victoria's dislike of him and knew that he could not expect her voluntarily to award him titles, wealth and office when she came to the throne. Now, supported by the Duchess, he tried to browbeat the Princess into signing a document promising him the post of private secretary when she should become queen. But, frail as she was, Victoria had an iron will and, with Lehzen's aid, firmly resisted. The governess, of course, came in for a good deal of bitter reproach from the Duchess and Conroy, but they dared not dismiss her as she held the confidence of the King, and they knew that, if she went, she would tell everything she knew of their machinations.

The year 1836 brought a mixture of happy and unhappy new experiences to the teenaged Princess. Two batches of German boy-cousins came over, ready to dance with her and walk with her and make her feel like a woman for the first time. One of them, Prince Albert, was designed by King Leopold to become Victoria's future consort – to the chagrin of King William, who had a candidate of his own for Victoria's hand – yet another Prince of Orange. When the British King tried to prevent the Coburg Princes' visit (which would overlap with the Dutchman's), the Belgian King was furious: "Now that slavery is abolished in the British colonies," Leopold wrote to Victoria, "I do not comprehend *why your lot alone should be to be kept a white little slavey in England*, for the pleasure of the Court."[11] In fact, William IV could not prevent Albert and his brother Ernest from making their visit to Kensington, and Victoria's obvious preference of her cousins to the Prince of Orange only added fuel to his burning resentment to the Duchess of Kent and her wiles.

In August that year, when Victoire grudgingly took her daughter to Windsor for the King's birthday celebrations, William took the opportunity of a public dinner to make a speech attacking his sister-in-law in the strongest possible terms:

> *I trust in God* [he declared] *that my life may be spared for nine months longer, after which period, in the event of my death, no regency could take place. I should then have the satisfaction of leaving the royal authority to the personal exercise of that young lady . . . , the heiress presumptive of the Crown, and not in the hands of a person now near me, who is surrounded by evil advisers and who is herself incompetent to act with propriety in the station in which she would be placed.*[12]

The Duchess, thus insulted, could only retaliate by keeping her daughter away from Windsor over the months that followed.

If fact, William IV was still living when Victoria attained her majority, in May 1837, and he used the customary formality of offering her an independent income to attempt to weaken her mother's influence. The Princess was to have £10,000 a year, which was to be administered on her behalf by a Crown servant, not by the Duchess, and she was to be allowed to choose her own ladies-in-waiting.

Inevitably, Conroy – and his pawn, the Duchess – could never agree to having Victoria made so independent of themselves; nor did they wish to have ladies brought into Kensington Palace who would observe – and probably gossip about – their treatment of Victoria. The Princess was forced to reply to her uncle at their dictation – but resolutely, and again with Lehzen's aid, she secretly wrote a document setting out the true facts of the matter. Tension mounted, and there were almost daily 'scenes' between the mother and daughter.

In many ways Victoria was still a child: she still slept in her mother's bedroom, still submitted to her mother's taste in choice of wardrobe, books and entertainment; she still looked to Lehzen for guidance where she could trust no one else – except Uncle Leopold, who was only just coming to understand his niece's problems; she still had 'crushes' on pretty opera-singers and trembled before eminent music-teachers; she still gushed and doted on her King Charles spaniel, "dear sweet little Dash". And yet the Princess was precociously mature in will-power on important issues, though her battles could not be fought without the inevitable resort to tears, and even while Conroy was attempting to persuade Cabinet ministers that the Princess was too childish, too unstable mentally and emotionally, to undertake the duties of a monarch, Victoria herself impressed these men as eminently suitable material for a sovereign.

In the last days of King William IV's life, that June of 1837, Sir John Conroy finally damned himself. He urged the Duchess of Kent to lock Victoria up until she had agreed to make him her private secretary – that is, to give him access to every state paper sent to her, to make him her go-between with ministers of state, to give him control of her personal role in government. But as Conroy's determination grew fiercer, the Duchess's weakened. Relations between herself and Victoria were at their most fragile: this final move might alienate her daughter from her for ever.

Then, less than a month after the need for the Duchess's regency had passed, and with Conroy despairing of ever ruling Britain and its empire through Victoria, King William IV died.

Early in the morning of the 20th June 1837, the Duchess of Kent woke her daughter and led her downstairs to receive the men who brought the news of her accession to the throne. But on the threshold Victoria stepped forward alone, leaving the Duchess outside, and for the rest of that day, and through all the days to come, Victoire was excluded from her daughter's councils. That very night, the Queen's bed was removed from her mother's room.

The Duchess was accorded a formal place in her daughter's Court, and Conroy could not wholly be ousted from sharing it – though he was refused admittance to Victoria's private apartments when she and her mother moved to Buckingham Palace, but relations between the Queen and her mother had dwindled to a polite exchange of trivialities, and the ogre of Kensington Palace was ignored. At the same time, while Uncle Leopold was tactfully allowed to understand that he must not interfere in British government affairs, though he would always be welcome on a personal basis in Victoria's home, even Lehzen was to be the royal confidante in domestic affairs only. In the business of government, Victoria would allow no one to usurp her own prerogatives, leaning on Prime Minister Melbourne alone for support in the trying first years of her reign.

It was to be several years before Victoria came to forgive her mother for the past. With Conroy's retirement (though not until after he had contrived to mar Victoria's popularity in the country by his meddling in a palace scandal), with the Duchess of Kent's tacit acceptance of her exclusion from power, with the waning influence of Lehzen and the growing influence of the Queen's husband – her cousin Albert, whom she married in February 1840, Victoria's emotions became more stable and she was able to look at her mother without remembering past wrongs. The Duchess of Kent proved a good mother-in-law and a perfect grandmother and at last settled thankfully into roles which Victoria could not resent.

When, in 1861, the Duchess died, the Queen was overcome with grief. "She was the gentlest, most tender and loving creature that one can ever imagine," Victoria wrote then.[13]

"Poor little Queen," wrote the great historian Thomas Carlyle on Victoria's coronation day, "she is at an age when a girl can hardly be trusted to choose a bonnet for herself; yet a task is laid upon her from which an archangel might shrink."

Victoria's inexperience did allow her to make mistakes, even grave mistakes, of judgement in the first years of her reign, and admittedly, under Lord Melbourne's tutelage, she was spared some of the rigours of paperwork and study which she later had to undertake – but from the first Victoria proved herself competent and, above all, conscientious, and, as an *ingénue* among sages, a young woman among old men, performed her role amid general satisfaction.

Inevitably the strains of her childhood told on her character. The Queen's emotions were volatile, especially in close personal relationships; she needed always to feel – as she had never done in adolescence before her accession – that her conduct was wholly approved; she needed to feel that those whom she loved – and especially her husband – put her first in their scheme of things; she needed to feel that she was in control of her public life – but at the same time revelled in her husband's masterful role at home. The insight which knowledge of the Queen's childhood gives, goes a long way towards explaining – perhaps even excusing – those facets of her life and character which so many biographers have criticized. We are accustomed today to forgiving delinquents their misdeeds if their psychologists can show evidence of their mistreatment or deprivation in childhood. Perhaps Queen Victoria may be allowed the same benefit.

"The grandmother of Europe"

The young Queen Victoria revelled in the fast-moving social life of her Court: she would dance into the small hours, eat ('gobble' some said) her way through vast banquets, attend opera and plays night after night – and still emerge fresh for duty each morning. By 1840, the third year of her reign, these pleasures had not palled but were given added zest by her sharing them with her bridegroom, Prince Albert, whom she married that February. Thus, when, within only a few weeks of her wedding, Victoria found that she was pregnant and must live more quietly, she was not pleased. When, a couple of months after the birth of her first child, she realized that she was already expecting a second, she was horrified and furious. In fact, between 1840 and 1857, the Queen would give birth to nine children.

Queen Victoria never overcame her distaste for the discomforts of pregnancy and the pains of childbirth, nor could she believe their end result adequate compensation for their horrors. "What you say of the pride of giving life to an immortal soul is very fine, dear," she wrote to her eldest daughter in 1858, "but I own I cannot enter into that; I think much more of our being like a cow or a dog at such moments; when our poor nature becomes so very animal and unecstatic. . . ."[1] Nor was Victoria ever particularly beguiled by small babies, "mere little plants for the first six months", she declared on one occasion[2] and on another wrote that "an ugly baby is a very nasty object – and the prettiest is frightful when undressed – till about four months; in short, as long as they have their big body and little limbs and that terrible froglike action".[3]

In fact, the Queen's confinements were never very difficult, never dangerous, and at the birth of her last two children she had the benefit of what she called "that blessed chloroform" to ease the pain.

Unlike so many mothers of large families in the nineteenth century, Victoria had the good fortune of rearing all her children to maturity, and all but one of them inherited her excellent constitution. The exception was the Queen's youngest son, Prince Leopold, the first member of the royal family to show the dreadful signs of haemophilia, a failure in blood coagulation by which a sufferer contracting even a minor cut or bruise may bleed to death. It is a rare disorder and one affecting only males, though it can be transmitted by a haemophiliac male or a female: three of Victoria's daughters were 'carriers' of haemophilia, spreading the fatal disorder into the royal dynasties of Europe by their marriages and those of their daughters.

The birth of the first royal child, Victoria, Princess Royal, in November 1840, gave the Queen's old governess, Baroness Lehzen, a new role, as head of the royal nursery. For some time past, Prince Albert has resented Lehzen's intimacy with the Queen and, already depressed and embittered by Victoria's refusal to share her government duties with him, now raged at what seemed like his exclusion from domestic authority, usurped by Lehzen. His chance to challenge her came at the beginning of 1842, when he and Victoria were becoming increasingly alarmed at the sight of their baby wasting away, unable to keep down any food.

At that time, the Queen was in the depths of post-natal depression (after the birth of her second child, the Prince of Wales), and Prince Albert was daily confronted with her tears and complaints, which he attempted to soothe with reason and caresses. But he did not scruple to lecture Victoria on her unwarranted confidence in Lehzen, who, he said, was responsible for their daughter's weakness. There were noisy quarrels, with Victoria in passionate tempers in defence of her friend, Albert quietly, patiently, trying to keep the peace but adamant in his insistence that Lehzen should go. Bitter words were said by both parties – Victoria that she regretted ever marrying, Albert that he could no longer endure to live at Court. However, it was Victoria who was largely in the wrong and Victoria who, horrified at the thought of losing her husband, made concessions in the end. With his characteristic tact, the Prince engineered Lehzen's departure. It was a sad end to her long years of devotion to Victoria – but justified by the improvement in the Princess Royal's health in the months that followed.

The royal marriage was not thereafter totally devoid of quarrels, for Victoria was of too volatile a temperament to be able to live entirely peacefully with those she loved the most. But Albert's tight control of his own emotions and his gentleness with his wife even in her blackest moods brought them through the worst times, and their home life was generally smooth and happy. After years of chafing at his exclusion from the Queen's state business, Albert at last carved himself a niche in public life and became Victoria's most valued assistant, but it was in domestic affairs that he was to prove himself first.

Victoria loved her children and never grudged them time and attention, but it was Albert who planned their studies, conferred with tutors,
arranged 'treats' and worried about moral development.

'Bertie' – Albert Edward, Prince of Wales, Victoria and Albert's
eldest son – was ten years old before he came to realize that it was he and
not his elder sister 'Vicky', Princess Royal, who was their mother's heir.
He could well be forgiven this ignorance, for not only had Victoria and
Albert taken care to shield their children from too full a realization of
their importance but Vicky was a born leader, showing a powerful in-
tellect and a strong will even from infancy, and always full of her own
importance. Beside her, Bertie made a poor showing: where Vicky was
quick in perception, he was slow; where the little Princess was diligent
and interested in her lessons, the Prince was lazy and easily distracted;
where Vicky advanced by leaps and bounds, Bertie plodded, and while
she accepted her (numerous) punishments with proud stoicism, her little
brother would scream and stamp in rage. Albert and Victoria made their
first mistake in letting Bertie feel his inadequacy compared with his
sister's brilliance: it was supposed to spur him on to self-improvement –
in fact, it only gave him an 'inferiority complex'. The will was there –
after his misdemeanours and failures the boy could be brought quickly
to penitence and to promises of reform and hard work, but nothing
could make the Prince of Wales as clever or as self-disciplined as his
elder sister.

Vicky was like Albert, Bertie like Victoria, and it may well be that the
Queen, who always deprecated her own shortcomings and elevated her
husband's virtues to sanctities, felt ashamed to see her own traits in her
son when he fell short of Albert's standards of perfection. One biographer after another has denounced Prince Albert for his harshness
towards Bertie, and Victoria for her continual carping criticism of him:
such denunciation is both understandable and to some extent apt, but
still one must understand the parents' viewpoint: both knew the
pressures on a monarch, the testing years which Bertie must undergo
when he came to the throne, the national contempt for those monarchs
who failed in their duty; it was their responsibility to Bertie, they felt, to
arm him against the future, and to the nation to give it a worthy ruler.
Their ideal was eminently praiseworthy; it was their methods which
were so cruel – depriving him of the company of his brother 'Affie',
who they thought distracted him from his work and encouraged him in
impudence, giving Bertie over to the charge of unsympathetic men who
were so anxious for royal approval of their charge's progress that they
'crammed' him mercilessly.

Nevertheless, this is to give too depressing a picture of the childhood

of the future King Edward VII: there was a very great deal in the domestic life of the royal family to make the boy happy, which he remembered with loving nostalgia into old age. And neither in childhood nor
later did Bertie ever resent his parents' well-meant but misguided efforts
on his behalf.

Their treatment of their eldest son apart, Victoria and Albert were
among the most loving and indulgent of nineteenth-century parents.
And nor was Albert the stern, unbending *paterfamilias* some biographers
have painted him: he was not above turning somersaults for his children's amusement, or running and jumping and rolling with them in
play. Just as it was Albert who spent serious hours planning out his children's curriculum of lessons and studying reports from their teachers, so
it was he who gave up his own precious leisure to rehearse them in plays
and tableaux, inventing fantastic costumes for their performances, he
who built snowmen and made them kites, who thought of having an old
bath dragged into the sea to encourage timid children to learn to swim;
and though it was not, as popular myth has it, Albert who introduced
the Christmas tree into Britain (a century earlier George III and Queen
Charlotte had regaled their offspring with German Christmas customs),
the Prince did make the Christmas festival one of such delight that
Windsor traditions were soon being copied in even the humblest homes
of the nation. Albert was at his best in the family circle.

There was little luxury in the lives of Victoria and Albert's children.
Their food was of the plainest, their bedrooms sparsely furnished and
rarely warmed by a coal fire; there was plenty of soap and water, plenty
of fresh air; even the royal children's clothes (except when they appeared on state occasions) were plainly made – and 'hand-me-downs'
were not unknown to the younger children; their pocket-money was
only a few pence each a week, out of which Christmas and birthday
presents for their parents, brothers and sisters and attendants were to be
bought.

Prince Albert's prime ideal for his children's upbringing was that they
should see as much of their parents as possible and be as close as possible
to them: he and Victoria paid several visits each day to nursery and
schoolroom, had the children into their sitting-room in the evenings,
occasionally dined with them and often saw them in bed; but it was on
holiday, in Scotland and on the Isle of Wight, that the Queen and Prince
saw most of the children.

At Balmoral, by the River Dee in Scotland, and at Osborne, on the
Isle of Wight, the royal family could enjoy privacy and freedom. Un-
observed, and largely unreported, they could take to horseback and
ride miles through lonely glens, picnicking in the heather and enjoying

the company of Highland crofters, who, they found, had none of the obsequious deference usually encountered in Victoria's subjects. ("The children will grow up under the strangest delusions as to what travelling means and the usual condition of people in England," Lady Lyttelton, the royal governess, had once written. "They must suppose one always finds them shouting and grinning and squeezing, surrounded by banners and garlands"⁴ – there was none of that in the Highland villages.) And at Osborne there was a large, well-fenced estate on which the children might roam unescorted, though as often as not their father accompanied them on their rambles, using every opportunity to interest them in nature study and encourage their collection of wild flowers, birds' eggs, shells, strange stones, fossils – all of which were carefully labelled and mounted for the family museum.

At Osborne too the children had their 'Swiss Cottage' – no mere playhouse but a real cottage in miniature, in which the girls were taught to cook and clean, where the boys had their workbenches for carpentry, overlooking the garden plots in which each Prince and Princess culti-vated vegetables which a royal gardener must certify as fit for consump-tion before they were 'purchased' for the table.

However, the royal children did not pass all their leisure out of the public eye. They knew, from an early age, what was expected of them when they went to Astley's Circus or the zoo, how to sit quietly on a public platform or in a drawing-room. Victoria and Albert were always shy of strangers, but Vicky at least was never timid: she had a 'presence' even in infancy which observers found droll but somewhat intimidat-ing; Bertie had a natural charm even as a boy. When the two elder children were taken to Paris, when their parents made a state visit to the Emperor Napoleon III in 1855 (the younger ones were in quarantine for scarlet fever), they were an instant success with their host and hostess, and Bertie was infatuated with the suave Bonaparte and his beautiful Spanish wife. When it came time to leave for home, the boy begged the Empress Eugénie to allow them to stay a little longer, ingenuously assur-ing her that he and his sister would not be missed, as "there are six more of us at home and they don't want us."⁵

At fourteen and thirteen years old, Vicky and Bertie were leaving childhood behind. That same year Prince Frederick William of Prussia (second in line to the Prussian throne) paid two visits to Britain expressly to woo the Princess Royal: on the second he proposed and was accepted. It was to be almost three years more before Victoria and Albert would allow the wedding to take place, but in that time Vicky was groomed for her future eminence – a matter for her mother's resent-ment, since Albert, envisaging his daughter's potential opportunities for bringing Prussia into nineteenth-century democracy, an influence over his beloved Germany and an ally for Britain, spent hours of his time on her instruction which the Queen was accustomed to having devoted to herself.

But while Vicky came closer to her father (it was only after her marriage that she struck up an intimacy with her mother, by correspondence), Bertie was increasingly divorced from the family circle. At White Lodge, Richmond, he had his own household, under the supervision first of his tutor, the Reverend Mr. Gibbs, an unsympathetic man who thought his duty began and ended with beating knowledge into the boy's head. By the summer of 1858, when the Prince of Wales was sixteen, it was obvious that Gibbs had failed to turn him into the paragon desired by the Prince Consort: the boy was not even fit to take the examination required for his planned entry into the army. Colonel Bruce, Gibbs's replacement, won Bertie's confidence, steered him through a successful Continental trip and a period at Oxford University (where he was segregated from his contemporaries, living not in college but in a mansion sufficiently removed from adolescent temptations) and accompanied the Prince when (unexamined) he began his army career. Bertie might have been an academic failure, but he took to army life with zest and zeal, and when, in 1860, his parents entrusted him with a 'goodwill' tour of Canada and a visit to the American president, he acquitted himself far better than anyone could have expected, enchanting the ladies, impressing the men and drawing appreciative 'reviews' from the international Press.

It was 'the ladies', however, who were to retard Bertie once again in his parents' estimation. While at army camp in Ireland in the autumn of 1861, the Prince of Wales met a pretty young actress, Nellie Clifden, and soon it was common gossip that they were lovers.

Remembering Bertie's heredity (his Coburg ancestors were as promiscuous as the Hanoverians) and in view of the licence accorded to most young aristocrats of his day, his 'fall' (as his mother was to call it) was not surprising. To the Queen, however, it seemed shameful, and to Albert it was disgusting – the Prince Consort was the strictest puritan in sexual matters. At the same time, both the young man's parents feared that if news of Bertie's affaire reached the Courts of Europe, his chances of a good marriage might be ruined – they already had a suitable princess in view.

It was a bad time for Prince Albert. The Queen had been in the lowest spirits all the past summer, deeply mourning the death of her mother; diplomatic relations with the USA were being strained to breaking-point, during the first phase of the American Civil War; he was overburdened with work for which, for the first time in nearly twenty years, he found he had little taste (Albert was a great statesman, but he had an obsessive conviction that he, and only he, could do anything right): and then, on the 22nd November, a day of pouring rain, he had to make the trip to Cambridge to confront Bertie with his sin. Already feverish and aching, Albert came home satisfied of his son's penitence – but not to rest; however, a few days later he gave in, taking to his bed. His doctors pronounced him sick of typhoid fever. On the evening of the 14th December 1861, he died.

The Queen was overwhelmed with grief. She cried and she raved; at times she even feared for her sanity. After selecting a spot in the grounds of Windsor Castle where she was to raise a mausoleum for Albert's tomb (and for her own – she was convinced she could not long survive him), Victoria retired to Osborne.

It was to be many months before the Queen could think of anything but her grief, years before she would consent to come out of seclusion, and she never gave up the sombre black of widow's weeds – topped by a white lace cap which the perceptive baby of the family, Princess Beatrice, dubbed 'the sad cap'.

The royal children had lost their father, but for a time it must have seemed to the younger ones that they had lost their mother too. Vicky, hastening to Britain from her home in Berlin, was admitted to the Queen's confidence, and the second daughter, Alice, was Victoria's mainstay, her go-between with the ministers whom the Queen could not face and with the household who rarely caught a glimpse of their mistress (Bertie, whom Victoria came to regard as partly responsible for 'worrying' his father into the grave, was kept at a distance), but Victoria could not bear to have her children round her *en masse* – they were occasionally admitted two at a time.

Later, the Queen looked to her children for comfort, and pledged herself to care for them as Albert had done – everything, she declared, was to be as Albert "would have wished". In fact, it was this which saved Princess Alice from being kept at home all her life, to serve Victoria, a task for which she seemed at one time to be fated – for Albert had chosen a husband for his second daughter (a German prince, Louis of Hesse), and so Victoria must honour his decision: Alice was married, privately, quietly, at Osborne, in the summer of 1862. Her place was taken by 'Lenchen', the Princess Helena, who was seventeen at her father's death.

It was a sadly depleted family which gathered round 'the widow of Windsor' in the 1860s. Vicky (herself a mother now) was in Prussia, Bertie (who married his Danish princess in 1863) had his own establishment, Affie was in the navy, Arthur away in the army, Alice starting her own family in Germany. The good Lenchen, a model of Victorian modesty and tranquillity, remained at home after her marriage in 1866 (to an inevitably German but landless prince who agreed to live in Britain); Louise – a difficult child, artistic but with no great talent, sharp and shrewd but not perceptive or sensitive, departed with a Scottish bridegroom at the end of the decade. Leopold (the haemophiliac) and 'Baby' Beatrice were left longest with their mother, the first to become one of her secretaries, the second to spend interminable hours in attendance on the Queen – she would not escape to marriage until 1885, and then only after a battle royal with her mother, conceded by Victoria only on condition that the Princess and her Henry of Battenberg make their home with her.

The gap in the ages of the eldest and youngest of Victoria and Albert's children made for some strange situations over the years. Vicky became a mother for the first time in 1858 when she was only eighteen – at which date her youngest sister, Beatrice, was only one year old. By the time Beatrice started her own family, in the mid-1880s, Vicky was already a grandmother.

The birth of grandchildren for Queen Victoria over a span of nearly thirty years meant that the Queen was generally surrounded by children in middle age, and in old age had the interest of a growing crowd of great-grandchildren, living in castles and palaces across the length and breadth of Europe. In fact, she came to be called 'the grandmother of Europe', with so many emperors and empresses, kings and queens among her descendants.

As often happens with unmaternal women, Victoria found more satisfaction and sympathy with her grandchildren than she ever did with her own children – Vicky could still annoy her mother on occasion with her arrogance; Alice was deemed 'worldly' and frivolous, until her death in 1878 'canonized' her; Bertie and Affie were regarded as irredeemable in their fashionable vices; Helena 'neglected' the Queen for her own brood; Louise criticized Victoria; Leopold worried and annoyed her by not taking due care of himself in his disability (he died, of his disease, in 1884); only docile Arthur and Beatrice (except during her disgrace when she wanted to marry) kept their mother's unqualified favour. Nevertheless, one or other of the royal children was generally to be found at Windsor, Balmoral or Osborne when the Queen was in residence there, bringing to 'Grandmamma' a host of English or German children, with their horde of governesses, nurses and maids.

Closest to the Queen were the children of Helena and Beatrice, who lived nearest her homes, but after Alice's death the Hesse children were often brought over to England to stay with their grandmother – who supervised their lives in Germany in a screed of letters, ordering their teachers, their clothes and their doses. The Prussian children were less often with her in their early years, for the old Kaiser their paternal grandfather and his anti-British minister Prince Bismarck mistrusted Victoria's influence – though 'Willy', the eldest of Vicky's children, who early lost sympathy with his liberal parents, always avowed the utmost respect and devotion for his English grandmother, which not even his hero Bismarck could mar.

Several of Queen Victoria's grandchildren (of whom only one, the nonagenarian Princess Alice, Countess of Athlone, Leopold's daughter, survives) have left memoirs, in which they describe their relations with and impressions of their grandmother.

The hush around Grandmamma's door [wrote Affie's daughter Marie, Queen of Romania] *was awe-inspiring, it was like approaching the mystery of some sanctuary. . . . Wonderful little old Grandmamma, who though such a small, unimposing little woman to look at should have known so extraordinarily how to inspire reverential fear. . . . When finally the door was opened, there sat Grandmamma not idol-like at all, not a bit frightening, smiling a kind little smile, almost as shy as us children, so that conversation was not very fluent on either side.*

Inquiry as to our morals and general behaviour made up a great part of it, and I well remember Grandmamma's shocked and yet amused little exclamations of horror when it was reported that one or the other of us had not been good. . . .

First and foremost there were portraits of Grandpapa [in the Queen's apartments], *portraits of every kind. Pictures and prints, statues, statuettes and photographs. There was Grandpapa in full general's uniform, Grandpapa in his robes of the Order of the Garter, Grandpapa in kilt, in plain clothes . . . on horseback, at his writing-table . . . with his dogs, with his children, in the garden, on the mountains . . . with important-looking papers in his hands . . . with his loving wife gazing enraptured up into his face. Grandpapa was certainly the first and foremost spirit of these rooms.*[6]

Princess Alice was more at home at Grandmamma's than her cousin Marie, who visited less often. Alice and her little brother Charles Edward would regularly be taken by their widowed mother to visit Victoria at Windsor, and after nursery tea their nanny would shepherd them into 'the presence' with the warning, "Mind you curtsey at the door and kiss Grandmamma's hand and don't make a noise and mind you are good."

She would be sitting writing at a diminutive table on which stood a small lamp with a green glass shade. We in the meantime would play with our toys and always built walls with her numerous despatch boxes. . . . If she were alone, one of her dressers would come in and remove her crisp tulle cap with streamers and put a funny little piece of lace over her tiny bun and often rub her legs from knee to heel, very gently.[7]

Formal portraits and photographs catch Queen Victoria's grand-children and great-grandchildren in solemn, prim attitudes, the boys in their sailor suits or kilts, the girls in white with their hair flowing or topped with huge beribboned hats, but their memoirs leave no doubt but that they were 'real' children, warm, lively and often mischievous. Grandmamma's disapproval may have been used as a warning to erring princes and princesses by parents and governesses, but childish pranks often 'amused' the Queen. On one occasion the small Prince George (Bertie's second son), after misbehaving at a family meal, was sent under the table in disgrace: he passed the time in removing every stitch of his clothing, to the horror, when he re-emerged, of all but his grandmother. But in fact this prince was the 'good boy' of the family – in contrast to his senior, Prince Eddy,* as wayward and difficult as ever his father had been but with a far less joyous and frank attitude to his adolescent vices. His parents were broken-hearted when he died, in his late twenties, in 1892, but certainly his brother George, a stalwart naval officer of little imagination but no real personal faults (beyond a hasty temper), made the better candidate for the throne.

Eddy, George and their sisters Louise, Victoria and Maud were hap-pier and more relaxed with their parents than their father, Bertie, the Prince of Wales, had been with his. He was always the most under-standing of fathers, approachable and sympathetic, while Princess Alex-andra, unhappy in her husband's frequent and flagrant infidelities, was a clinging, possessive mother – 'Motherdear' her children called her, even when they were themselves middle-aged. At home the children were noisy and often rough; in public they were timid – 'the whispering Waleses' the girls were called. They had not the *savoir faire* of their next-ranking cousins, Affie of Edinburgh's brood, who had a Russian Grand Duchess for a mother and had travelled to Russia and Germany and all

* Victoria had always intended that her successors on the throne should bear the name of her beloved husband. Bertie should become Albert I, his son Albert Victor (Eddy) Albert II, and so on. In fact, Bertie chose to become Edward VII, and he was succeeded not by Eddy but by George – as George V. In the next generation, George's son Edward Albert (born in 1894) was 'David' in the family and became Edward VIII, and his brother Albert, who succeeded him on his abdication in 1936, though always 'Bertie' at home, became George VI, so the old Queen's wish was never fulfilled.

over the Mediterranean by the time they entered their teens.

By the end of the century, princes were at last being freed from the home-tutoring system and being sent to public schools – Prince Leopold's son 'Charlie' and his Battenberg and Schleswig-Holstein cousins, and in the next generation the future George V's sons Henry and George. Then came training in army or navy and perhaps a spell at Oxford or Cambridge and (until 1914) a German university, though always under the vigilant eye of 'Grandmamma'.

The time-honoured system for princesses was not abandoned, however.

> *Young girls were educated at home* [reminisced Marie Louise, one of Princess Helena's daughters, many years later]. *Governesses superintended and taught them and, carefully chaperoned by these 'govies', as we used to call them, the young ladies, when they reached the age of fifteen or sixteen, were allowed to attend lectures on art or literature, and if they showed any talent for music or drawing they received the necessary instruction from special carefully-selected masters.*[8]

All Queen Victoria'a grandchildren growing up in England were cosmopolitan in outlook, accustomed to foreign travel and the life of the Continental Courts, equally fluent in English, German and French, and the majority of the princesses made foreign marriages, taking Victorian influence and virtues into the Courts of Europe (and English milk-puddings and sanitation into palace nurseries from St. Petersburg to Madrid).

The death of the Queen, in January 1901, shocked the nation – the majority of her subjects could remember no other monarch. But now at last Bertie was king (already in his sixtieth year), and, despite his mother's long foreboding, he did not disgrace himself. He still kept a string of mistresses, still enjoyed the thrills of the turf and the card-table, still over-indulged in rich food and wines, but his pitiful inexperience of government (Victoria had always refused to delegate real responsibility to her heir) did not stand in the way of his application to his new duties. However, his reign was short, and in 1910 George V succeeded Edward VII.

George had married his distant cousin Mary of Teck (a great-granddaughter of George III), and they proved fine monarchs, thoroughly appreciated by the nation, especially after their display of fortitude and sympathy during the First World War; but as parents there was something lacking.

They had five sons and one daughter, born between 1894 and 1905 (the youngest Prince, John, was subject to epileptic fits and rarely seen in public; he died in 1919, aged thirteen). The King and Queen were shy with their children, reserved and undemonstrative. King George was subject to violent rages when his sons annoyed him – which the eldest especially frequently did, and the second Prince, Albert's stammering speech may certainly be attributable to his nervousness with his parents. George V and his brother had been cadets in the Royal Navy, and the King could imagine no finer training for his own elder sons. He had forgotten by then the trials and teasing he had suffered from his contemporaries, from which his more sensitive sons shied, and never really understood that the spartan life at Osborne College did not suit his boys. Nor was either of the princes a particularly good student, and their regular mediocre or downright shameful reports inevitably brought them to their father's desk in well-warranted expectation of 'dressing-down' and 'wigging'.

Not surprisingly, in manhood, the Prince of Wales never fitted into the home circle but dismayed and worried his parents with his nervously frenetic 'fast' living and his sophisticated, expensive circle of friends. Albert, Duke of York, shy and introspective, was more domesticated, happy in the family life created for him by his Scottish wife. But it was only in the difficult years after his accession to the throne (after his elder brother's abdication) that a bond of sympathy was forged between him and his mother. In fact, King George V and Queen Mary showed more real affection for and interest in their grandchildren than they ever had for their own children.

The 'Victorian Age', as far as the upbringing of children was concerned, ended when George V's children grew up, just as the Victorian ethos waned before the new manners and morals of the years after the First World War. Nevertheless, neither Victoria nor Albert would have disapproved of the sensible upbringing and training of the child who was to be the next Queen of Great Britain. . . .

The Modern Age
1914 – today

Teenyboppers and teenagers

The Victorians lingered over childhood, prolonging it into adolescence by keeping children free from responsibility, under parental authority, as long as possible. In the modern age, childhood is as brief as in the Middle Ages – though for different reasons and with very different results. Today, children pass swiftly from dolls and trains and games to the 'toys' of adolescence, records and clothes and gimcrack novelties, even before they enter their teens and begin the social interplay, the courting of sexual attention and the bids for independence formerly associated with the late teens.

This is a development of the past thirty years, since the concentration of 'big business' on the child and adolescent (the 'teenybopper' and teenager) as consumers of mass-market products: vast sums are expended in advertising to encourage them to put pressure on parents to buy products without which they would feel 'inferior' to their contemporaries, outsiders in the group.

And it is the approval of their peer-group, rather than of parents and teachers, which product-advertising urges them to seek: competitiveness in material possessions is good for business. At the same time, teenagers have come to see themselves as an identifiable group within society, rebelling against school uniforms but inevitably clad in their own chosen uniform of jeans and T-shirt. They form sub-groups, again for self-expression and group-identification: from the 'Teddy boys' and 'beatniks' of the 1950s, through 'mods' and 'rockers' and 'hippies' to the 'punks' of the late 1970s.

All this is a phenomenon of the years since the end of the Second World War. In the inter-war years there was no such long transitional period between childhood and maturity. Almost overnight, on leaving school, a child was transformed into an adult, with adult responsibilities, sharing fashions in clothes and tastes in entertainment with the older generation, as well as an outlook on life and ambitions for domesticity.

Nevertheless, the first half of the century did lay a foundation for one of the major developments of post-war Britain: the sharing of parental responsibility with the state. The nineteenth century had seen the beginning of the trend, with state acceptance of the duty to provide access to education, then enforcement of education, for all children, and in the first four decades of the twentieth century advances were made in the provision of free medical and dental inspection for schoolchildren, free or subsidized meals for the children of the poor and later a daily issue of free milk, and the extension of libraries and sports facilities.

The Second World War was a watershed in state participation in child care. Thousands of children were offered the chance of evacuation from town to country, away from the danger of air-raids (though 7,736 children were killed and 7,623 wounded by bombing between 1939 and 1945), and their hosts were recompensed from national resources with a cash allowance to cover their guests' expenses. The rationing of food during the war controlled the type of food consumed by the majority of children, and the fact that child health actually improved during this period revealed the extent of malnutrition and of unwise eating habits before the war.

The social welfare schemes introduced immediately after the Second World War, improving conditions for the poorest families by supplementing inadequate wages, produced not only a 'family allowance' intended specifically for children's needs and new facilities for baby and child health but a new system of education, in which, after primary schooling to the age of eleven, each child in the state system was to be tested for aptitude and ability and sent to a grammar, technical or secondary modern school. Undoubtedly this system did provide unprecedented opportunities for the academically-suited child, with a chance to proceed to higher education, but in the decade after the introduction of the eleven-plus examination, government statistics showed that it was the middle-class child who still profited most and that the child of the working-class family, especially in 'deprived' areas of the country, was most likely to suffer from inadequate school buildings, poor teaching and limited extra-curricular facilities. While private education, especially in the expensive public schools, continued to give pupils the greatest chance of university entrance (and of the best job opportunities), the grammar schools, catering for the academic élite in the state system, had become the financial and teaching priority with public authorities, to the disadvantage of other types of secondary school.

The ideal of comprehensive education, ending the division of children into academic and non-academic at eleven, began to find advocates in the late 1950s, and in the 1960s was introduced by a Labour government. In theory, the end of the eleven-plus testing and the collection of children in a school on the principle of locality rather than ability, was to give children equal education opportunities in which they could find their own level (and to eliminate the psychological branding of children through life as 'successes' and failures' as a result of one examination). In practice, evasion of 'comprehensivization' by some local authorities, the unsuitability of existing buildings to the scheme, the problems of slum areas in providing adequate staffing and building of schools, and a set-back in the national economy, forcing the limitation of government spending on education, has contributed to the only qualified success of the comprehensive system, though it has yet to be proved that it is a direct cause of the lowering of education standards noticed and decried in recent years.

The range of subjects provided for schoolchildren in this century has broadened immeasurably, with almost every child now taught sciences and foreign languages as well as the basic three Rs, history and geography. Educational theorists ever since the end of the nineteenth century have sought to reorientate education away from the presentation of facts and ideas to a study of the community and world into which the child must fit. Children are taught to question and reappraise, to look beyond their own locality into a world which is faster-changing than ever before in world history. It is now a well-established attitude to education but one open to many criticisms, not the least being those which deplore the supposedly low priority placed on basic literacy and the many opportunities for the unmotivated child to evade instruction.

There has been truancy from the enforced educational system ever since its inception, but truancy in secondary schools today has reached high proportions, and classroom violence in frustration and rebellion against 'boring' lessons and 'weak' teachers continues to grow, as a result of lax or over-liberal discipline. With a minimum school-leaving age now of sixteen, by which time most pupils regard themselves as adults, eager for work and wage, the problem is only likely to increase unless academic goals are lowered and schooling is directed more towards preparation for employment and productive leisure.

Television is often blamed for children's lack of interest in educational activities today – though it is never blamed for inhibiting interest in active sports, which have an increasing attraction. Though television undoubtedly offers unprecedented opportunities for seeing distant parts of the world, for sharing new ideas, for cultural appreciation and study, it is blamed throughout society for stultifying the mind with trivial, mass-market 'sex and violence' programmes. It is also blamed for the child's lack of interest in books – though the 'comic' had captured the bulk of the child market in literature long before television entered every home. (Nevertheless, while television and comics may have inhibited children's reading habits, for those children who do read, their literature is of a higher standard than that of pre-war years, when unrealistic adventure stories and tales of public school life dominated the market.)

Television has not drastically curbed children's membership of clubs and interest groups. The Boy Scout and Girl Guide movements, originated by Baden-Powell before the First World War, reathed their peak in the 1950s, but today there is a far broader range of social activities to attract children, and horse-riding and ballet-dancing classes are always filled. Holiday centres catering for children's sports proliferate.

While the child remains a child, before the onset of teenage independence and emergence into 'pop-culture', the toy-market offers a wider range of products than ever before – though all mass-produced and devoid of individuality. The traditional toys, balls and dolls and so on, are still the staple of every child's collection, but the old tin soldiers have become plastic, realistic, replicas of modern commandos, with every sort of weapon from hand-grenade to tank, and modern electronics provide working models not only of trains but of 'planes and helicopters. A less stable market caters for periodic crazes: the pogo-stick, the hoolah-hoop and, recently, the skate-board. Again, the desire for possession of such toys brings children early into the 'consumer society'.

With so much provided for children, in and out of school, with interest and concern for deprived children and generous state finance to answer their needs, bewilderment over increasing juvenile delinquency is growing. Theorists offer a wide range of explanations and excuses: the breakdown of so many marriages resulting in children's insecurity, the example of violence and greed offered in television programmes, the materialistic ethic on which modern society turns, the failure of traditional culture to satisfy, the decline in religious faith – even the lack of wars to provide an outlet for violent feelings. No one explanation offers the whole reason, nor can one reform offer society a panacea.

Each adult generation re-makes the civilization it has inherited, failing in as much as it succeeds, and each following generation despises the efforts of its predecessors. The 'angry young men' of the 1950s had their chance to build a utopia but erected instead a concrete jungle; the iconoclasts of the 1960s had their chance to root out prejudice and inequalities but only entrenched them by the violence of their actions; the 'new poor' of the 1970s, hit by inflation and unemployment, have their chance to adapt to 'plain living, high thinking' but instead look forward to an oil bonanza in which everyone will become rich without effort. And so it is the world which adults have created in which today's children live, and the responsibility of today's children to give tomorrow's children the world of our dreams.

"Lilibet"

"I pray to God that my eldest son will never marry and have children," declared King George V a few weeks before his death in January 1936, "and that nothing will come between Bertie and Lilibet and the throne."[1]

In fact, it was to be the marriage of George V's eldest son which precipitated 'Bertie' to the throne, as King George VI, and 'Lilibet', his elder daughter, to the status of heiress presumptive to the crown.

For some time before his father's death, the then Prince of Wales had been contemplating marriage with an American socialite, Mrs. Simpson, but he knew that his father would not allow it, and there was a restraint within the royal family which prevented discussion of the matter. Thus, it was only after his accession that Edward VIII began negotiations with Church and Government for his marriage. By the early autumn of 1936, with the British Press breaking its tactful silence on the matter, the nation was being informed that there was one insuperable obstacle to the royal marriage: Mrs. Simpson had divorced one husband and was in the process of divorcing another – and the Church of England, of which the monarch is always Head, would not countenance the sanctified remarriage of *divorcés*. Church, Government and the bulk of public opinion urged the King to give up his plans, but he would not. Rather than lose the woman he loved, he would renounce the throne. On the 10th December 1936 King Edward VIII signed an Instrument of Abdication, and the reign of his brother, George VI, began.

At a house in London's Piccadilly, a ten-year-old girl wrote the words 'ABDICATION DAY' in her exercise book before starting her homework. She had more reason than any other child in Britain to take note of the occasion, though even then its full import may not have struck her. She was 'Lilibet', the Princess Elizabeth, the elder daughter of King George VI, heiress presumptive and future Queen Elizabeth II.

Royal children had been born in strange places and in unusual circumstances in past centuries, but Elizabeth was the first to be born in a street of numbered houses. She arrived at three o'clock in the morning of the 21st April 1926 at 17 Bruton Street, Berkeley Square, the first child of the Duke and Duchess of York and first member of the new generation of the royal family. Christened 'Elizabeth Alexandra Mary', as soon as she could talk she called herself 'Lilibet'. Four years later, she was joined by a little sister, Princess Margaret Rose, whom she quickly named 'Bud' – "You see, she isn't a real rose yet, only a bud."[2] However, though 'Bud' was soon replaced by the formal 'Margaret' in the royal nursery, the elder Princess was always 'Lilibet' in the family.

The children's first years were spent out of the limelight, even though, stimulated by the popular Press, there was quite a cult for them through the nation, and their photographs appeared frequently in the newspapers. In Bruton Street and later in Piccadilly, they were brought up quietly by a trained nanny, Mrs. Knight ('Alah') and began their education under the superintendence of a sensible, humorous Scotswoman, Marion Crawford – 'Crawfie'.

'Uncle David', the then Prince of Wales, was a gay and amusing visitor to the Princesses' nursery, and with her granddaughters Queen Mary was by no means the cold disciplinarian she had seemed to her own children – but it was the old King, George V, who was most unlike his usual self in the little girls' company, unbending in a manner which surprised his sons. 'Lilibet' especially featured continually in the royal diary for this period, and when the King suffered a serious illness in 1930, and his doctors ordered him off to the seaside, at Bognor, to recuperate, the child's company figured on their prescription for his treatment. At four, this was Elizabeth's first visit to the sea.

The funeral of the King, in January 1936, marked the Princess's first major appearance in public (though she had accompanied her mother on less serious occasions over the previous year), and she felt her grandfather's loss keenly. But the furore over King Edward VIII's marriage of the next months was not allowed to intrude into the nursery: newspapers were kept well away from the Princesses. In fact, though the circumstances were explained in part to the ten-year-old Elizabeth when her father became King, the most noticeable change in the small girls' life was their removal from Piccadilly to Buckingham Palace. Intensely fond of home, Princess Elizabeth begged for an underground passage to link the Palace with '145', so that at least she could go back to her own room to sleep. With the new need for security, rambles and games in the Palace gardens had to replace earlier walks in parks and play in Hamilton Gardens.

On Coronation Day, 1937, Elizabeth and Margaret drove to the Abbey in a coach with their grandmother, Queen Mary. Dressed

exactly alike in beribboned lace dresses, ermine-edged capes and coro-
nets, they played a small part in the ceremony, processing down the aisle
and watching the service from a small gallery. But it was a long day, and
there had been some anxiety as to how the six-year-old Princess Margaret would behave: "She was wonderful . . . ," Elizabeth reported to
their governess that evening, "I only had to nudge her once or twice
when she played with the prayer-books too loudly."[2]

By then the new routine was established: weekdays at Buckingham
Palace, weekends at Windsor, where there was more freedom for running about in the Home Park and a more relaxed home life. Though the
elder Princess could only ever be 'heiress presumptive' – on the possibility that her mother could still give birth to a male heir who would
displace her in the royal succession, there were plans afoot to have her
prepared for a career as her father's successor. When she was thirteen,
Elizabeth was introduced to Sir Henry Marten, Provost of Eton College, who was to teach her constitutional history. A formidable man to
the boys of the college, erudite and dignified, he held no terrors for the
Princess: he had an endearingly sweet tooth and the habit of chewing his
handkerchief when pondering a problem. She visited him once a week
and, like Queen Victoria with her Uncle Leopold, King of the Belgians,
corresponded with her mentor on her reading and observations.

From earliest childhood, both Princesses displayed a passionate love of
animals, especially horses and dogs (corgis predominated at the Palace,
snapping and chewing strange trouser-legs). At four Elizabeth had her
first Shetland pony, learning to groom him as well as to ride, but even in
the nursery she would play 'horse-games': she would pretend that she
was herself a horse, pawing the carpet with her feet, snorting and nuz-
zling her head against her governess's pockets as if for sugar; in fact, the
first sight Miss Crawford had of her charge was of the Princess (then
aged only five) sitting up in bed with her dressing-gown cords tied to
the end, 'driving her team'.

The publication, in 1950, of Marion Crawford's memoirs of life in the
royal household caused some coldness in relations between 'the Palace'
and herself, as did the printing of more reminiscences in the children's
magazine 'Sunny Stories' from 1953. In the Princesses' childhood,
formal photographs had been released to the Press at frequent intervals,
and there had always been a photographer ready to 'snap' them when
they emerged from the Palace, but for the most part they had been protected from the inquisitive. Now, for the first time, a royal servant had
broken that unwritten rule of silence. (Queen Victoria had herself
offered for publication her private diaries of her family's life in the
Highlands, with informal glimpses of her children, but it was only after

her death that her attendants had published their own memoirs of royal life.) Though the Crawford 'revelations' were entirely idolatory, they did constitute a formidable breach of the confidence the royal family had placed in her.

Nevertheless, for biographers of the Queen and her sister Miss Crawford's memoirs are a boon. From them we have a full picture of the lives of the two little Princesses: they pursue falling leaves in autumn, in the age-old children's game of 'catching happy days'; they play Red Indians and hide-and-seek in the vast gardens of Buckingham Palace; they collect farm animals, bought for a few pence at Woolworth's; they practise housekeeping at 'Y Bwthyn Bach', the miniature house near Royal Lodge, Windsor, a gift from the people of Wales; they detest milk puddings and dislike going to bed for a noon-day rest; occasionally they wrangle and fight, snapping the elastic on each other's hats; they take their first rides on the top deck of a London bus and in the Underground; they play with selected contemporaries at dancing-classes and Girl Guide meetings. Several books, well illustrated with photographs, appeared on the lives of the 'little Princesses' in the late forties and early fifties, but none with so intimate a view of their home life as Marion Crawford's.

Again according to the royal governess, the Princesses' relations with their parents were perfect: the shy, diffident King George VI, overwhelmed by the burden so suddenly thrust upon him (and totally unprepared for the work of a monarch in government), was at his happiest at home with his wife and children, riding, working in the gardens at Windsor, on holiday at Balmoral and Sandringham; and, if his elder daughter was his chief source of pride, the demonstrativeness of the younger, while it half-embarrassed him, was his delight. But it was his Scottish Queen (the former Lady Elizabeth Bowes-Lyon, herself the ninth of ten children) who was the rock of the family, soothing her husband's fears in the troublous days of 1936 and through the fifteen years of his reign. To Elizabeth and Margaret, 'Papa' and 'Mummy' were the centre of their lives.

Three years after George VI's accession, however, Britain was at war with Germany, and in the following five years the Princesses, like so many children in Britain had to acclimatize themselves to an unnatural way of life, often apart from their parents.

The outbreak of war found them in Scotland, at Queen Victoria's beloved Balmoral, which the royal family visited for some weeks at the end of every summer. But that year the holiday, at least for the girls, was prolonged, and months after their parents had gone south, they were still in the Highlands, delighted by the early snow and the household trials of cold rooms and frozen water-supply which only discomforted their attendants. And there were more children to play with, at the local Girl Guides and in the houses nearby, which had been opened to take in evacuees from Glasgow's slums. There was talk, in government and Press, of the Princesses being sent abroad, perhaps to Canada, out of danger, but the Queen vetoed the idea firmly. "The children could not go without me," she said, "and I could not possibly leave the King."[3] So, for the duration, the ancient stronghold of Windsor Castle became their home. There they continued their lessons in the gloomy Victorian apartments (a twentieth-century 'maidenhall'), with vast areas of windows covered by black-out curtains each night, practising with their gas-masks, listening to 'Itma' and throwing cushions at the wireless when they heard the infuriating tones of 'Lord Haw-Haw', donning siren-suits to run to the dungeons during air-raids, 'digging for victory' in their own plots of land.

On the 13th October 1940, Princess Elizabeth, aged fourteen, made her first broadcast, with a short talk to the children of the Empire. It was a fine (much rehearsed) performance, infinitely moving to the parents of children away from home, as it ended:

> I can truthfully say to you all that we children at home are full of cheerfulness and courage. We are trying to do all we can to help our gallant sailors, soldiers and airmen, and we are trying, too, to bear our own share of the danger and sadness of war. We know, every one of us, that in the end all will be well.

Then a hesitation: "Come on, Margaret, say goodnight," and the clear "Goodnight, children," from the little sister.

Though the war isolated the Princesses in some ways (their loss of Palace distractions delighted their governess, who was able, for five years, to teach them uninterrupted), in others they had unprecedented opportunities for meeting people who would otherwise never have crossed their path – like the Glaswegian evacuees at Balmoral, and the Cockney children evacuated from the East End of London, who shared their games at Windsor, with cries of "Lilibet, Lilibet" following the Princess through gardens which had once witnessed prim promenades of princesses, a 'decent' distance from gawping sightseers. Both Elizabeth and Margaret were always fascinated by new people, and their parents never allowed them to be shy with strangers. Elizabeth particularly had the knack of putting the shy at ease: on one occasion, at an official reception, she spotted an Indian guest standing alone, ill at ease – whereupon she went up to him and put a question about Indian elephants as if he were the one person in the room whom she had been seeking out.

In London, day after day, bombs were falling, and parts of Buckingham Palace were destroyed in air-raids while the King and Queen
were in residence there. No one, not even the watchful governess, could
guess how deep were the elder Princess's fears that family tragedy would
bring her the crown while she was still a child.

One of the wartime emergency statutes demanded the registration for
national service of every girl when she reached the age of sixteen, and
duly, on her sixteenth birthday, Princess Elizabeth 'signed on'. It was
nearly two years, however, before the King could be induced to allow
his daughter to leave her safety and her studies to join other girls in war-
work, but her own persistence won his permission to join the ATS (the
Auxiliary Territorial Service), and just after her eighteenth birthday she
was commissioned as a Second Subaltern, to be trained in motor main-
tenance and driving. A few months later, she proudly displayed the results of her new studies to her parents and sister, during their visit to her
depot at Camberley, where, covered in oil, she was stripping down an
engine in a thoroughly professional manner.

At the same time, the Princess was now a member of the Council of
State, the body functioning for the monarch in his absence (King
George was away reviewing his troops in the Mediterranean during the
summer of 1944).

Then came the victory in Europe, and in May 1945 the Princesses took
their place with their parents and Winston Churchill on the balcony at
Buckingham Palace as crowds surged outside the railings as if they
would not stop cheering all night. On that occasion, and two months
later, on VJ night, Elizabeth and Margaret went down among the
crowds and walked around unrecognized.

Princess Elizabeth was nineteen years old when the war ended, Princess Margaret only fifteen, but both by now were busy with public
duties and charitable enterprises, both heading (if only nominally for the
time being) committees and funds, especially those in aid of children.
And for Princess Elizabeth there was an increasing round of social engagements.

In the autumn of 1946 came the first rumours of a royal romance.
Prince Philip of Greece (like the Princess a descendant of Queen Victoria), who had served in the British navy during the war, was strongly
tipped to marry the King's elder daughter, and only an official denial by
the Palace dampened speculation in the Press. In fact, the rumours were
well-founded, for it was only the caution of the King and Queen which
postponed the engagement of Elizabeth and Philip.

They had first met many years earlier, on a royal visit to Dartmouth

Naval College, where the Prince was a student. Even then, with Elizabeth only thirteen years old, Philip already eighteen, there was an attraction between them, which had deepened in their meetings when the Prince visited the Palace on leave from his ship. But the King demanded a test of the couple's feelings, using the royal visit to South Africa of 1947 to postpone their, and his, decision. Nevertheless, on the family's return, both Elizabeth and Philip were still firm in their resolve, and in November 1947 the then twenty-one-year-old Princess married Prince Philip, who took British nationality and was created Duke of Edinburgh. Now, with Princess Elizabeth a wife and soon a mother, and with Princess Margaret in her late teens, a vivacious member of fashionable society and busy with public duties, the royal childhood was over.

New days, new ways

For hundreds of years the prospect of a royal birth had seen the fore-gathering of dignitaries of Church and State at castle or palace, as witnesses to the true birth of a potential heir to the throne. In antiquity, crowds of statesmen and courtiers had thronged the delivery-chamber, their personal germs adding to the risks of infection of mother and child but their testimony valued in preventing risks of allegations of chicanery. (Though the fact that many people had witnessed the birth of James II's heir in 1688 had not precluded the 'warming-pan' rumours.) By the nineteenth century feminine modesty had been respected sufficiently for representatives of the government to wait in an antechamber. But it was only on the birth of Prince Charles in 1948 that his grandfather, King George VI, ended the tradition once and for all, signifying to his government that the presence of the Home Secretary (the customary observer) would not be required.

Prince Charles was born on the evening of Sunday, 14th November, at Buckingham Palace – rather late, in fact, for he had been expected at the end of October. The usual 'mother and child doing well' notice was issued at the Palace gates, but that did not prevent jubilant crowds waiting on into the night, until an appeal was made for quiet. Within hours the news of the royal birth had gone round the world: this latest heir to the throne had been born into an age of publicity. It was something that was to dog him, his sister and brothers throughout childhood.

The second royal child of the new generation was born on the 15th August 1950, this time a girl: Princess Anne. Then there was to be a gap of ten years before the appearance of another prince, joined by the last of the quartet in 1964. A two-tier family.

The royal decision to employ a nanny for the children was inevitable. Not only was the handing over of children to a mother-substitute a long tradition in royal and aristocratic families but it was obviously impossible for Princess Elizabeth, Duchess of Edinburgh, to devote herself full-time to the care of her children. 'Still only heiress-presumptive in name, it was certain that she would succeed her father on the throne, and her engagements, both in Britain and abroad, were not to be shirked. Indeed, she and her husband were away for weeks in 1951, on a long tour of Canada, and a Commonwealth tour of 1952 was planned which would keep the couple away from home for months. But they had gone only as far as Kenya when a message came, that February, telling of the death of King George VI. Queen Elizabeth II flew home to her kingdom.

His advancement to status of heir-apparent entitled Prince Charles to the dukedom of Cornwall: he was not to become Prince of Wales (a title awarded at the discretion of the monarch) until July 1958. Nor, at the age of three, would his mother's accession mean anything to him – though he was allowed to sit with his grandmother in the Abbey on Coronation Day, and showed lively interest in the ceremony. Charles and Anne both appeared with their parents on the balcony of Buckingham Palace later in the day.

The Prince's first lessons were begun when he was five years old, by Miss Katherine Peebles, a Scotswoman like 'Crawfie', and like her predecessor the new royal governess was soon taking the children on outings in London. It was 1955 before the – to the family – momentous step was taken of sending the boy to school. When the plan was announced, it inevitably drew public comment and criticism (to balance the earlier criticism of 'democrats' who demanded that he go to a state primary school). The school chosen for the Prince was Hill House, in Chelsea, less than a mile from Buckingham Palace, a newish 'private' school for the sons of London business and professional men. Charles was happy there: Hill House had a relaxed atmosphere but firm discipline, and the Prince made friends there.

His second school (this time a boarding-school) was somewhat less successful. Prince Philip had been a pupil at Cheam School (then in Surrey) as a child, and in all his time there had never been bothered by his superior rank (as a prince of Greece); his son, on the other hand, already had an uncomfortable awareness of his peculiarity, not helped by the initial mistrust and 'stand-offishness' of his contemporaries, who unwarrantedly suspected him of 'side'. Nor did the Press help: the Queen had begged newspapers to keep their coverage of the Prince's schooldays to a minimum, but there were British journalists who could not resist hovering nearby, foreign photographers who scaled the walls, and even ordinary sightseers who flocked to nearby villages. Guards on the Prince were increased. Even so, though often tense and nervous, Charles managed to do quite well at Cheam and to make friends.

There was no dearth of opinion, asked and unasked, as to the public school to which he should proceed, but again the Duke of Edinburgh had his choice – though his son was given the final decision.

Gordonstoun, until then, had never been counted in the first rank of British public schools. It was comparatively new, of German origin, placing more emphasis on sport and character-building than on scholarship. It had been the brainchild of an innovatory educationist, Dr Kurt Hahn, in the 1920s, and, with the help of a prince of Baden (a connection of Prince Philip), it had been set up at Salem in Bavaria. The Greek Prince had been a pupil there, and later in Scotland, to which the Jewish Hahn was forced to move his establishment with the rise of Nazism. In 1961, when Prince Charles was sent there, there was an outcry in the Press against subjecting the boy to 'austerity', 'spartan conditions' and even 'forced labour' at this 'advanced' establishment.

The Gordonstoun regime was certainly rigorous, involving cold baths, marathon hikes and so on, and Prince Charles took some time in settling down there. But he was allowed to develop his love for music at Gordonstoun and, again after initial resistance, won respect and friendship. He even, in the end, became something of the Gordonstoun 'type', ready to enter into any activity, take any responsibility, on his own initiative.

Again, however, the bugbear was the Press. Two incidents in Charles's Gordonstoun career entrenched the royal family's mistrust of newspapermen – with good reason, The first was the 'cherry brandy incident'. The Prince and some friends, with a teacher, had been touring the Highlands and Islands, and were in a Scottish hotel one day when, in the master's temporary absence, a crowd collected to stare at Charles. In embarrassment he retreated into the hotel bar, where, to the delight of journalists, he ordered a cherry brandy – at fourteen, several years under the age required by law for drinking in licensed premises. The fact that the Palace denied the incident, only to have to retract the denial later, prolonged the furore. Then there was the business of the royal exercise book, a set of essays secretly purloined from the Prince's desk and published in foreign magazines. It is scarcely surprising, therefore, that newspapermen have come in for the rough side of Prince Philip's tongue on many occasions, and that the royal family cling to any privacy they can find.

Princess Anne had difficulties different from her brother's. Though she had been educated at home until she was thirteen, she was 'a good mixer', extrovert, not too sensitive to criticism, and went eagerly to her public school, Benenden. But she had problems of her own character: she would not submit easily to discipline, or apply herself wholeheartedly to academic subjects, and though she found her own circle of friends, she was coolly and effectively scornful of anyone whom she suspected of 'toadying', which gave her a reputation for arrogance. It was riding which moulded Princess Anne's character, rather than any imposed authority. She, like her mother, had loved horses from childhood, and in her early teens set herself high standards of professionalism involving a good deal of self-sacrifice and self-discipline.

Both Prince Charles and Princess Anne achieved good results in their General Certificate examinations – the Prince despite a break in his Gordonstoun career, when he was seventeen, when he was sent for some months to school in the Australian outback. But he had gained from the experience, coming home far more self-confident than he had left. His years at university (at Cambridge and Aberystwyth) rounded him off, as he emerged as a social personality, with a wide range of interests, from polo and yachting to music and drama, and a fascination with his family history to humanize the constitutional studies his future career dictated.

The gap in age between the Queen's elder and younger pairs of children was at its widest in the early 1960s, when Prince Andrew and Prince Edward were at home, their brother and sister at school. But that gap is narrowing, as the younger princes proceed through their schooling.

Prince Andrew has few of the inbuilt disadvantages suffered by his elder brother. Not being heir to the throne, there is less pressure on him, and, at least until recently, he was less pursued by the Press. He took to Gordonstoun keenly, excelling at sports, cheerfully accepting every challenge, though, very much like his sister, not always amenable to authority, and gaining a reputation for aggressiveness. Prince Edward is more like Prince Charles was at his age, introspective and self-absorbed, happier quietly fishing or watching birds than in 'joining in'. But he too faces Gordonstoun.

The traditional pattern of royal childhood may have been broken by the education of the children of Elizabeth II at school rather than at home, but as they emerge from childhood the age-old careers in the armed forces and public service continue. The Prince of Wales took a commission in the Royal Navy, until royal duties swamped him; Prince Andrew is to do the same. Princess Anne, with less taste for public duties, has been allowed latitude for her career as a show-jumper and, more recently, for motherhood: it seems likely that if feminist agitation should ever bring about a change in the law regarding the succession to the throne (placing her before her younger brothers, directly after the Prince of Wales), as an extension of 'equal opportunities', the increased burden of responsibility, real and potential, will not please her. As it is, however, she and her younger brothers are free from the rigorous preparation for kingship which Prince Charles undergoes.

Despite the efforts made by the Queen and her consort to bring up their children in a 'natural' atmosphere, despite their school years and their integration into the social round of the aristocracy (from which their personal friends are almost entirely drawn), the royal children are still 'apart'. Threats against their lives by political extremists and cranks, their hounding by the Press, their continual travelling and public appearances, are unique pressures. Politicians choose to enter the public arena; media 'personalities' and pop-stars welcome publicity; criminals sell their life-stories to newspapers: royal children are born into the glare of the limelight and must fight for every moment of privacy. It is a problem not suffered before this century – or at least, not on this scale (the sons of George III made complaints against publicity very similar to those of modern princes, but then the Press had rather more excuse for submitting royal conduct to scrutiny and criticism).

In a century in which the crowns of Europe have tumbled in war and revolution, the fact that the monarchy has not only survived in Britain but maintained undamaged its prestige and popularity, is due as much to the high standard of personal conduct and service of its members as to the stability of national institutions. The direct power of the monarchy has diminished, but the role of the monarch as leader in national endeavour and focus for loyalty remains largely unchallenged. It is difficult, therefore, to envisage a future in which royal children may be free of the pressures imposed on this generation, hard to imagine a time in which they may be free to walk unmolested in a London street and socialize without public comment. While there are yet great privileges and luxuries inherent in royal birth, demands on members of the royal family, even on the children, have only changed, not decreased, over the centuries.

A royal genealogy

William, Duke of Normandy (born *c.* 1028), became King of England by conquest in 1066 and reigned until his death in 1087. He married Matilda of Flanders (1031–83) in 1052.

Their children:
    Robert, Duke of Normandy (*c.* 1053–1134) married (1090) Sybilla of
        Conversano
    Richard (*c.* 1054–*c.* 1075)
    William II, King of England (born *c.* 1056, reigned 1087–1100)
    Henry I, King of England – *see below*
    Cecily, Abbess of Caen (*c.* 1055–1127)
    Constance (*c.* 1057–90) married (1086) Alan, Count of Brittany
        (d. 1119)
    Adela (*c.* 1062–1127) married (1080) Stephen, Count of Blois
        (d. 1101) and became the mother of, among others, King Stephen –
        see page 194
    Adelicia
    Agatha
    Matilda (d. *c.* 1080)

Henry I, King of England (born 1068, reigned 1100–35), married first (1100) Matilda of Scotland (*c.* 1079–1118) and secondly (1121) Adelicia of Louvain (1102–51), who was childless.

The children of Henry and Matilda:
    William (1102–20) married (1119) Isabelle of Anjou
    Matilda (1104–67) married first (1114) the Holy Roman Emperor
        Henry V (d. 1126) and secondly (1127) Geoffrey, Count of Anjou
        (1111–50)

At the death of Henry I in 1135, the throne of England was disputed between the King's daughter Matilda and her cousin Stephen of Blois. For almost two decades there was civil war in England, with sometimes

Stephen, occasionally Matilda, triumphant. For the most part, however, Stephen was recognized as king.

Stephen, King of England (born 1097, reigned 1135–54), married (c. 1124) Matilda of Boulogne (1103–52).

Their children:
Baldwin
Eustace, Count of Boulogne (1135–54), married Constance of France
William, Count of Mortain and Boulogne (d. 1160), married Isabel de Warenne
Matilda (1134–6)
Mary (1136–82) married (1160) Matthew of Flanders (divorced 1169)

In the last year of his life, King Stephen agreed to pass over his sons' claims to the throne in favour of Matilda's eldest son Henry (by Geoffrey of Anjou), who at Stephen's death in 1154 became King Henry II.

Henry II, King of England (born 1133, reigned 1154–89), married (1152) Eleanor of Aquitaine (1122–1204).

Their children:
William (1152–6)
Henry (1155–83) married (1165) Marguerite of France (d. 1197)
Richard I, King of England (b. 1157, reigned 1189–99), married (1191) Berengaria of Navarre (d. c. 1230), who was childless.
Geoffrey, Duke of Brittany (1158–85) married (1165) Constance, heiress of Brittany (d. 1201) and had a son and daughter, Arthur (1185–1203) and Eleanor (d. 1241). At the death of Richard I, Arthur's claim to the throne was passed over in favour of his Uncle John.
John, King of England – *see below*
Matilda (1156–89) married (1167) Henry, Duke of Saxony and Bavaria (1129–95)
Eleanor (1161–1214) married (1170) Alfonso VIII, King of Castile (1158–1214)
Joan (1165–99) married first (1177) William II, King of Sicily (1154–89) and secondly (1196) Raimond VI, Count of Toulouse (1156–1221)

John, King of England (born 1166, reigned 1199–1216), married first (1189) Isabel (Avisa) of Gloucester and divorced her (1200) to marry

Isabelle of Angoulême (*c.* 1187–1246). The first marriage was childless, but by Isabelle John had children:

Henry III, King of England – *see below*

Richard, Earl of Cornwall, King of the Romans (1208–72), who married first (1229) Isabel Marshall (1199–1240), secondly (1243) Sanchia of Provence (d. 1261), thirdly (1269) Beatrix of Falkenberg (d. 1277)

Joan (*c.* 1203–38) married (1221) Alexander II, King of Scotland (1198–1249)

Isabel (1214–41) married (1235) the Holy Roman Emperor Frederick II (1194–1250)

Eleanor (1215–75) married first (1224) William Marshall, Earl of Pembroke (d. 1231) and secondly (1238) Simon de Montfort, Earl of Leicester (d. 1265)

Henry III, King of England (born 1207, reigned 1216–72) married (1236) Eleanor of Provence (d. 1291).

Their children:

Edward I, King of England – *see below*

Edmund, Earl of Lancaster (1244–96) married first (1270) Aveline de Forz (d. 1270) and secondly (1275) Blanche of Artois (d. 1302)

Richard

John

William

Henry

Margaret (1240–75) married (1251) Alexander III, King of Scotland (1241–85)

Beatrice (1242–75) married (1260) John, Duke of Brittany (1248–1305)

Catherine (1253–7)

Edward I, King of England (born 1239, reigned 1272–1307) married first (1254) Eleanor of Castile (*c.* 1244–90), secondly (1299) Marguerite of France (*c.* 1282–1317).

The children of Edward and Eleanor:

John (1265–71)

Henry (1267–74)

Alfonso (1273–84)

Edward II, King of England – *see page 196*

Eleanor (*c.* 1264–98) married first (1282) Alfonso III, King of Aragon

(d. 1291), secondly (1293) Henry, Count of Bar (d. 1302)

Joan (1271–1307) married first (1290) Gilbert de Clare, Earl of
Gloucester (d. 1295), secondly (1297) Ralph de Monthermer

Margaret (1275–1318) married (1290) John, Duke of Lorraine
(d. 1312)

Berengaria (1276)

Mary (1278–1332)

Elizabeth (1282–1316) married first (1297) John, Count of Holland
(d. 1299), secondly (1320) Humphrey de Bohun, Earl of Hereford
and Essex (d. 1322)

Isabel

Beatrice

Blanche

The children of Edward and Marguerite:

Thomas, Earl of Norfolk (1300–1338) married first Alice Halys,
secondly Mary de Braose

Edmund, Earl of Kent (1301–30) married Margaret Wake (d. 1349)

Eleanor (1306–11)

Margaret

Edward II, King of England (born 1284, reigned 1307–27) married
(1308) Isabelle of France (1292–1358) by whom he had children:

Edward III, King of England – *see below*

John, Earl of Cornwall (1316–36)

Eleanor, (1318–55) married (1332) Rainald, Duke of Guelders
(d. 1343)

Joan (1321–62) married (1328) David II, King of Scotland (1324–71)

Edward III, King of England (born 1312, reigned 1327–77) married
(1328) Philippa of Hainault (1314–69).

Their children:

Edward, Prince of Wales (1330–76) married (1361) Joan of Kent
(1328–85), by whom he became father of Edward (1365–70) and
Richard II – *see page 197*

William (1335–6)

Lionel of Antwerp, Duke of Clarence (1338–68) married first (1359)
Elizabeth de Burgh (d. 1363), secondly (1368) Violante Visconti

John of Gaunt, Duke of Lancaster (1340–99) married first (1359)
Blanche, heiress of Lancaster (1347–69), secondly (1371) Costanza
of Castile (1347–94), thirdly (1396) Catherine Swynford

(c. 1356–1403). By his first wife John was the father of King Henry IV – *see below*; by his third ancestor of the House of Beaufort from which Henry Tudor derived his claim to the throne.

Edmund of Langley, Duke of York (1341–1402) married first (1371) Isabel of Castile (1355–94) secondly (1395) Joan Holland (d. 1434)

William (1349)

Thomas of Woodstock, Duke of Gloucester (1355–97) married (c. 1375) Eleanor de Bohun (d. 1399)

Isabel of Castile (1355–94), secondly (1395) Joan Holland (d. 1434)

ford (1339–97)

Joan (1333–48)

Blanche (1342)

Mary (1344–61) married (1361) John de Montfort, Duke of Brittany (d. 1399)

Margaret (1346–61) married (1359) John Hastings, Earl of Pembroke (d. 1375)

Richard II, King of England (born 1367, reigned 1377–99, died 1400) – grandson of Edward III; son of Edward, Prince of Wales – married first (1382) Anne of Bohemia (1366–94) and secondly (1396) Isabelle of France (1389–1409). Both queens were childless. In 1399 Richard was overthrown by his cousin Henry, Duke of Lancaster, son of John of Gaunt, who reigned as

Henry IV, King of England (born 1366, reigned 1399–1413). Henry married first (1380) Mary de Bohun (c. 1370–94) and secondly (1403) Joanna of Navarre (c. 1370–1437), who was childless.

The children of Henry and Mary:

Henry V, King of England – *see below*

Thomas, Duke of Clarence (1388–1421) married (1412) Margaret Holland

John, Duke of Bedford (1389–1435) married first (1423) Anne of Burgundy (d. 1430) and secondly (1433) Jacquetta of St. Pol (d. 1472)

Humphrey, Duke of Gloucester (1390–1447) married first (1422) Jacqueline of Hainault (divorced 1428) and secondly (1428) Eleanor Cobham (d. c. 1446)

Blanche (1392–1409) married (1402) Louis, Duke of Bavaria (d. 1436)

Philippa (1393–1430) married (1406) Eric X, King of Denmark (d. 1459)

Henry V, King of England (born 1386, reigned 1413–22) married

(1420) Catherine of France (1401–37), by whom he was the father of one child:

Henry VI, King of England (born 1422, reigned 1422–61, 1470–71), who married (1445) Margaret of Anjou (1430–82), who gave him one son:

Edward, Prince of Wales (1453–71) who married (1471) Anne Neville (1456–85)

With Henry VI's inability to rule, his right to the throne was challenged by his cousin Richard, Duke of York (descendant of Edward III's sons Lionel of Antwerp and Edmund of Langley). Richard was killed in battle (1460), but his claim was taken up by his son Edward, who overthrew Henry VI in 1461 and ruled (apart from a brief period in 1470–71, when Henry was restored) as Edward IV.

Edward IV, King of England (born 1442, reigned 1461–83) married (1464) Elizabeth Woodville (c. 1437–92).

Their children:
  Edward V, King of England – *see below*
  Richard, Duke of York (1472– ?83)
  Elizabeth (1465–1503) married (1486) Henry VII, King of England –
  see page 199
  Mary (1466–82)
  Cecily (1469–1507) married first (1487) John, Viscount Welles (d.
  1498) and secondly Thomas Kyme
  Margaret (1472)
  Anne (1475–1511) married (1495) Thomas Howard, Duke of Nor-
  folk (d. 1554)
  Catherine (1479–1527) married (1495) William Courtenay, Earl of
  Devon (d. 1509)
  Bridget (1480–1517)

Edward V, King of England (born 1470) reigned briefly after his father's death in 1483 but was displaced, and possibly murdered, by his uncle the Duke of Gloucester, who reigned as

Richard III, King of England (born 1452, reigned 1483–5), who married Anne Neville (1456–85), widow of Edward of Lancaster, Prince of Wales (see above), by whom he had one child:

Edward, Prince of Wales (1476–84)

In 1485 Richard III was defeated in battle by his cousin Henry Tudor (a descendant of Edward III, through John of Gaunt's third marriage), who became King Henry VII.

Henry VII, King of England (born 1457, reigned 1485–1509) married (1486) Elizabeth of York (1465–1503) – *see above*.

Their children:
> Arthur, Prince of Wales (1486–1502) married (1501) Catherine of Aragon (1485–1536)
> Henry VIII, King of England – *see below*
> Edmund (1498–9)
> Margaret (1489–1541) married first (1503) James IV, King of Scotland (1473–1513), secondly (1514) Archibald Douglas, Earl of Angus (c. 1489–1557, divorced 1526), thirdly (1528) Henry Stewart, Lord Methven (c. 1495–c. 1551)
> Elizabeth (1493–6)
> Mary (1498–1533) married first (1514) Louis XII, King of France (1462–1515), secondly (1515) Charles Brandon, Duke of Suffolk (1485–1545)
> Catherine (1503)

Henry VIII, King of England (born 1491, reigned 1509–47) married first (1509) Catherine of Aragon, his late brother's widow (*see above*), whom he divorced in 1533, secondly (1533) Anne Boleyn (c. 1507–36), thirdly (1536) Jane Seymour (1509–37), fourthly (1540) Anne of Cleves (1515–57, divorced 1540), fifthly (1540) Catherine Howard (c. 1526–42), sixthly (1543) Catherine Parr (1512–48). The last three queens were childless.

The children of Henry and Catherine of Aragon:
> Henry (1512)
> Mary I, Queen of England – *see page 200*

The child of Henry and Anne Boleyn:
> Elizabeth I, Queen of England – *see page 200*

The child of Henry and Jane Seymour:
> Edward VI, King of England – *see below*

Edward VI, King of England (born 1537, reigned 1547–53) – died unmarried.

At the death of Edward VI in 1553, the throne was usurped by his cousin **Lady Jane Grey** (1537–54), great-granddaughter of Henry VII, through Mary Tudor's marriage to the Duke of Suffolk. Her reign lasted only a few days, on the assertion of the rights of

Mary I, Queen of England (born 1516, reigned 1553–8), who married Philip II, King of Spain (d. 1598) and was childless. She was succeeded by her half-sister

Elizabeth I, Queen of England (born 1533, reigned 1558–1603), who died unmarried.

Elizabeth was succeeded by a descendant of Henry VII, through Margaret Tudor's marriage to James IV, King of Scotland:

James VI, King of Scotland (born 1566, reigned 1567–1625) as **James I, King of England** (reigned 1603–25). He married (1589) Anne of Denmark (1574–1619).

Their children:
  Henry Frederick, Prince of Wales (1594–1612)
  Charles I, King of England – *see below*
  Robert (1602)
  Elizabeth (1596–1662) married (1613) Frederick, Elector Palatine, later King of Bohemia (1596–1632)
  Margaret (1598–1600)
  Mary (1605–7)
  Sophia (1606)

Charles I, King of England and Scotland (born 1600, reigned 1625–49) married (1625) Henrietta Maria of France (1609–69).

Their children:
  Charles (1628)
  Charles II, King of England and Scotland – *see page 201*
  James II, King of England and Scotland – *see page 201*
  Henry, Duke of Gloucester (1639–60)
  Mary (1631–60) married (1641) William II, Prince of Orange (1626–50) and had one son, who became William III, King of England (William II, King of Scotland) – *see page 201*
  Elizabeth (1635–50)
  Anne (1637–40)

Henrietta Anne (1644–70) married (1661) Philippe of France, Duke of Orleans (1640–71)

Charles II, King of England and Scotland (born 1630), fell heir to his father's kingdom in 1649 but lived in exile until the downfall of the Commonwealth brought him home in 1660, to reign until his death in 1685. He married (1662) Catherine of Braganza (1638–1705), who was childless. He was succeeded by his brother as

James II, King of England, VII, King of Scotland (born 1633, reigned 1685–8, died 1701), who married first (1660) Anne Hyde (1637–71) and secondly (1673) Maria Beatrice of Modena (1658–1718).

The children of James and Anne:
James (1663–7)
Edgar (1666–72)
Mary II, Queen of England and Scotland – *see below*
Anne, Queen of Great Britain – *see below*
Catherine (1671–2)

The children of James and Maria Beatrice:
Charles (1677)
James Francis Edward, Prince of Wales – 'King James III' (1688–1766) married (1719) Maria Clementina Sobieska (1702–35), through which marriage the Stuart line of pretenders to the British throne continued until 1807.
Catherine Laura (1675)
Isabella (1676–81)
Charlotte Mary (1682)
Louise Marie (1692–1712)

James II was overthrown in 1688 and succeeded on the throne by his daughter Mary and son-in-law/nephew William of Orange (*see above*) who reigned as

William III, King of England, II King of Scotland (born 1650, reigned 1689–1702), and **Mary II, Queen of England and Scotland** (born 1662, reigned 1689–94). They were childless, and William was succeeded by Mary's sister

Anne, Queen of Great Britain (born 1665, reigned 1702–14), who married (1683) George of Denmark (1653–1708). Of their seventeen children only one survived infancy:

William, Duke of Gloucester (1689–1700)

At the death of Queen Anne in 1702, the throne passed to the Stuarts' nearest Protestant relation, George, Elector of Hanover (a descendant of King James I/VI through his daughter Elizabeth), who became

George I, King of Great Britain (born 1660, reigned 1714–27). He had married (1682) Sophia Dorothea of Celle (1666–1726, divorced 1694).

Their children:
  George II, King of Great Britain – *see below*
Sophia Dorothea (1687–1757) married (1706) Frederick William I, King of Prussia (1688–1740)

George II, King of Great Britain (born 1683, reigned 1727–60) married (1705) Caroline of Anspach (1683–1737).

Their children:
  Frederick Lewis, Prince of Wales (1707–51) married (1736) Augusta of Saxe-Gotha (1719–72) – for their children, *see below*
  George William (1717–18)
  William, Duke of Cumberland (1721–65)
  Anne (1709–59) married (1734) William IV, Prince of Orange
  Amelia (1711–86)
  Caroline (1713–57)
  Mary (1722–72) married (1740) Frederick II, Landgrave of Hesse-Cassel (d. 1785)
  Louisa (1724–51) married (1743) Frederick V, King of Denmark (1723–66)

The children of Frederick Lewis, Prince of Wales, and his wife, Augusta of Saxe-Gotha:
  George III, King of Great Britain and Hanover – *see page 203*
  Edward, Duke of York (1739–67)
  William, Duke of Gloucester (1743–1805) married (1766) Maria Walpole (1736–1807)
  Henry, Duke of Cumberland (1745–90) married (1771) Anne Luttrell (1742–1808)
  Frederick (1750–65)
  Augusta (1737–1813) married (1764) Charles, Duke of Brunswick-Wolfenbuttel (1735–1806)

Elizabeth (1741–59)

Louisa (1749–68)

Caroline Matilda (1751–75) married (1766) Christian VII, King of Denmark (1749–1808)

George III, King of Great Britain and Hanover (born 1738, reigned in Britain 1760–1820, in Hanover 1814–20) married (1761) Charlotte of Mecklenburg-Strelitz (1744–1818).

Their children:

George IV, King of Great Britain and Hanover – *see below*

Frederick, Duke of York (1763–1827) married (1791) Frederica of Prussia (1767–1820)

William IV, King of Great Britain and Hanover – *see page 204*

Edward, Duke of Kent (1767–1820) married (1818) Victoire of Saxe-Coburg-Saalfeld (1786–1861), by whom he had one child, Queen Victoria – *see page 204*

Ernest Augustus, Duke of Cumberland (1771–1851), King of Hanover (reigned 1837–51), married (1815) Frederica of Mecklenburg-Strelitz (1778–1841)

Augustus, Duke of Sussex (1773–1843), married first (1793) Augusta Murray (1768–1830), and secondly (1831) Cecilia Buggin (1785–1873)

Adolphus, Duke of Cambridge (1774–1850), married (1818) Augusta of Hesse-Cassel (1797–1889)

Octavius (1779–83)

Alfred (1780–82)

Charlotte (1766–1828) married (1797) Frederick I, King of Württemberg (1734–1816)

Augusta (1768–1840)

Elizabeth (1770–1840) married (1818) Frederick IV, Landgrave of Hesse-Homburg (1769–1829)

Mary (1776–1857) married (1816) her cousin William, Duke of Gloucester (1776–1834)

Sophia (1777–1848)

Amelia (1783–1810)

George IV, King of Great Britain and Hanover (born 1762, reigned 1820–30) married (1795) Caroline of Brunswick-Wolfenbuttel (1768–1821).

Their child:

Charlotte (1796–1817) married (1816) Leopold of Saxe-Coburg-

Saalfeld (1790–1865)
George was succeeded by his brother

William IV, King of Great Britain and Hanover (born 1765, reigned 1830–37), who married (1818) Adelaide of Saxe-Meiningen (1792–1849).

Their children:
  Charlotte (1819)
  Elizabeth (1820–21)
William was succeeded by his niece (the daughter of Edward, Duke of Kent)

Victoria, Queen of Great Britain, Empress of India etc. (born 1819, reigned 1837–1901), who married (1840) Albert of Saxe-Coburg-Gotha (1819–61).

Their children:
  Edward VII, King of Great Britain etc. – *see below*
  Alfred, Duke of Edinburgh (1844–1900) married (1874) Marie of
    Russia (1853–1940) – one son, four daughters
  Arthur, Duke of Connaught (1850–1942) married (1879) Louise of
    Prussia (1860–1917) – one son, two daughters
  Leopold, Duke of Albany (1853–84) married (1882) Helena of Wal-
    deck-Pyrmont (1861–1922) – one son, one daughter
  Victoria (1840–1901) married (1858) Frederick, Kaiser of Germany
    (1831–88) – four sons, four daughters
  Alice (1843–78) married (1862) Ludwig IV, Grand Duke of Hesse
    (1837–92) – two sons, five daughters
  Helena (1846–1923) married (1866) Prince Christian of Schleswig-
    Holstein (1831–1917) – two sons, two daughters
  Louise (1848–1939) married (1871) John Campbell, Duke of Argyll
    (1845–1914) – childless
  Beatrice (1857–1944) married (1885) Prince Henry of Battenberg
    (1858–96) – three sons, one daughter

Edward VII, King of Great Britain etc. (born 1841, reigned 1901–10) married (1863) Alexandra of Denmark (1844–1925).

Their children:
  Albert Victor, Duke of Clarence (1864–92)
  George V, King of Great Britain etc – *see page 205*
  Alexander (1871)

Louise (1867–1931) married (1889) Alexander Duff, Duke of Fife (1840–1912)

Victoria (1868–1935)

Maud (1869–1938) married (1896) Haakon VII, King of Norway (1872–1973)

George V, King of Great Britain etc. (born 1865, reigned 1910–36) married (1893) Mary of Teck (1867–1953).

Their children:

Edward VIII, King of Great Britain etc. – *see below*

George VI, King of Great Britain etc. – *see below*

Henry, Duke of Gloucester (1900–1972) married (1935) Alice Montagu-Douglas-Scott (born 1901)

George, Duke of Kent (1902–42), married (1934) Marina of Greece (1906–68)

John (1905–19)

Mary (1897–1965) married (1922) Henry Lascelles, Earl of Harewood (1882–1947)

Edward VIII, King of Great Britain etc (1894–1972) reigned briefly in 1936 and abdicated in favour of his brother George VI – *see below*. As Duke of Windsor he married (1937) Wallis Warfield Simpson (born 1897).

George VI, King of Great Britain etc. (born 1895, reigned 1936–52) married (1923) Elizabeth Bowes-Lyon (born 1900).

Their children:

Elizabeth II, Queen of Great Britain etc. – *see below*

Margaret (born 1930) married (1960, divorced 1978) Antony Armstrong-Jones, Earl of Snowdon (born 1927)

Elizabeth II, Queen of Great Britain etc. (born 1926, reigning since 1952) married (1947) Philip Mountbatten, Duke of Edinburgh (born 1921).

Their children:

Charles, Prince of Wales (born 1948)

Andrew (born 1960)

Edward (born 1964)

Anne (born 1950) married (1975) Mark Phillips (born 1948)

Sources and Bibliography

The sources cited here, referring to numbered quotations within the text, are drawn mainly from primary sources, some of them published centuries ago, others within copyright (for which acknowledgement is made on pages 9–10). Such sources are not invariably listed in the bibliography, which is rather a suggestion for further reading on specific persons or periods. Only books available to the general reader, in print or obtainable from public libraries, are listed in the pages which follow, a small fraction of the works consulted during the preparation of this book.

Sources

THE MIDDLE AGES
"*They love an apple more than gold*"
1. *Medieval Lore* (a shortened version of Bartholomew the Englishman, *On the Properties of Things*), ed. R. Steele (1893), p. 32
2. Bartholomew, *On the Properties of Things*, trs. J. Trevisa (1535), book VI, p. lxii
3. *Medieval Lore, op. cit.*, p. 46
4. *A relation, or rather true account, of the island of England*, trs. C. A. Sneyd (Camden Society, volume 37, 1847), pp. 24–5
5. *Stans puer ad mensam* in *Early English meals and manners*, ed. E. Furnivall (Early English Text Society, 1868), p. 32
6. *How the good wife taught her daughter* in *The Babees' book*, ed. E. Rickert from E. Furnivall's translation (Chatto & Windus, 1908), p. 32
7. *The little children's book* in *The Babees' book, op. cit.*, p. 20

"*Virtuous learning . . . honest disports*"
1. J. Leland, *De rebus Britannicis Collectanea*, trs. T. Hearne (1770), volume IV, p. 179
2. Sir C. Markham, *Richard III* (Smith Elder, 1906), pp. 4–5
3. *A collection of ordinances and regulations for the government of the royal household* (Society of Antiquaries, 1790), pp. 27–8
4. M. A. E. Green, *Lives of the Princesses of England* (1851), volume III, p. 423
5. *The Chronicles of Froissart*, trans. Sir J. Bouchier, Lord Berners (Tudor Translations, ed. W. E. Henley, 1903), volume VI, p. 159
6. M. A. E. Green, *op. cit.*, volume III, pp. 257–8
7. *Ibid.*, volume III, pp. 327–8
8. M. Paris, *English History, 1233–73*, trs. J. A. Giles (1853), volume II, p. 465
9. *Ibid.*, volume II, p. 88

The medieval boy-kings
1. A. Strickland, *Lives of the Queens of England* (1857), volume I, p. 502
2. *Ibid.*, p. 507
3. T. Walsingham, *Chronicon Angliae, 1322–88*, ed. E. M. Thompson (Rolls Series, 1874), p. 155
4. *Froissart's Chronicles*, ed. and trans. J. Joliffe (Harvill Press, 1967), p. 246

5. C. Oman, *The Great Revolt of 1381* (Clarendon Press, 1906), p. 200
6. *Froissart's Chronicles*, ed. J. Joliffe, *op. cit.*, p. 250
7. *Proceedings and Ordinances of the Privy Council of England*, ed. N. H. Nicholas (1834–7), volume III, p. 297
8. *Ibid.*
9. *State Papers and Manuscripts . . . Milan*, ed. A. B. Hinds (H.M.S.O., 1912), volume I, pp. 117–18

THE TUDOR AGE
"What, hast smutched thy nose?"
1. R. Whitford, *A Work for Householders* (1531) – no pagination
2. H. Rhodes, *Book of Nurture, or School of Good Manners* (1577) – no pagination
3. R. Weigall, 'An Elizabethan gentlewoman' in *Quarterly Review* (volume 215, no. 428, July 1911), p. 122
4. P. Erondell, *The French Garden* (1605) – no pagination

Tudor see-saw
1. *The Epistles of Erasmus*, ed. J. Nichols (1840), volume I, p. 201
2. *Ibid.*
3. A. Strickland, *op.cit.*, volume III, pp. 312–13
4. *Ibid.*, p. 331
5. *Letters and Papers, Foreign and Domestic, of the Reign of Henry VIII*, ed. J. Brewer *et al.* (1862–1932), volume VI, p. 472
6. *Ibid.*, volume IX, p. 90

The last boy-king
1. *The Literary Remains of Edward VI*, ed. J. G. Nichols (1857), volume I, p. 59
2. *The Chronicle of King Henry VIII of England*, ed. M. A. S. Hume (1889), p. 187
3. *Literary Remains. . . , op. cit.*, volume II, p. xx
4. *Original Letters*, ed. H. Robinson (1846), volume II, p. 47
5. G. Pollini, *Historia ecclesiastica della revoluzione d'Inghilterra* (1594), p. 297
6. R. Ascham, *The Schoolmaster* (1570), pp. 11–12
7. *Ibid.*
8. R. Baker, *Chronicle* (1653), p. 90
9. M. Florio, *Historia della vita . . . Giovanna Graia* (1607), p. 60
10. A. Strickland, *The Lives of the Tudor and Stuart Princesses* (1888), p. 215

THE STUART AGE
"The thing is called Bridget"
1. M. Blundell, *Cavalier* (Longmans Green, 1933), p. 79
2. A. Jessopp, *The Lives of the Norths* (1890), volume III, p. 215
3. R. Braithwaite, *The English Gentlewoman* (1631) – no pagination
4. B. Makin, *An essay to revive the ancient education of a gentlewoman* (1631 edition), p. 33
5. H. Woolley, *The Gentlewoman's Companion* (1675), p. 17
6. L. Stone, *Crisis of the Aristocracy* (Oxford University Press, abridged edition, 1967), p. 275

Intrigue and complicity
1. *The Memoirs of Robert Carey*, ed. F. H. Mares (Oxford University Press, 1972), p. 69
2. *Original Letters Illustrative of English History*, ed. H. Ellis (1824), volume III, p. 92
3. Sir John Harington, *Nugae Antiquae* (1779 edition), volume I, p. 371
4. J. Nichols, *The Progresses, Processions and Magnificent Festivities of King James I* . . . (1828), volume II, p. 485
5. *Letters of Henrietta Maria*, ed. M. A. E. Wood (1857), p. 18
6. British Museum: Harleian Manuscript 6988 f95
7. *The Autobiography of Anne, Lady Halkett*, ed. J. G. Nichols (Camden Society, 1875, new series, volume XIII), p. 22
8. J. Nalson, *A True Copy of the Journal of the High Court of Justice for the Trial of King Charles I* (1684), pp. 105–7

The dynasty dwindles
1. Blenheim Palace: G-I-8
2. *Letters of Two Queens*, ed. B. Bathurst (Robert Holden, 1924), p. 44
3. Althorp: Marlborough manuscripts, book A

THE GEORGIAN AGE
Idealists and philanthropists
1. C. Aspinall-Oglander, *Admiral's Wife* (Longmans Green, 1940)
2. Jane Austen, *Emma* (first published in 1816; innumerable later editions), chapter 3.

Family feuds
1. R. L. Arkell, *Caroline of Anspach* (Oxford University Press, 1939), p. 46

2. *Ibid.*, p. 107
3. Lord Hervey, *Some materials towards memoirs of the reign of George II*, ed. R. Sedgwick (Eyre & Spottiswoode, 1931), volume III, p. 278
4. *Ibid.*, pp. 762–3
5. *The Letters and Journals of Lady Mary Coke* (1889), volume I, p. lxxxv
6. *Ibid.*
7. Sir George Young, *Poor Fred: the People's Prince* (Oxford University Press, 1937), pp. 172–5

Happy families
1. *The diary and letters of Mme d'Arblay* (Fanny Burney) – (1842), volume II, p. 392
2. George Keppel, Earl of Albemarle, *Fifty years of my life . . .* (1876), volume I, p. 273
3. The Farington diary, ed. J. Grieg (Hutchinson, 1922–8), volume IV, p. 142
4. G. Keppel, *op. cit.*, volume I, p. 312
5. *Letters of the Princess Charlotte, 1811–17*, ed. A. Aspinall (Home & van Thal, 1949)

THE VICTORIAN AGE
"The happiest days of your life"
1. Flora Thompson, *Lark Rise to Candleford* (Oxford University Press, 1939–43 and later editions), chapter XL

"Poor Vicky"
1. W. W. Tulloch, *The Story of the Life of Queen Victoria* (J. Nisbet, 1901), p. 6
2. D. Duff, *Edward of Kent* (Stanley Paul, 1938), p. 267
3. C. Grey, *The Early Life of the Prince Consort* (1867), p. 23
4. *The Letters of Queen Victoria, 1837–61*, ed. A. C. Benson and Viscount Esher (John Murray, 1907), volume I, pp. 17–18
5. L. Hunt, *The Old Court Suburb* (1855), volume II, p. 175
6. G. Keppel, Earl of Albemarle, *op. cit.*, volume II, p. 310
7. *The Letters of Queen Victoria, 1837–61*, *op. cit.*, volume I, p. 18
8. H. Cathcart, *Royal Bedside Book* (W. H. Allen, 1969), p. 24
9. *The Letters of Queen Victoria, 1837–61*, *op. cit.*, volume I, pp. 49–50
10. *Ibid.*, volume I, pp. 85–6
11. *Ibid.*, volume I, p. 61
12. *The Greville Memoirs*, ed. H. Reeve (1874–87) volume I, part iii, p. 367

13. *Further Letters of Queen Victoria*, ed. H. Bolitho (Thornton-Butterworth, 1938), p. 117

"The grandmother of Europe"
1. *Dearest Child*, ed. R. Fulford (Evans Brothers, 1965), p. 115
2. *Ibid.*, p. 144
3. *Ibid.*, p. 191
4. *Correspondence of Sarah Spencer, Lady Lyttelton, 1787–1870*, ed. H. Wyndham (John Murray, 1912), p. 333
5. *The Greville Memoirs, 1814–40*, ed. L. Strachey and R. Fulford (Macmillan, 1938), volume VII, p. 157
6. Marie, Queen of Romania, *The Story of my Life* (Cassell, 1934), volume I, pp. 19–20
7. H.R.H. Princess Alice, Countess of Athlone, *For My Grandchildren* (Evans Brothers, 1966), pp. 68–9
8. H.R.H. Princess Marie Louise, *My Memories of Six Reigns* (Evans Brothers, 1956), p. 38

THE MODERN AGE
"Lilibet"
1. Mabel, Countess of Airlie, *Thatched with Gold* (Hutchinson, 1962), p. 197
2. C. Birt, *The Royal Sisters* (Pitkin, 1949), p. 4
3. M. Crawford, *The Little Princesses* (Cassell, 1950), p. 45
4. *Ibid.*, p. 66

Bibliography

GENERAL BOOKS ON THE HISTORY OF CHILDHOOD

R. Bayne-Powell, *The English Child in the Eighteenth Century* (John Murray, 1939)

M. C. Borer, *Willingly to School* (Lutterworth, 1976)

P. Cunningham and A. Buck, *Children's Costume in England, 1300–1900* (Adam & Charles Black, 1965)

L. Daiken, *Children's Games Throughout the Year* (Batsford, 1949)

——, *Children's Toys Throughout the Ages* (Batsford, 1953)

F. J. H. Darton, *Children's Books in England* (Cambridge University Press, 1932)

O. Dunlop, *English Apprenticeship and Child Labour* (T. Fisher Unwin, 1912)

P. W. R. Foot, *The Child in the Twentieth Century* (Cassell, 1968)

E. Godfrey, *English Children in the Olden Time* (Methuen, 1907)

C. Hole, *English Home Life, 1500 to 1800* (Batsford, 1947)

J. Kamm, *Hope Deferred: Girls' Education in English History* (Methuen, 1965)

D. Kennedy, *Children* (Batsford, 1971)

M. King-Hall, *The Story of the Nursery* (Routledge & Kegan Paul, 1958)

J. Latham, *Happy Families: Growing Up in the Eighteenth and Nineteenth Centuries* (Adam & Charles Black, 1974)

S. Lynd, *English Children* (William Collins, 1942)

I. Pinchbeck and M. Hewitt, *Children in English Society* – two volumes (Routledge & Kegan Paul, 1969)

F. G. Roe, *The Georgian Child* (Phoenix House, 1961)

——, *The Victorian Child* (Phoenix House, 1959)

THE MIDDLE AGES

So little mention is made of royal children in medieval works that the information is widely diffused, and research for this chapter proved difficult – but fascinating. It would be tedious to name all the chronicles, collections of documents, biographies etc used for this chapter, and even the books listed below may be hard for the general reader to find now, though there is much interesting material in them which adds to the picture of royal childhood in the Middle Ages.

M. A. E. Green well researched *The Lives of the Princesses of England* (volumes I to IV, 1850–52): it is a shame that there is no companion series on the princes. Agnes Strickland adds a little more in *Lives of the Queens of England* (volumes I and II, 1857).

A fine picture of Edward III's family is drawn in B. C. Hardy's *Philippa of Hainault and Her Times* (John Long, 1910). A good deal of this book is based on Froissart's chronicles: the fullest English version of them is still Lord Berners' translation, edited by W. E. Henley (Tudor Translations, 1903) – there are several more recent editions, though much abbreviated.

Royal Palaces, by Olwen Hedley (Robert Hale, 1972) provides an excellent background to royal home-life in the Middle Ages and in the later periods.

Further reading on the child-kings of medieval England could well include the following:

For Richard II – A. Steel, *Richard II* (Cambridge University Press, 1941); M. Collis, *The Hurling Time* (Faber, 1958); H. F. Hutchinson, *The Hollow Crown* (Eyre & Spottiswoode, 1961).

There is no full biography of Henry VI; the best survey of his life and reign appears in R. L. Storey's *The End of the House of Lancaster* (Barrie & Rockliff, 1966).

The brief reign of Edward V is fully covered in the relevant chapters of P. M. Kendall's *Richard III* (George Allen & Unwin, 1971).

THE TUDOR AGE

Marie-Louise Bruce's *The Youth of Henry VIII* (Collins, 1978) is a fine assessment of the King's early development.

His daughter Mary's childhood is chronicled in Agnes Strickland's *Lives of the Queens of England* (volume III), Elizabeth's in the same series (volume IV, 1857). The best modern work on Mary is H. F. M. Prescott's *Mary Tudor* (Eyre & Spottiswoode, 1940). Of the many books on Elizabeth I, Alison Plowden's *The Young Elizabeth* (Macmillan, 1971) is the most relevant here.

The personal life of Edward VI has been best described by H. W. Chapman in *The Last Tudor King* (Jonathan Cape, 1958); the background to the reign is dealt with more fully in *Edward VI: the Young King* and *Edward VI: the Threshold of Power*, by W. K. Jordon (George Allen & Unwin, 1968 and 1970).

Again, H. W. Chapman gives an illuminating picture of Lady Jane Grey (Jonathan Cape, 1962), which may be supplemented by

D. Mathew's *Lady Jane Grey: the Setting of the Reign* (Eyre Methuen, 1972).

An interesting character outside the scope of this book is Lady Arbella Stuart, a cousin of the Tudors who was brought up as a potential heiress to Elizabeth I – though in the event no one seriously considered her claim. Her remarkable childhood is described by P. Handover (Eyre & Spottiswoode, 1957).

The bibliographies of these books list contemporary works consulted for this book.

THE STUART AGE

There is ample recently-published material on the lives of the Stuart monarchs and their families, comprising books whose bibliographies list the contemporary works (memoirs, letters, etc.) consulted for this book but usually inaccessible to the general reader.

James (VI and) I: biographies by Hugh Ross Williamson (Duckworth, 1936); D. H. Willson (Jonathan Cape, 1956); W. McElwee, (Faber & Faber, 1958); D. Mathew (Eyre & Spottiswoode, 1967).

Charles I: C. Hibbert (Weidenfeld & Nicolson, 1968); John Bowle (Weidenfeld & Nicolson, 1975).

Charles II: Arthur Bryant (Longmans Green, 1931), with H. W. Chapman, *The Tragedy of Charles II* (Jonathan Cape, 1964).

James II: F. C. Turner (Eyre & Spottiswoode, 1948); M. Ashley (Dent, 1977).

William III: S. Baxter (Longmans, 1966); N. A. Robb (Heinemann, 1962–6).

Mary II: H. W. Chapman (Jonathan Cape, 1953); E. Hamilton (Hamish Hamilton, 1972) – with a biography of William and Mary together by H. and B. van der Zee (Macmillan, 1973).

Anne: D. Green (Collins, 1970).

For other members of the royal family, the following books are useful: P. Handover, *Anne of Denmark* (Longman, 1970); C. Oman, *Henrietta Maria* (Hodder & Stoughton, 1936); C. Oman, *Mary of Modena* (Hodder & Stoughton, 1962); C. H. Hartmann, *The King My Brother* – Henrietta Anne and Charles II (Heinemann, 1954); C. Oman, *Elizabeth of Bohemia* (Hodder & Stoughton, 1938); H. W. Chapman, *Queen Anne's Son* (André Deutsch, 1954).

THE GEORGIAN AGE

The circumstances of George II's unfortunate childhood are outlined in *Sophie, Electress of Hanover,* by M. Kroll (Gollancz, 1973) and *Sophie Dorothea* by Ruth Jordan (Constable, 1971). The development of the feud with his father, the loss of his children and his relationship with his eldest son are examined in *George II* by C. Chevenix Trench (Allen Lane, 1973) and also in the biography of Caroline of Anspach by R. L. Arkell (Oxford University Press, 1939).

The main biographies of Frederick Lewis, Prince of Wales, are those by Sir George Young – *Poor Fred, the People's Prince* (Oxford University Press, 1937), A. Edwards (Staples Press, 1947) and M. Marples – *Poor Fred and the Butcher* (Michael Joseph, 1970).

The only formal biography of Augusta of Saxe-Gotha, Princess of Wales, appears in *Princess of Wales* by D. M. Ashdown (John Murray, 1979). Her relations with her eldest son and influence on him are studied in biographies of George III named below. The King's correspondence with Lord Bute was edited for publication by R. Sedgwick (Macmillan, 1939).

Among the Court memoirs of the period, the most interesting are those of Lord Hervey – *Some Materials Towards Memoirs of the Reign of George II,* edited by R. Sedgwick (Eyre & Spottiswoode, 1931) and Horace Walpole, edited most recently by M. Hodgart (Batsford, 1963).

Two books give a broad view of Court and royal family life under George III: C. Hibbert, *The Court at Windsor* (Longmans, 1964) and N. Pain, *George III at Home* (Eyre Methuen, 1975).

The best biographies of the King are those by J. Brooke (Constable, 1972) and S. Ayling (Collins, 1972) and of Queen Charlotte by O. Hedley (John Murray, 1975).

An excellent book on the individual younger sons of George III is *Royal Dukes* by R. Fulford (Duckworth, 1933 – and later editions), and there are two interesting books on the princesses by D. M. Stuart – *The Daughters of George III* (Macmillan, 1939) and M. Marples – *Six Royal Sisters* (Michael Joseph, 1969).

Two ladies attached to George III's household have left fascinating memoirs of their observations of the royal family: Fanny Burney, whose journals and letters were edited by J. Hemlow *et al.* (Oxford University Press, 1972), and Mrs Delany, whose papers have been edited by R. B. Johnston (Stanley Paul, 1925).

Relations between the future King George IV and his wife, and theirs with their daughter, are examined in the fine two-volume biography of the King by C. Hibbert (Longman, 1972; Allen Lane, 1975), in the biographies of Caroline by E. Parry (Benn, 1930) and E. E. P. Tisdall –

Wanton Queen (Stanley Paul, 1939) and in *The Disastrous Marriage* by
J. Richardson (Jonathan Cape, 1960).

There are two excellent biographies of Princess Charlotte, by
D. M. Stuart – *Daughter of England* (Macmillan, 1951) and D. Creston –
The Regent and His Daughter (Thornton Butterworth, 1932). The Princess's letters, 1811–17, were edited by A. Aspinall (Home & van Thal,
1949), and a first-hand observation of her tribulations, *The Autobiography of Miss Knight*, has been edited by R. Fulford (William
Kimber, 1960).

THE VICTORIAN AGE

Of the many biographies of Queen Victoria, only three are outstanding
in their originality of research and treatment: Lytton Strachey's (Chatto
& Windus, 1921 and later editions); Elizabeth Longford (Weidenfeld &
Nicolson, 1967) and Cecil Woodham-Smith – as yet only volume I,
1819–61, published (Hamish Hamilton, 1972).

The Girlhood of Queen Victoria is an edition of her journal, 1832–40, by
A. C. Buckle (John Murray, 1904), and her letters have been edited –
first series, 1837–61 but including earlier correspondence also – by
A. C. Benson and Viscount Esher (John Murray, 1907).

On Victoria's father there is *Edward of Kent* by David Duff (Stanley
Paul, 1938), and there are two books on her mother, by D. M. Stuart
(Macmillan, 1942) and D. M. Ashdown (Robert Hale, 1974). The best
biography of the Queen's Uncle Leopold is *My Dearest Uncle* by J.
Richardson (Jonathan Cape, 1961) and of William IV the work by P.
Ziegler (Collins, 1971).

The account, from her letters, of Duchess Augusta of
Saxe-Coburg-Saalfeld's visit to England in 1826, may be found in *A
Royal Bedside Book* by Helen Cathcart (W. H. Allen, 1969).

The best biographies of Prince Albert, the Prince Consort, are by
H. Bolitho (David Bruce & Watson, 1970) and R. Fulford (Macmillan,
1949), with David Duff's *Albert and Victoria* (Muller, 1972).

Dozens of books on and memoirs of Queen Victoria's children and
grandchildren have appeared in the years since her death. Their family
life, and a full bibliography, appear in my book *Queen Victoria's Family*
(Robert Hale, 1975). For the later generation of the British royal family,
see *A King's Story*, the memoirs of H.R.H. the Duke of Windsor, formerly King Edward VIII (Cassell, 1960) and his book *A Family Album*
(Cassell, 1960), with *The Windsor Tapestry* by C. Mackenzie (Rich &
Cowan, 1938) and the King's biography by F. Donaldson (Weidenfeld

& Nicolson, 1974). The main biography of King George VI is by Sir John Wheeler-Bennett (Macmillan, 1958).

THE MODERN AGE

The main source for the childhood of H. M. Queen Elizabeth II and her sister is Marion Crawford's *The Little Princesses* (Cassell, 1950), used and supplemented by many more recent biographers.

Of the many books on the life of their mother, H. M. Queen Elizabeth the Queen Mother, the best is by David Duff (Muller, 1965) and of their father, King George VI, the work by Sir John Wheeler-Bennett already cited.

Dozens of books about the present royal children have appeared in the last two decades and are easily obtainable from the biography sections of public libraries. Particularly noteworthy are *The Heir Apparent* by Geoffrey Wakeford (Robert Hale, 1967), *To Be A King* by Dermot Morrah (Hutchinson, 1968), *Anne, Portrait of a Princess* by Judith Campbell (Cassell, 1970) and *The Queen's Children* by Donald Edgar (Arthur Barker, 1978).

Index

140–1, 150–61, 162–73, 183, 184
Victoria, Princess Royal, 163–7, 168, 169
Victoria, Princess, 171
Villiers, Lady Frances, 104–5, 107
Villiers, George, Duke of Buckingham, 93, 94
Vives, Juan Luis, 61

Walpole, Sir Robert, 123
Walworth, William, 42
Waring, Johanna, 24
Wesley, Charles and John, 117
Whittington, Sir Richard, 30
Wilhelm II, Kaiser, 130, 170
William I, King of England, 26, 31, 32
William III, King of England and Scotland, Prince of Orange, 102, 105–11
William IV, King of Great Britain etc., 133, 140, 153, 155–9

William, Prince, Duke of Cumberland, 124, 125, 128
William, Prince, Duke of Gloucester (son of Queen Anne), 108–9
William, Prince, Duke of Gloucester (nephew/son-in-law of George III), 135
William, Prince, 23–4
William II, Prince of Orange, 95, 96, 106,
William IV, Prince of Orange, 128, 140
William V, Prince of Orange, 139
William, Count of Hainault, 38
Woodville, Anthony, 47
Woodville, Elizabeth, Queen Consort, 48
Woolley, Hannah, 86
Wykeham, William of, 18–19

Yonge, Charlotte M., 147